ME
KEEPER

Jackie Kohnstamm grew up in North London, where she still lives. She studied an ancient Jewish community in France for her PhD, never guessing how the skills acquired then would later help her delve into her own family story. She has lectured in higher education and written short stories and plays for BBC radio and the stage. Jackie is nourished by lengthy meals with friends and by her garden on the wild side. If she hits a winning shot at tennis, that's a bonus. *The Memory Keeper* is her first book.

THE MEMORY KEEPER

A JOURNEY INTO THE PAST TO UNEARTH FAMILY SECRETS

JACKIE KOHNSTAMM

CANONGATE

This paperback edition published in 2024 by Canongate Books

First published in Great Britain in 2023 by Canongate Books Ltd,
14 High Street, Edinburgh EH1 1TE

canongate.co.uk

1

Epigraph excerpted from 'The Unloved' by Kathleen Raine, © Kathleen Raine, 1952,
from *The Collected Poems* by Kathleen Raine, published by Faber and Faber Ltd, 2001

Lines on p. 36 excerpted from 'In meinen Träumen läutet es Sturm' by Mascha Kaléko
© Mascha Kaléko, 1977, dtv Verlagsgesellschaft mbH & Co. KG, München

All images courtesy of the author with the exception of those listed below

Image on p. 22 courtesy of Roni G. Ronen (Rosner)

Image on p. 195 from Brandenburgisches Landeshauptarchiv (BLHA),
Rep. 36A Oberfinanzpräsident Berlin-Brandenburg Nr. 5039

Image on p. 241 courtesy of Lonnie Zwerin

Image on p. 251 from the Arolsen Archives

Image on p. 293 from National Archives, Prague, Registers of Jewish religious
communities in the Czech regions, Death certificates – Ghetto Terezín;
Rychwalski Max, volume 74

British Library Cataloguing-in-Publication Data
A catalogue record for this book is available on
request from the British Library

ISBN 978 1 83885 805 6

Typeset in Garamond Premier Pro by Palimpsest Book Production Ltd,
Falkirk, Stirlingshire

Printed and bound by CPI Group (UK) Ltd, Croydon CR0 4YY

Dedicated to the memory of my grandparents, Max and Mally Rychwalski, and of my whole shadow family.

CONTENTS

Author's Note   ix
Family Trees   x

December 2005   3

PART 1: Berlin, January 2006   17

Reaching Through the Wallpaper   19
Meeting My Grandparents   29
Connections   43
Tilting   58

PART 2: Hearing Their Voices   67

The First Letters   69
Money   77
Ten Years of *Stolpersteine*   88
Cracking the Code   117
The Dam Bursts   130
Crucial Months   145
Chancing It   156
War   160

PART 3: Into the Fog of In-Between   177

'What are Jews?'   179
The Family in Public   187
Thresholds   202
Transgression   215
Crossing the Road   220

PART 4: The Cupboard Is Aired   253

The Cost of Claiming   255
Reconnecting   267
A Different Roll of the Dice   273
Meeting Myself   280
The Last Threshold   289
Back to the Beginning   294

Sources   299
Appendix   305
Acknowledgements   307

AUTHOR'S NOTE

Some names have been changed to protect privacy, and on occasion two individuals conflated into one for narrative simplicity.

The word *Stolpersteine* is usually translated into English as 'stumbling stones'. Gunter Demnig, the artist who created them, intends passers-by to stumble upon them by chance, not link the term to tripping over them. To keep the term more abstract, I call them 'stumble stones'.

THE MESERITZ FAMILY

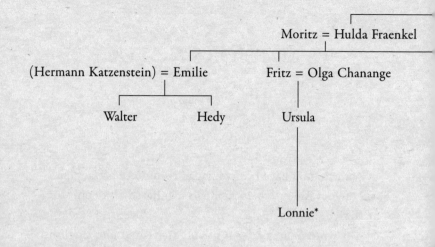

Moritz = Hulda Fraenkel

(Hermann Katzenstein) = Emilie   Fritz = Olga Chanange

Walter   Hedy   Ursula

Lonnie*

THE RYCHWALSKI FAMILY

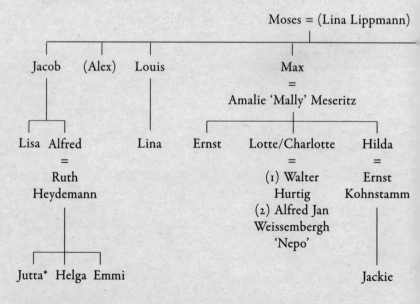

Moses = (Lina Lippmann)

Jacob   (Alex)   Louis   Max
                                =
                        Amalie 'Mally' Meseritz

Lisa Alfred   Lina   Ernst   Lotte/Charlotte   Hilda
        =   =   =
      Ruth   (1) Walter   Ernst
    Heydemann   Hurtig   Kohnstamm
                                    (2) Alfred Jan
                                    Weissembergh
                                        'Nepo'

Jutta* Helga Emmi   Jackie

Note:
Names with asterisks — Lonnie* — are referred to, not named in the book
Names in brackets — (Georg) — show relationships; they do not feature in the book

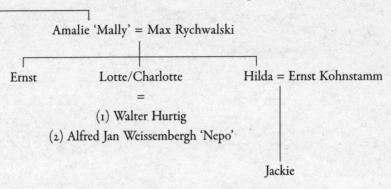

Josephine 'Findel' Fraenkel

Amalie 'Mally' = Max Rychwalski

Ernst   Lotte/Charlotte   Hilda = Ernst Kohnstamm

=

(1) Walter Hurtig

(2) Alfred Jan Weissembergh 'Nepo'

Jackie

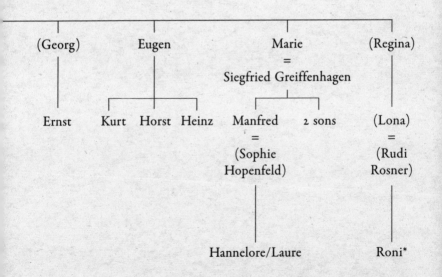

(Georg)   Eugen   Marie   (Regina)

=

Siegfried Greiffenhagen

Ernst   Kurt   Horst   Heinz   Manfred   2 sons   (Lona)

=

(Sophie

Hopenfeld)

=

(Rudi

Rosner)

Hannelore/Laure   Roni*

Rychwalski family, 1908. Middle row standing: Moses Rychwalski (centre); on his right Max, Mally, Siegfried and Marie Greiffenhagen

DECEMBER 2005

Restless. I was feeling restless. Unable to settle to anything. Then a chance happening set things off. That's the only way I can explain it. Serendipity.

* * *

I am standing by the garden door holding a pair of trousers that have lost a button. I really want to be outside, but what can you do in a garden in early December? Shrubs are waiting for the sun to come out long enough to reach their roots and nudge them into life. As am I.

It's been more than two weeks since I wore these trousers. If it was a question of cooking, I'd have done it straight away. I find cooking meditative, the rhythm of chopping soothing. My mind takes wing, floats, and there's a meal at the end of it. But sewing I hate.

So I go to the kitchen, open the fridge, clear out the veg drawer and throw into a saucepan carrots, onion, celeriac, leeks, potatoes, all the winter root stuff, plus dried herbs because the fresh ones have withered to nothing – another good reason for spring to roll on – pour in stock and add garlic for zing. While the soup is simmering, I step out into the last sad patch of daylight and plan for spring.

Hard to imagine that rose stump will send out shoots, or the jasmine skeleton spill over the fence, full and fragrant once again, or that only a couple of months ago I ate my own figs. Does the fig need repotting or is it best left? At least it's hardy, unlike the geranium which I wrap in more fleece and tuck back against the wall.

Now it's completely dark. I go inside and eat my soup.

If it was the Middle Ages, I'd piss in my pot, chuck it out the window, snuff out the candle and go to bed. Darkness would have come as a relief. Electricity and technology give us too many choices and I don't fancy any of them, certainly not sewing. So I turn on the TV to distract me. That's the best way. Catch myself offguard and deal with that button before I realise I've done it.

I grab the remote and land on Channel 4 just as a large man steps into the boot of a car and – presumably of his own free will because he is smiling at the camera – folds himself up and allows himself to be shut inside. The camera then pans over lines of cars until all we see is a giant car park full of parked cars. No one allowed in or out as that would spoil the game. Channel 4 has challenged a group of psychics to find the very car with the man inside it.

This is just the kind of distraction I need to help me concentrate on threading the needle. I glance at the television as, one by one, the psychics succeed, almost succeed, just fail or fail miserably. In between smug psychics and cross psychics come commercial breaks and mini psychic tests for us, the viewers, at home. I jab the needle in and out of the cloth, do every test and score two out of ten. What else did I expect? I have never felt even slightly psychic. By now the button is more or less on, so I go to bed.

Actually, I don't. I mean to, but on the way – and this is the odd thing, as I've really no idea why I choose this particular moment – I turn on the computer and type into Google my mother's maiden name: Rychwalski. An unusual name in England but not in Eastern Europe, nor the USA. I have searched before, not in any purposeful way, more like surfing for anybody I might have heard of, even though common sense tells me by now they must all be dead.

I scroll down until two entries bring me up short: Max and Amalie Rychwalski. My grandparents. What on earth are they doing on my screen? I click and enter the website of the district in Berlin where they used to live. Bleibtreustrasse, number 32. I read that two '*Stolpersteine*' have been placed in the pavement outside their block of flats. What on earth are *Stolpersteine*?

Another click. A picture unfurls and I am back in the cinema of the 1950s watching *The Ten Commandments* with Moses – Charlton Heston – brandishing two tablets of stone hot off the press from God. But, instead of ten Thou Shalt Nots, I read on one:

HIER WOHNTE
AMALIE RYCHWALSKI GEB. MESERITZ
JG. 1878
DEPORTIERT 1942 THERESIENSTADT
ERMORDET 13.11.1942

(HERE LIVED
AMALIE RYCHWALSKI NÉE MESERITZ
DATE OF BIRTH 1878
DEPORTED 1942 THERESIENSTADT
MURDERED 13.11.1942)

and on the other:

HIER WOHNTE
MAX RYCHWALSKI
JG. 1864
DEPORTIERT 1942 THERESIENSTADT
ERMORDET 31.01.1943

(HERE LIVED
MAX RYCHWALSKI
DATE OF BIRTH 1864
DEPORTED 1942 THERESIENSTADT
MURDERED 31.01.1943)

I stare at the screen, shocked by this sudden meeting with my grandparents, shocked by the word 'murdered' ('*ermordet*'). My parents had never used it. 'Died', they would say on the rare occasions the fact was mentioned. Or 'perished'. But not 'murdered'. 'Murdered' is such a stark word.

You'd think after fifty years I might be used to it. Getting on with life, walking down the street, queueing at the checkout, thoughts of bulldozed bodies nowhere near the surface of my mind, when suddenly a picture, a headline, a phrase overheard in passing and whoosh! My grandparents appear.

I was eleven when I found out the truth. I had already

realised my maternal grandparents must have died, but didn't know where or how, unlike my father's father who had dropped dead of a heart attack before I was born. No mystery there. He and my paternal grandmother – the only grandparent I knew – had managed to escape from Germany to England in the nick of time.

'At least they weren't killed there,' my mother had commented, implying there were degrees of severity to death in a concentration camp. Theresienstadt was a transit camp; it had no gas chambers, and her parents were not shot, so no single action had ended their lives. It would be many more years before I found out what had actually happened to them.

I dash to a long-closed cupboard, extract a file of family papers and rummage till I find two yellowed Red Cross death certificates. Back at the computer I compare dates. They tally exactly. Then I see something else: 'Dedicated 30 November 2005.' Today is 4 December 2005. Their *Stolpersteine* were placed last Wednesday. Only four days ago.

Now, look. I am willing to believe there are people who really are psychic – in fact, I have a friend who says she gets premonitions in the form of images – but not me. I have always been down to earth. Sensible. Logical. I was like it as a child, from birth for all I know. Surely this is simply a coincidence?

Recently I had been thinking about my mother's family more than I had done for years. Only a week earlier I had got out her family photos, as if looking at them might help me put my finger on something – a sense of unbelonging that I have had all my life and which latterly I had been feeling more strongly. Maybe this time the photos would help me get to grips with it. I had gazed at my grandmother, soon to be married, exquisitely dressed in figure-hugging white lace, the height of fashion in 1903. In another photo my grandfather is deep in conversation with my mother. By then he must have been in his seventies, bearded, with thick eyebrows and deep furrows down his cheeks. Even under his homburg hat he looks like an Old Testament prophet.

Hilda and Max

The unbelonging felt like a block of ice lodged in my gut. Much of the time I was unaware of it. But every now and then while I was growing up that feeling would surge through me, and looking at the photos helped to shift it. They were kept in a shoebox in the cupboard under the TV set. I would take them out and spread around me a whole black-and-white family of great-aunts, great-uncles and cousins. My doll-like baby mother, Hilda, with her older brother Ernst and sister Charlotte. My grandparents, Max and Mally, always referred to by their first names. Mally was short for Amalie. Her older sister had been named Emilie. How odd, I thought. Emilie and Amalie. Like Tweedledum and Tweedledee.

I watched Mally change from wild-haired girl in fancy dress through wasp-waisted bride to plump young woman in plus-fours and stylish jacket posing next to Max, one foot on the rung of a toboggan. Later still she became a stout matron, carefully dressed in matching hat, gloves and handbag, but with deep shadows under sad eyes.

Mally and Max

My grandfather Max changed less than she did, constantly tall, bearded and balding. He rarely looked at the camera except in the posed shots. I liked catching him engrossed in the newspaper or reading a postcard he had just written. In one tiny snap he and Mally stand by the sea. In the foreground a striped towelling robe lies crumpled on the sand. I doubted it belonged to Max; in his suit and bow tie, he was hardly about to strip and swim. In any case, if Max had owned such a robe, it would have been folded and crumple-free. Tidy and fastidious was how my mother described him, with a special cup to keep his moustache and beard clean. His hands were sweet-smelling, nails well cared for.

As a child I used to crouch over the shoebox and stare until the figures jerked into motion, like a newsreel that had stuck and restarted. I imagined stroking the fur of Mally's collar, holding Max's large hand, so like my mother's. At such times my black-and-white grandparents seemed more colourful than the family among whom I was growing up.

That included my mother, the monochrome version consistently more fun than the one I lived with, usually too tired, busy with chores or struck down by a migraine to join in my games. Only in the shoebox could I be sure of finding the ironic, energetic woman who pulled faces, turned cartwheels, wore jaunty hats, posed in palazzo pants and halter-neck swimsuits by sunny Berlin lakesides in the days before England.

Hilda

Three separate eras marked my childhood landscape. My parents had survived the exciting, glamorous, dangerous world of Before – escaping Nazi Germany, meeting in England as refugees and dodging the Luftwaffe's bombs – whereas I was born in the grey, dull, safe, post-war era of After. Gradually I became aware of a third period, shadowy and hard to locate, which came after Before but before After and, as far as I could tell, only affected us, not the families of my schoolfriends. They, born like me after the Second World War to parents who had lived through it, remained untouched by that third era which could lower the temperature at home by several degrees.

That icy world of In-Between, although rarely mentioned and hard to grasp, shaped my everyday life. If I felt angry or fed up, I tried not to show it and eventually, by biting my lip – or, more often than not, feeling bad because I failed to bite it – I began to lose touch with strong, loud, multi-coloured feelings that were bound to be awful. Good feelings were bland, beige and unthreatening. I refrained from asking the one question about my grandparents I most wanted to ask. And then, one Saturday when I was eleven, I asked it.

Normally I took awkward questions to my mother, like could the rumour spread by the boys at school about sexual intercourse actually be true? I tackled her with that the following morning while she was cleaning the fireplace, and she confirmed it while still sweeping the ashes. Might, then, she and my father have another go at giving me a brother or sister? Apparently not.

This question, though, I had to ask my father. He was sitting on the bottom stair, his shoes lined up before him ready for their weekly clean. I dithered by the front door as he opened the tin of black Cherry Blossom. I waited till he'd done the first pair, the next pair, the last . . . 'Mummy's parents!' I blurted out. 'What happened to them?'

He scooped out a dollop of polish that even I could see was far too big and smeared it on, spreading it round and round. Some stuck to the laces. 'They were taken to Theresienstadt,' he muttered without looking up. 'We didn't know much during the war. The news didn't get through. It came afterwards.' He tried to wipe off the excess polish and got it all over his hands. Savage brushing followed. 'I hid the articles from Mum, of course.' Suddenly he stood up, leaving shoes and cleaning stuff in a heap, and went into the kitchen.

I found them whispering by the sink. My mother gave me the swiftest glance before continuing to scrape potatoes. 'It wasn't the worst camp,' she said. 'At least they weren't killed there.'

'So if they weren't killed,' the question burst out before I could stop it, 'how did they die?'

She put down the knife, her shoulders hunched and rigid. 'They had no food!' she said, her voice unusually shrill. 'They starved.'

Half an hour later we sat down to lunch. Fish, peas, new potatoes. I tried not to think of my grandparents' hands – those caressing hands I liked to imagine holding me close – reaching for scraps. Not the worst camp. Please let starving be better. I stared at my plate and chewed and chewed, but swallowing was hard.

* * *

And suddenly here they are, my starved and murdered grandparents, on my computer screen. I don't know how long I stare at their names, as if waiting for them to tell me what they're doing there. What are *Stolpersteine* anyway? I click and learn that the word is an invented one. It translates literally as 'stumble stones'. The artist who created them, Gunter Demnig, is my contemporary, born in Berlin in 1947, his work inspired by anger at the crimes committed by his father's generation. In an earlier project he had laid a ribbon of brass across Cologne to remind inhabitants of the deportation route of their former Roma and Sinti neighbours, neighbours they had meanwhile seemingly forgotten or chosen to forget.

Stolpersteine honour the individual. They are small, square, brass-covered blocks inserted in the pavement outside the front door of Holocaust victims' homes. Passers-by come upon them by chance and, by pausing to read the inscriptions, bring the murdered person back from oblivion to the very spot where they last lived and walked freely.

I wonder if someone is doing that right now for Max and Mally. What time is it? Nearly midnight here in London, the early hours of Monday morning in Berlin. Freezing cold, I should think. Bleibtreustrasse lit up and empty. I imagine a young couple wrapped around one another walking unsteadily along the street. She drops . . . what? Keys. Giggles. Tries to pick them up but he's quicker and holds them out of reach. She's still looking at the spot where the keys landed, a small brass square in the pavement etched with an inscription. She reads it and the one next to it. 'Look!' she says.

'Yes!' I shout at the screen. For the first time since they were deported, my grandparents have been brought back to their rightful home.

In 1995, when Gunter Demnig laid his first *Stolperstein*, it was an act of defiance. Anti-authority. Anti-bureaucracy. A cloak-and-dagger job. Drilling into the pavement without permission. But in the meantime town councils throughout Germany have embraced and supported the project. Anyone can commission *Stolpersteine* – a surviving relative, the current resident of a victim's house, anyone.

So who commissioned my grandparents' ones?

A contact number is given next to their entry on the local municipal website. The following morning I phone. A woman answers. I tell her my name, 'but that won't mean anything to you. My grandparents were Rychwalski, Max and Amalie, known as Mally . . .' I tail off. Why doesn't she say anything? 'So I wondered: who could have arranged this? I'm their only grandchild, you see. There isn't anyone else. The end of their line, you might say.'

I hear a sound like a deep sigh, as if she had been holding her breath until she could hold it no longer. 'We only just placed them!'

'But who are you?'

Another silence.

'Hello?'

No answer. She seems to have gone away.

Then a man comes to the phone. 'Knoll.'

Herr Knoll tells me . . . Quite honestly, I don't know what he's telling me. I'm trying to listen, but a voice in my head keeps butting in: 'This is incredible. Who'd have thought it? A complete stranger doing this for Max and Mally. Really, who'd have thought it?'

'Why did you pick my grandparents?' I eventually say out loud.

Herr Knoll must be repeating what I missed the first time round, and he is speaking very slowly. He is a Freemason. So was Max – that's news to me – both members of the same Lodge. A Lodge founded by gentiles and Jews. Many were victims of the Nazis. Herr Knoll is placing *Stolpersteine* for all of them. And their wives. 'If only I'd known about you. But there was no way I could have done.' He pauses. 'Have you any family photos? Can you send them? We only have names and dates. Birth and deportation. Sometimes of death. If known.'

Lists of absences. That's all he has. He needs to fill the emptiness. Of course he does. 'Yes, I'll send you photos.'

An hour later I receive an email from a Frau Lenck of the Coordination Office Stolpersteine Berlin.

'Dear Frau Kohnstamm, I handle *Stolpersteine* requests for the 12 districts of Berlin and liaise with volunteers who do the research in each one. Herr Knoll now looks after Wilmersdorf/Charlottenburg, the district where your grandparents used to live.'

She goes on to say that *Stolpersteine* are mushrooming throughout Germany, with more requests now received from the current residents of a building where victims once lived than from surviving relatives and descendants.

Amazing. After decades of silence, of keeping off the subject because those days are over and done with so let's sweep them under the carpet, Germans are now rolling up that carpet to take a good look. Ordinary people are getting to grips with the grim, haunted by their legacy. Until now I had been completely alone with mine.

'Please be assured,' Frau Lenck concludes, 'that in this city where your family suffered so much, they are not forgotten.'

I burst into tears.

PART 1:
BERLIN, JANUARY 2006

REACHING THROUGH
THE WALLPAPER

'There are known knowns. There are things we know we know.' At a press conference in 2002 Donald Rumsfeld, the then US Secretary of Defense, was fielding questions on Iraq's supposed possession of weapons of mass destruction. 'We also know there are known unknowns,' he went on. 'That is to say we know there are some things we do not know.' Then came the punchline: 'But there are also unknown unknowns, the ones we don't know we don't know.'

His much quoted, much mocked answer made perfect sense to me. It captured exactly my growing awareness of the fates of my grandparents and much of the shoebox family. Until I was eleven and tackled my father while he was cleaning his shoes, the world of In-Between was a colossal unknown unknown. Trying to steer clear – of what? – I sometimes unwittingly put my foot right in it and caused my mother to explode. In those early days of After she had not yet completely screwed down the lid on her cauldron of rage. But as soon as I had learned the bald facts, unknown unknown progressed to known unknown. From then on I was impelled to find out more, while keeping a weather eye open for signs of steam escaping from under my mother's lid.

I developed extraordinarily sensitive antennae, on high alert when my parents, huddled together, muttered in German. Until I was twelve and started learning it at school, German was the language of secrets from Before and In-Between – apart from a few children's stories and songs that they taught me – my mother taking short, tense drags on her cigarette, my father sitting on the edge of his armchair, crouched over the old Royal type-writer balanced on the pouffe while he pounded away on its keys.

After I had discovered Max and Mally's fate, I asked my mother if she still had any of their letters. 'No,' she replied, leading me to believe that in the three years between her arrival in London in December 1936 and the outbreak of war there had only been the odd phone call.

Many years later – in October 1987 to be exact – I learned that couldn't be true. An Israeli cousin had phoned me early one morning with the news that my uncle Ernst had suddenly died, and I immediately booked a flight to Tel Aviv. Neither of his sisters came to his funeral, although I wasn't entirely surprised. Both my mother and Charlotte used to grumble about how uncommunicative their brother was, lazy and difficult to be with. And by then my mother herself was frail. Yet their lack of sadness at his death, of any show of regret, I found shocking.

I was the closest family member there – Ernst had never married and had no children. In his flat after the burial I felt uncomfortable going through the belongings of such a private person. At the bottom of one cupboard I came across a folder entitled *Alte Briefe* (*Old Letters*). Inside was a sheaf of correspondence in *Sütterlin*.

Ludwig Sütterlin had developed his script from older cursive ones, and from the late nineteenth century it was widely taught in German schools. Apart from marked distinctions between upper- and lower-case letters, a lower-case letter might also be written differently depending where it appeared. For example, the 's' has three versions – for the beginning, middle and end of a word.

The only bits I could read were dates and signatures in modern script. *1938 . . . 1939 . . . Vater . . . Mutter . . .* I shivered. Max and Mally had come to meet me at last. That is when I realised: if their pre-war letters to Ernst had got through, my mother must also have received some.

Back in London I dithered. Had enough time passed? Should I show them to her? Might it even do her good by providing some catharsis? I picked one letter at random – but, oh boy, what a mistake that was. The very sight of their handwriting sent her scuttling deep inside herself. So I stuffed the letters into my own cupboard, and for the next eighteen years there they stayed, waiting for Herr Knoll to commission my grandparents' *Stolpersteine* and for me to stumble across them.

The deaths then came every two and a half years: my father in 1990, and then in 1992, aged seventy-seven, my mother. Hers was a slow decline from cancer. While she still had the strength, she began to talk about her childhood during the safe years before Hitler. I suggested recording her memories, and she was happy to talk on tape. As usual, I avoided the Nazi era, but then, to my surprise – and perhaps because she knew she didn't have much time left – she approached it herself. She described a much older cousin whom she had liked. 'Alfred wore a patch because he lost an eye in the First World War, and I kept trying to pull it when he played with me. He gave me an orange, and I thought it was a ball because I'd never seen an orange before. He married a country girl, and they had one child after another. All perished.'

Alfred Rychwalski

'Your family was really decimated,' I said.

'Yes, well, I worked out how many . . .' Out poured a list of parents, uncles, aunts and cousins. At one point she hesitated, and I prompted her: 'Aunt Marie?' She shook her head. 'She comes later. I do the uncles first.' In that moment I realised she was recalling them in strict order of age, first Max's side, then Mally's, slotting in the corresponding cousins as she went along. We counted a total of twenty-two. 'And that's only the immediate family,' she said. 'There were also many friends, people you were close to. Yes, quite a handful.'

Afterwards we sat together in a new kind of silence. I have never forgotten that silence, the privilege of sharing it with her. For the first and last time my mother had revealed to me her private litany of the murdered. Twenty-two members of her closest family.

Clearing the house after her death, I found not so much as a postcard from Max and Mally. All she had kept from Before was the trunk that had carried her own belongings from Berlin to London.

In February 1995 I flew to the USA to say goodbye to her sister Charlotte. Matter-of-fact as ever, even though terminally ill with cancer, she greeted me with two plastic bags bulging with papers. 'You're the family archivist,' was all she said. 'Here you are.' No explanation. No nothing. I flicked through her teenage diaries, mountains of love letters, some letters from my mother, a few impenetrable ones from Max and Mally, and their faded birth, marriage and, finally, death certificates issued after the war by the Red Cross. One month later Charlotte herself was dead.

Then a strange thing happened. Having spent my life straining to pick up clues about my grandparents and the shadow family, I found myself with a whole hodgepodge of material and couldn't bear to look at it. Most of the papers I was unable to fathom anyway, and now that everyone who could have guided me through them was gone, I didn't know what to do. Sometimes I took the folders out, but each time felt a great weight descend on my head. So much loss. Everyone dead. The ones I had known and those I was never able to know. Even my mother's silly schoolgirl notes to her sister didn't help. '*I'm sitting in boring biology. We're doing mammals with teats and suchlike. What's more, I've an enormous pimple on my chin – look!*', with a lurid illustration. I had loved it when that light-hearted mother popped up in my world too, dashing into the garden to hang toffees from branches of 'The Sweetie Tree' for my friend Michael who ran straight to it every time he came to tea. Meanwhile all I seemed able to do was stare at the papers, frozen, before pushing them back into the cupboard. Over the next ten years, there they stayed.

Now, though, my grandparents' fates no longer belong to me alone. Herr Knoll wants to know what kind of people they were. Isn't that what I've always wanted, too? Max and Mally deserve to be known at last as the *Menschen* – human beings – they used to be.

He's asked for photos. Photos are easy. I've been looking at their photos since childhood. I pick out one of Max and Mally's wedding day, another of the whole family by the seaside.

Next I go to the cupboard, then stop myself. Yet last night I hadn't hesitated. As soon as my grandparents flashed onto my screen, I ran to it without thinking and pulled out their death certificates to compare dates. But now, in the cold light of day, I can feel the old tightening of my stomach at the thought of unearthing it all. Do it fast, I tell myself. That's the only way.

I yank open the door and empty everything out. I'm looking for something in my uncle Ernst's papers that I know I once managed to read. My grandparents' last Red Cross message saying goodbye.

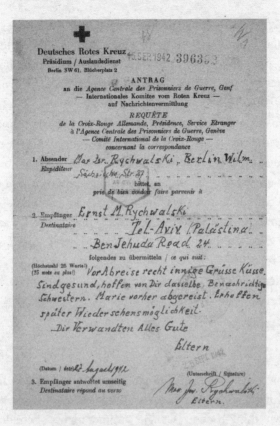

'*Before departure fondest greetings kisses. Are well, hope you too,*' Max wrote in clear, modern lettering shortly before they were shipped off to the city the Führer 'gave' the Jews, as a notorious 1944 propaganda film referred to Theresienstadt. '*Tell sisters. Marie left earlier. Hope possible meet again. Best wishes to you, relatives. Parents.*' Twenty-five words exactly, the maximum allowed by the Red Cross.

'*Are well . . . Marie left earlier . . .*', as if they were about to join Max's sister Marie on holiday. The Nazi Government had told them veterans of the Great War and the privileged elderly would continue living normal lives, breathing fresh air, playing cards, listening to music and dancing. They all wanted to believe this final lie. So they packed their best clothes and best shoes, bought train tickets as instructed and waited to be collected.

This is a first for me. I've dived into the cupboard's darkest corners, pored over the bleakest piece of paper and not been overwhelmed. Because at last I've got someone to share it with. An unknown couple in Berlin have seen fit to commemorate my grandparents. Am I simply to send information and leave it there? No, that won't do at all. Now that I've finally started moving, I can't stop. I shall have to send me.

I arrange a date to meet Herr Knoll and book a flight to Berlin.

*   *   *

A few weeks later, on a bright morning in January 2006, watching clouds cast shadows on a snow-capped forest far below, I think back to the light summer nights of childhood as, wide awake, I stared at the pink roses, green leaves and gold stems of my bedroom wallpaper. I would listen to our neighbour mow his lawn, my mother clatter saucepans in the kitchen, my father sing the *Pearl Fishers* duet with Jussi Björling or laugh as he poured drinks for friends. Life was continuing downstairs without me, so this was my time to get to know Max and Mally, and for them to get to know me.

Max I imagined as the God we learned about at school but who had no place in our home. The problem was, if he was all-seeing and all-powerful, he might see into my mind and know my every thought. That made me uncomfortable, especially as my mother had told me Max was stern and a stickler for tidiness. He was bound to disapprove of something. Had I left my knickers on the floor? I sat up and checked. No, the floor was clear.

Anyway, tidy or not, he'd love me if he could only know me, wouldn't he? After all, I was his only grandchild. And Mally looked like a cuddly sort of grandmother with a lap you could settle in.

I half shut my eyes till the wallpaper quivered. With just the right gap between upper and lower lids, if I peeped through my eyelashes, I could imagine the rose buds opening and the stems beginning to sprout tendrils that snaked down to the living room to draw my grandparents out of their shoebox and pull them back upstairs.

At first, I heard distant muttering in German and a cough from my grandfather. Some hesitation behind the roses. Finally the stems parted, they squeezed themselves into my room and looked around. I willed Max to hold out those large hands and sweep me up so I could stroke his beard. I imagined sinking into Mally's softness and kissing her round face. Again and again I reached out to them, but my fingers always closed on emptiness. Eventually, sadly, my grandparents would melt back through the roses and drift down to their shoebox.

* * *

This same January in 2006 the NASA spacecraft *Stardust* shoots a capsule back to earth to land in the desert of Utah. It is the end of a seven-year mission to collect particles from the tail of a comet. Analysis of the dust is about to challenge current scientific theories about the beginnings of the solar system – that comets were formed in its icy outer reaches – by revealing minerals that could only have been produced at its centre by the intense heat of the sun. A hot, turbulent whole, the scientists will conclude, had suddenly fragmented and been hurled out into space to form smaller, frozen bodies.

As the plane lands at Tegel Airport I am still unaware of *Stardust*'s mission, its collecting probe like a giant tennis racquet at the end of an outstretched arm sweeping through space to trap comet dust. All I know is my own world has shifted. For the first time ever, I have reached into icy nothingness and found my hand seized in a warm grasp.

MEETING MY GRANDPARENTS

I arrive at the hotel at lunchtime. Herr Knoll I shall meet tomorrow when he takes me on a tour of my family's addresses. This afternoon Frau Lenck from the Coordination Office Stolpersteine Berlin is going to introduce me to my grandparents' memorials.

With three hours to go before she is due and Bleibtreustrasse only a couple of streets away, I could easily go and find the stumble stones for myself, but my old default mode – do it alone because there's no other option – has become redundant. So I leave my case in the room and set off in the opposite direction in search of a lunch that doesn't need chewing.

A week ago, shortly after booking my flight, I had woken up in the middle of the night with throbbing toothache, three quadrants of my mouth vying for attention. Here we go, I thought. Why does some part of my body always have to protest when I'm dealing with something emotional? Ironic, yet fitting, that this time it's my teeth.

I owe my existence to dentistry. Dentistry enabled my mother to survive the Nazis. She was nearly eighteen and in her last year at school when the Nazis came to power. Barred from higher education, she did a secretarial course and found a job with a Jewish dentist who in 1936 emigrated to Willesden Green. He brought her over on a domestic visa – practically the only way single women were allowed into the UK – to cook, clean, look after his children and eventually work again in his surgery. It was in Willesden Green that she first clapped eyes on my father, or rather on his teeth.

Fortunately, I had managed to get an emergency appointment. But when the dentist injected, he missed his target, numbed my ear, and pain shot up to sinuses and down to feet. Had he drilled into my brain? Thank goodness by the time I boarded the plane my teeth had settled down.

At an intersection along the Kurfürstendamm a food stall wrapped in see-through plastic offers *Erbseneintopf mit Würstchen*. Just the job. I dive into the warm pocket of the stall for a steaming bowl of pea soup, chunks of sausage to be tackled carefully and a roll, fortunately soft.

'Just like my mother used to make,' I tell the elderly bottle blonde with bright red lipstick as she ladles it out.

'So enjoy it.' She speaks in the broad Berlin dialect my mother occasionally unleashed, its sharp vowels and the sardonic merging of consonants perfect for teasing me or for shouting at the cat when he was sick on the carpet.

The soup is tasty and I eke it out, in no hurry to exchange my warm bubble for the bitter cold. A glance at my watch tells me I still have plenty of time. Returning to the counter for a coffee, I can hardly miss a pyramid of chocolate-covered mounds right by the till. 'What's that?'

'Don't you know? *Janz lecker. Negerkuss.*'

Oh please. A negro's kiss? Even if it's not the 'n' word, even if it has always been called that, even if the image that leaps to my mind isn't in hers, within two hours of landing in Berlin my visit has a racist edge.

'Want to try? Here. My treat.' She plonks one on a plate.

'Er . . . *danke*.' I am searching for something else to say but can't quite get to it. Years ago, arranging student exchanges, I spoke German more frequently, but right now it feels as if I have put on a crumpled old jacket with a jumble of words stuck in creases that I need to shake out.

I continue sitting in the warm fug and watch passers-by dodge icy clumps of snow. Food, I think as I nibble the chocolate biscuit and picture our table at home awash with 'foreign muck', as a friend of my parents called it, not that that stopped him from tucking in. Salami, Westphalian ham and *Leberwurst* brought home by my father from his weekly pilgrimage to Schmidt's, the German deli in Charlotte Street. Our far-from-kosher home saw my mother serve up typical Jewish chicken soup with *matzo* dumplings one week, hefty German potato soup with *Knackwurst* the next, interspersed with good old English bacon and eggs at weekends. Although my father travelled to Germany on business, as a family we avoided the country. When a summer holiday in Switzerland saw us having to motor through a section to get there, we hardly stopped for breath until we reached the Swiss border. With one exception: an Aladdin's cave of a German kitchen shop where my mother stocked up on indestructible casseroles, a fearsome implement to shoot stones out of cherries, and a set of Arzberg blue-and-white-flowered crockery. When it came to cars, however, my parents were purists, my father buying exclusively British models – two Austins, one Wolseley and a Triumph – even though he yearned for a BMW. Only food, it seemed, familiar and comforting food remained untainted by the country from which it came. Food was the one acceptable way of spanning Before and After and must have played a major part in making me me.

'You're English,' my father once told me. 'Your mother and I were naturalised, which means we can only ever be British, but you're also English because you were born here. You're both English and British.' According to him, I arrived in the world with roots as firmly planted in the northwest London clay of our home as the roses. But did I? Surrounded by the aromas and tastes of childhood, I'm no longer so sure.

I leave the food tent. The icy air slaps my face and stings my lungs. Given that I owe my existence to Hitler as well as to dentistry, the familiarity of German food and language is troubling as well as nostalgic.

While waiting amongst a crowd of muffled-up Berliners to cross the road I look left and right. Not a car in sight, the red man illuminated for eternity, yet no one will move until he turns green. Suddenly I step out, solitary and defiant, as if reclaiming my Britishness.

Frau Lenck arrives bang on time. She is earnest and a little breathless from clearing the ice off Max and Mally's stumble stones to prepare them for our first meeting. I'm glad that I did not sneak a preview and spoil the moment.

It is dark by the time we turn down Bleibtreustrasse, an elegant street off Kurfürstendamm. Mounds of frozen snow glisten along the pavement. Boutique shop windows display exquisite clothes with no price tag: one fur-lined leather coat draped over an antique chair, a red chiffon dress floating in mid air.

Surely that huge pink-and-grey block of flats can't be

number 32? I was here briefly once before with my parents, thirty years ago when the city was still divided, but the building my memory dredges up was much smaller and shabbier. I don't remember shops on either side of the main entrance either. To the left is another boutique with designer clothes, to the right an art gallery. Above rise four storeys with delicate patterns chiselled in the stonework around the windows. The date 1909 is embossed on a stone shield above the door. Below, looking tiny in an expanse of dark grey pavement, are the two gleaming brass squares.

Frau Lenck stands to one side to give me my own moment with my grandparents. I walk towards them and feel . . . I don't know what I feel.

The last time I was here, in 1975, I was already an adult and rarely holidayed with my parents any more. But this was special. Two years previously my mother, stuffed to the gills with Valium, had returned to Berlin for the very first time since 1936 to complete the sale of this block of flats. No sooner was the contract signed than, much to her own surprise, she began to enjoy herself, and both she and my father wanted to come back with me.

We did the zoo, nature, art, political satire in a few cabarets and crossed to the East to see a Brecht play. The one thing we steered clear of was family history. Except one day my father said: 'We're near Bleibtreustrasse.' I believe we stopped further along on the other side of the street and shuffled about for an uncomfortable few minutes. Maybe I remember the building as being smaller because we saw it at an angle. I don't know what I felt then either, other than disbelief actually to be here and unease as to how it would affect my mother. My own emotions? They never had a chance to get going because the only person really entitled to feel anything and show me the way revealed absolutely nothing.

Wording on stumble stones is carefully chosen to quash euphemism and make up for the Nazi massaging of language to cover up and mollify – for *protective custody* read *incarceration*; for *resettled* read *expelled*. I walk up to my grandparents' *Stolpersteine* and bend over them. *Max . . . Amalie . . . murdered . . .* The blunt word *ermordet* leaves no room for quibbling about whether starving is better than gassing or shooting.

AMALIE. Known to the family as Mally. My grandmother. *YEAR OF BIRTH 1878. DEPORTED 1942. MURDERED 13.11.1942.*

I take a deep breath. A wave surges up from my belly, then stops in mid surge.

Max. YEAR OF BIRTH 1864. How can I have a grandfather born almost 150 years ago? It's so remote. Yet I did, and here he is. Was. *MURDERED 31.01.1943.*

I gulp in more air, bend lower over both *Stolpersteine,* but the wave still won't break. Yet I know it can. It did so once at Yad Vashem in Jerusalem. I was a student, on my first visit to Uncle Ernst and Israel. The simplicity of the memorial, a plaque for each concentration camp, affected me as nothing else ever had. As I stood by the Theresienstadt plaque, tears spurted out, a hot stream rolling down my cheeks that took me completely by surprise. Violent sobbing followed. I was horrified. It made no sense. How could I be crying, and so noisily, for grandparents I'd never known? Pull yourself together, I told myself, but it was no use. The wall separating In-Between from After had suddenly been breached. Only that was half a lifetime ago.

I imagine Max and Mally walking home and pausing at this very spot to take out their keys. As I stare at the two brass squares in the pavement, I want to feel more connected to them, but don't. Not really. And yet. And yet. This is very different from the time my parents and I stole a look from across the street. I have a right to be here now. Because their names are inscribed for all to see. Because I am their only surviving descendant. Because their lives – and deaths – have affected me deeply.

'Hello,' I say at last, 'it's me.'

Frau Lenck joins me. We stand in silence for a moment, then go up to the front door to peer through glass panels into the entrance of Max, Mally and my mother's last family home. At the end of a marble hallway another door leads out into a courtyard. The block, much bigger than it appears from the street, must have four wings – front, back and two at the side. Judging by the rows of round, brass buzzers, it contains about forty flats. There seems little chance of discovering which was theirs.

There is nothing more we can do here. And yet we are both reluctant to leave, as if doing so might break this fragile connection to my grandparents.

Sitting in the warmth of a local café we talk about the distortion of language; how the word *Zigeuner* (gypsy) became unacceptable after the Nazis perverted it to mean subhuman. I mention the chocolate *Negerkuss*.

'A woman of her generation wouldn't have realised. It's not PC, but not meant maliciously.'

Frau Lenck tells me she has only recently started working on the *Stolpersteine* project. Shyly, she pushes a package across the table. I unwrap it to find a collection of poems by Mascha Kaléko, a Jewish refugee who had difficulty adjusting to life in exile. A bookmark indicates 'The Street Is Called Bleibtreu', a poem inspired by her return to Berlin forty years after fleeing her home in this very street. As she stands outside, she hears the rattle of the S-Bahn and recalls the Nazis in the bar next door bellowing out the Horst Wessel song. The last four lines read:

> *Was blieb davon?*
> *Die rosa Petunien auf dem Balkon.*
> *Der kleine Schreibwarenladen*
> *Und eine alte Wunde, unvernarbt.**
> (What's left of it?
> The pink petunias on the balcony.
> The little stationery shop,
> And an old wound that never healed.)

I try to imagine meeting a public servant in similar circumstances in the UK, but there can be no similar circumstances. The offer to accompany me had seemed to me to be a kind gesture from the stumble stones office, but this is different, personal, a gift from someone of my generation reaching across the divide filled with the ghosts of my family and of her whole country.

On my way back I dawdle outside number 32. The street is busy with people hurrying home from work. I glance up at the façade, wondering which windows my grandparents looked out of and who lives there now.

---

* Please see Appendix for full poem text.

'*An old wound that never healed.*' I take out a tissue, wipe Max and Mally's stumble stones and stand amongst the hurly-burly, enclosing their names between my feet.

* * *

The extended family I grew up with was small and almost exclusively my father's. He grew up in Nuremberg – epicentre of the Nazi rallies, where local Jews were known and targeted. As a law student in the 1920s he had learned to box so he could fight off Brownshirts, 'although' he added, 'I usually ran away as they hunted Jews in packs.' After graduating, he worked for the family hop business – not helpful for securing work and a visa to the UK, or indeed to anywhere else. His brother Otto, a doctor, had come to the UK as early as 1933 to requalify before setting up as a GP in Willesden Green, around the corner from Dr Rosenkranz's dental practice.

As my father and I stomped across Hampstead Heath in the safe world of After, he would describe tramping the streets of London in search of work while time ticked by and his three-month temporary visa elapsed, forcing him to return to Nuremberg again and again. I imagined myself with him at 6 a.m. on that damp, misty morning in September 1937, as he pushed his way through a crowd of commuters to board the train for his final journey to England. This time he would be allowed to stay, which was just as well, because in desperation he had tried to smuggle money out of Germany and been betrayed. Barely an hour later the police arrived at the family home and hammered on the door to arrest him.

Compared to my father's tales of escape and of his own parents' eventual last-minute flight to England, the fate of my mother's family was glossed over, so I assumed there was something embarrassing, even shameful about it. Perhaps Max and Mally only had themselves to blame for ignoring the signs that had been glaringly obvious to their children who got out. Ferreting out what had happened to them would be my way of trying to make sense of it. But the opposite was the case for my parents. Mentioning it brought discomfort and a quick change of subject. Mentioning it was in bad taste. We were British now, after all. Stiff upper lip and all that.

Those members of my mother's family who had escaped and survived were spread around the world – Israel, Belgium, Switzerland, Brazil, Peru and the USA. When I was a child they wrote frequently, their envelopes plastered with exotic flowers and birds-of-paradise on stamps which I collected in my album, but we rarely, if ever, saw the writers who had stuck them on in the first place.

Of Max and Mally's three children – Ernst, Charlotte and Hilda – my mother was the youngest. I loved to watch her put on a glamorous evening dress for a night at the opera with my father. Just like Cinderella going to the ball, unlike most days when she was plain old Cinders cleaning out the grate.

My aunt Charlotte, on the other hand, was permanently glamorous. From the late 1940s, before moving to New York with husband number three in the early 1950s, she lived in Paris and periodically exploded through our front door in London in a cloud of Guerlain's Mitsouko, dangling earrings, a fox fur and carrying a hat box. I followed her everywhere, even standing guard outside the toilet in case she disappeared. As she peed I learned my first words of French:

> *J'fais pipi sur le gazon*
> *pour emmerder les coccinelles,*
> *J'fais pipi sur le gazon*
> *pour emmerder les papillons.*
> (I'm doing a wee-wee on the lawn
> to piss off the ladybirds,
> I'm doing a wee-wee on the lawn
> to piss off the butterflies.)

Charlotte

Until I was twelve, all I knew of my uncle Ernst was that he lived in Israel and every winter sent us a crate of Jaffa grapefruit. Then he finally came to visit. Unlike his slim sisters, who resembled one another but no one else in the shoebox, Ernst looked like Mally – fair-skinned, shortish and round. I had hoped for the same hilarity to break out as when the sisters got together, but no such luck. He was quiet and tiptoed about the house, yet the air crackled with tension, causing my mother to keel over with migraines and my father to haul Ernst off for long walks on Hampstead Heath.

Ernst

The one constant presence in my childhood from my mother's side of the family was 'Auntie' Hedy, a cousin who worked as a bookkeeper and lived in a room in someone else's flat – 'poor soul, she's had a hard life'. She did exquisite embroidery, which she spectacularly failed to teach me, but she more than made up for that by giving me her love. We were now, after all, her closest family in the UK. Much older than my mother but a child at heart, Hedy and I would head for the top deck of the bus to get the full force of the Christmas lights along Regent and Oxford Streets. Our annual panto outing to the Golders Green Hippodrome delivered yet more bling, with Arthur Askey as the Dame in rhinestone-encrusted glasses.

Max's family was huge. He was one of six brothers and two sisters born and brought up in Tirschtiegel (now called Trzciel), a small market town on the Obra river in East Prussia, a part of Germany that after 1945 would be incorporated into Poland.

Mally's much smaller family consisted of one sister (Auntie Hedy's mother), who died before the war, and a brother, Fritz, a kind man with pebble-lensed glasses and the same round face as Mally. He lived in Hamburg with his fragrant wife Olga, who – my mother said – left a trace of freshness as she wafted through their house.

I have my mother to thank for those family sketches, recorded in our sessions at the end of her life. When I read the transcripts now, the remark I made that prompted her to reveal her private litany of the murdered troubles me. 'Your family was really decimated,' I said. *Your* family. Not *our* family.

I have been in Berlin for less than a day, yet already suspect this short trip is the start of a longer journey. Ever since stumbling across Max and Mally's stones, I have occasionally had the sensation you get in the sea when swimming through a warm current. It has just happened again with Frau Lenck. As if the people I am meeting, and have yet to meet, are rooting for me, as if they instinctively understand what I'm struggling towards because they, too, have grown up hungry for information. Information that was withheld, suppressed, hidden and is only now, especially since the fall of the Wall, beginning to resurface.

Maybe there is more to my visit than just meeting my grandparents' *Stolpersteine* and finding a way into the contents of my cupboard. I sense wider horizons. Not that I have the faintest idea what lies beyond them. All I know is that being here feels right. As right as it did to sit quietly with my dying mother after she had voiced the extent of her losses, when I had my first fleeting sensation those losses might also be mine.

CONNECTIONS

Next morning, while waiting for Herr Knoll to pick me up from the hotel, I notice the receptionist keeps glancing at me. She is young, startlingly pale and comes from Eastern Europe.

'Have you been to the Holocaust Memorial?' she asks eventually.

'Not yet. I'm going later.'

'I thought so,' she says, satisfied.

My father used much the same tactics in the 1960s when we holidayed abroad, walking, swimming, breathing the pure air of the Alps and Dolomites. Hearing couples their age speak German he would strike up a breezy conversation – 'Wonderful scenery. D'you know the area well?' – to unearth their background. With former refugees there was an instant understanding. With others he sniffed the air for essence of Nazi, although what could they do to him now? In any case, not everyone had supported the Third Reich. He never forgot the wife of a schoolfriend who had waved him off to England, a gesture that could have got her locked up. But as there was no knowing what these people might have done, best give them a wide berth for my mother's sake.

The receptionist tells me that her family left Ukraine

because of worsening post-Chernobyl contamination, uncontrolled selling of vegetables at local markets, more and more cancers. And here, she warns me, anti-Semitism is once again on the rise.

Yet Berlin has become her refuge.

Everything in this city is on a grand scale: buildings, streets, Wolfgang Knoll's car, the man himself. His large frame, bursting with energy, seems to contain an even bigger person struggling to escape. Even his hair is ebullient, each white strand straining to break free. He is about to celebrate his seventieth birthday and keen to tell me that both Mally and he were born in Fürstenwalde-an-der-Spree, about 50 km southeast of Berlin. There he spent his boyhood alone with his mother while his father fought on the Eastern Front and was captured by the Russians. One day at school in the early 1950s he wrote an enthusiastic piece about Speakers' Corner, and a fellow pupil denounced him to the East German police. They pulled him in for questioning and upon release he fled to West Berlin. He was sixteen years old.

It is a short drive to Emser Strasse, a quiet tree-lined street, and we park in front of the Freemasons' headquarters, a heavy grey structure that also survived Allied bombing. Herr Knoll strikes me as an unusual mason. Admittedly I know zilch about it but assume the organisation to be steeped in conformity, ritual and secrecy, whereas Herr Knoll is outspoken and impulsive.

'Why did you become a mason?' I ask.

'I thought any organisation the Nazis banned must be good.' From his briefcase he produces two sheets of paper and hands them to me.

His Lodge, Zum Spiegel der Wahrheit, was established exactly one hundred years earlier. 'Look into the mirror to seek the truth and become a better person' seems to be the general idea. The founding document, dated January 1906, contains the signatures of all those who set it up, and Max was one of them. I follow his signature with my finger, the initial 'M' and capital 'R' a confident flourish of whirls and tails.

'How did you find all this out? That my grandfather was a member? That he and the others were killed?'

'After the Wall came down you could at last get hold of former GDR files that had been taken to Moscow. I discovered the Nazis had killed eleven Jewish *Brüder* and seven of their wives. Then I read in the paper about Gunter Demnig's project and decided that was how I wanted to commemorate them.'

We tour displays of portraits, banners, robes and insignia, baffling to me but as familiar to Herr Knoll as they would have been to my grandfather. Our perspectives could not be more different, yet we are united by a similar compulsion: to bring human beings out of the shadows and back to their world.

Each Berlin district has its own council, and Wilmersdorf-Charlottenburg is the one where Max, Mally and many of the murdered had lived. When no one would take responsibility for the stumble stones, Herr Knoll formed a project group.

'The council sent me a contract. It was a farce. They wanted me to sign a third-party liability clause in case someone slipped and injured themselves. We tried to explain that you stumble *upon* the stones, not *over* them;

they are flush with the pavement, they won't trip you up. But the council continued to interpret "stumble" literally. They were afraid they would be held responsible for accidents and sued. Meanwhile relatives were coming from the USA, Britain and South Africa to dedicate stumble stones they had sponsored. In the end I wrote to the council and said: "The survivors and their descendants know their relatives were murdered thanks to the efficiency of German bureaucracy. Now German bureaucracy is preventing those victims from being commemorated.'" Pregnant pause. 'I immediately got a call asking me to come in.'

'I wish I could have been a fly on the wall when they read your letter.'

He grins.

As we leave the building, Herr Knoll points out a nearby stumble stone and explains how much research goes into each one. 'You can't use the last known address. That's probably where the victim was forced to live before deportation. It must be their real home, where they could still come and go freely.'

'How do people react when they see one in front of their house?'

'It's varied. I often accompany Gunter Demnig. On one occasion he needed to drill into the pavement, so I went into the house to ask if we could plug in the extension lead. "Stumble stones? Of course. Come in. Would you like tea? Coffee?" But it's not always like that. There was a woman in Kreuzberg who came out of her house during a dedication ceremony. "Hasn't enough money already been spent on the Jews? And now these stones? Unbelievable." I said to her: "While people like you are still around, there'll always be a need."' Herr Knoll sighs, then bursts out: 'And it's not only the Nazis who object. The Munich Jewish community refuses to let *Stolpersteine* be placed in the pavement, even when survivors make a request. Apparently it's "disrespectful" if people tread on them!'

He yanks the car door open in exasperation. As I get in, I drop my pen under the seat. Fishing around for it, I pull out a truncheon. Herr Knoll glances at it and shrugs. 'Some get defaced. There've been threats.'

So is the pale receptionist right? Is anti-Semitism once more on the rise? We drive off in silence.

'Nazi shits!' he shouts, his eyes full of tears.

We bowl along the massively wide Strasse des 17. Juni, circle the victory column in the middle of the Grosser Stern roundabout and keep heading west. Skirting the Tiergarten, an expanse of green mainly hidden under a snowy blanket, we arrive at my mother's birthplace, 22 Siegmunds Hof, to find it no longer exists. The last house in the street is number 20. Three trees and a couple of parked cars occupy the space where number 22 used to be.

Max and Mally had thought their family was complete until, in 1915, with the First World War in full swing, my mother came along. 'The station was opposite the balcony. You could see the trains,' my mother told me when recalling her first childhood home. And sure enough, directly across the road from the trees is the raised S-Bahn with a sign on the bridge: *Tiergarten.* 'I was only a baby during the First World War, but they told me the trains stopped running at night to save power and they couldn't sleep because it was too quiet.'

I picture the balcony amongst the topmost branches. The maid had told Charlotte if she placed two sugar cubes on it, Mally would have twins. Some days later, feeling hungry and deciding one baby would do, she retrieved one cube – by now covered in soot from the surrounding chimneys – and ate it. 'Which is why I'm not a twin.'

Nine-year-old Ernst, excited by real soldiers – much better than his toy ones – jumped up and down on that same balcony to shout 'Hoorah!' at the Kaiser leading his troops in a deafening clatter of hooves and boots over the cobbles below. Twenty years later, by then a graphic artist, he took his collection of First World War posters to the Promised Land, where I found them after his death. They are chillingly fine examples of his profession. Like Kitchener, whose pointing finger exhorted Brits that *'Your country needs you!'*, heroic German soldiers stand amongst flames and proclaim: *Dein Vaterland ist in Gefahr – Melde Dich!* (*Your Fatherland is in danger! Enlist!*). And enlist they did, willingly, both sides losing a whole generation but only one suffering defeat. Enter the far right and a different pointing finger. Who to blame for German humiliation, inflation, unemployment? Who else but the 2,000-year-old scapegoat, the Jew.

My grandparents, steeped in the language and literature of Goethe and Schiller and proud of their German nationality, identified with its values and *Kultur*. Twenty years before Hitler confiscated their valuables, they were content with an iron medal in exchange for gold to fund the Kaiser's last stand. The inscription reads: *Gold gab ich zur Wehr, Eisen nahm ich zur Ehr* (*I donated gold for our defence and was honoured by iron*). As wave upon wave of young men leaped from Ernst's posters into the trenches, as Max and Mally lay awake to the sound of no trains, their milky new daughter slept.

GOLD
GAB ICH ZUR
WEHR EISEN
NAHM ICH ZUR
EHR

Honoured by iron

On the bridge a train thunders to a standstill and brings me back to the present. Herr Knoll is waiting patiently nearby, just as Frau Lenck did yesterday while I bent over my grandparents' *Stolpersteine*.

Next we head to the district where Max and his sister Marie, also his business partner, had their tie factory. Max had founded the company together with Marie's husband, and when he died suddenly she took his place. Ten years younger than her brother, she seems to have injected new energy into the business and become its driving force.

'Aunt Marie ran the workroom and Max organised the salesmen,' my mother recalled in our taped talks. 'Mally might take Charlotte or me along when she needed material. Aunt Marie liked seeing us nieces as she only had sons. She dyed her hair red and wore make-up. In those days, a woman no longer young . . . she was noticeable.'

Wasn't it unusual, I wondered, that a Victorian patriarch such as Max should be in business with a woman, even if she was his sister? 'They got on well,' my mother explained, 'plus she was a very good businesswoman.' In the end, that is what counted for Max. If you showed flair and were go-ahead, you earned his respect.

I imagine my human dynamo of a great-aunt supervising the factory, three sons and her chauffeur Otto – Max travelled by public transport – a woman who more than held her own in a man's world.

Marie

I know before we arrive that Neue Friedrichstrasse, the street with the factory, no longer exists. Pulverised in the war, it was rebuilt under a new name. Herr Knoll slows down, but we don't stop. There is no way of telling where the workroom and offices once stood.

Our third destination is where red-haired Marie lived, in Schöneberg's Bavarian quarter. Another number 22, this time Heilbronner Strasse. I hope we find this building still standing, as it must have been splendid, with white marble walls and a glass lift that slowly carried you up five floors. If you wanted to sit down during the ride, you could perch on a red velvet-covered bench and enjoy the view.

The streets around here are quiet. Green spaces where nannies used to wheel large prams. But once again, no joy. A modern housing development has replaced turn-of-the-century buildings. The Allies must have done another thorough job on the whole street, and now it's hard to tell where Marie's house stood.

Herr Knoll produces another sheet of paper.

'What's this?'

'A list of those deported from your great-aunt Marie's house. It was a *Judenhaus*.'

Before deportation the Nazis forced Jews to move into designated houses so as to mop them up more easily. A letter from Charlotte that had puzzled me during one quick foray into the cupboard now makes sense. '*I went hot and cold when I heard that Jews are obliged to move into specified areas,*' she wrote to Ernst in the summer of 1939. '*For once they've forced them into ghettos, they can unleash real pogroms and burn down their houses without endangering a single pure-blooded German. So I don't understand how Aunt Marie can still be in possession of her house, as are some other Jews.*'

Not even clear-sighted Charlotte foresaw the system and scale of annihilation. Seventy-two Jews passed through Marie's house on their way to death, including its 'noticeable' red-haired owner. Suddenly I no longer mind that it was blown to kingdom come.

In the car I show Herr Knoll copies of a few of my grandparents' letters in the hope he might speed-read them, but he shakes his head. 'I never learned that old script. Barbara can read it, though. My wife. Leave them with me.'

He drives me back to Max and Mally's *Stolpersteine*. At least one family address still exists. And even though the others don't, travelling between the absences has helped give me a sense of their lives here. Max and his sister, far sighted when it came to business, remained resolutely blind to the growing threat of Hitler. Their success enabled them to buy this block of flats, which eventually they were forced to sell. The *Schwanefeld'sche Sterbekasse* (Schwanefeld Burial Society) snapped it up. What an appropriate name. The Insurers of Death.

We turn down Bleibtreustrasse and park. Herr Knoll gives me yet more papers: annual lists of the block's inhabitants before and during the war. I see that Max and Marie remained the registered owners until 1939, when the Insurers of Death took over.

We get out of the car. Saturday lunchtime, the street full of shoppers. My grandparents' brass plaques wink in the sunshine. Herr Knoll and I stand together and look down at them.

'If you had searched any earlier, you wouldn't have found anything,' he says. 'I only uploaded the information the evening before you phoned.'

'Exactly when I looked. Sunday 4th December.'

And that's not the only coincidence.

'I wanted to ask you about this,' he says, handing me a page of testimony from Jerusalem's Yad Vashem database of Holocaust victims. 'I found it on the internet. Do you know her?'

On the sheet of paper are details of the deportation and murder of Marie's eldest son, Manfred. His daughter Hannelore, who survived the Holocaust, had filled in the form by hand. '*Greiffenhagen, Manfred. Date of birth: July 20, 1896*.' The next column is headed '*Approx. age at death*'. Manfred was forty-eight. Approximately. No way of knowing exactly. Sucked into nothingness, just the way the Nazis liked it. '*Place of death*: *Dachau*.' His daughter knew that much, if not the manner or date of his death – she had written '*gassed or died?*' with a question mark. Her lettering is round and open, almost childlike: '*deported from Holland (Westerbork) never came back*'.

'Hannelore is Marie's granddaughter,' I explain. 'I never met her. After the war she moved to Texas. As a surviving heir of Marie, she was also part-owner of this block of flats. But her side of the family disagreed about the sale of the building, and afterwards there was a rift. I didn't even know she was still alive.' I suddenly notice the date on the testimony. 'Good grief, Herr Knoll! Look when she did this.'

Together we pore over her signature and the date – 3 December 2005.

'One day before you and me!'

Rooted to the pavement, like two rocks in a river of pedestrians, we stare at one another in disbelief. Actually, that isn't strictly true. I'm the stunned one. Herr Knoll's eyes, clear as clear, don't express any surprise whatsoever. Maybe this happens to him all the time.

'Can you send me a family tree?' he asks at last. 'I'd like to place everyone.' He holds out his hand. When I shake it, he bows. I don't think anyone has bowed to me since a teenage bout of ballroom dancing. What an unusual mixture he is; formal, frank and unexpected – who else keeps a truncheon under their car seat?

'Herr Knoll . . . Wolfgang . . . do you think we could call each other by our first names?'

He grins, squashes me in an enormous hug, gets back in his car and drives off.

I stay to take photos of the building. While dodging between passers-by to get a clear view, I see a young man let himself in and rush up to him before the door shuts. 'Please may I step inside? You see those two *Stolpersteine*? They were my grandparents.'

'Come in, come in.'

Soon I am sipping tea in Hans and Dieter's exquisite flat, one of those at the front with a bay window overlooking the street. The doors are high and wide with delicate carvings and etched brass handles. They offer me a ride in the wood-panelled lift. 'It's the original one. See the date? 1908. Your grandparents will have gone up and down in it. Do you want to see the garage?'

I want to see everything.

The garage takes up the entire basement and is empty apart from dustbins, a few cars and a rack of bicycles. 'In the war they used it as an air raid shelter,' Dieter says. Then he points to a large concrete patch in the brick wall. 'They broke through to the house next door in case of a direct hit. The hole was filled in after the war.'

A steep cobbled ramp leads up to street level. I shiver. The whole space feels hostile.

The door rumbles open and a man comes down for his bicycle. Dieter introduces us and explains my relationship to the stumble stones.

'Oh right. An old lady lived opposite me in the side wing till a few years back. Frau Steinke. She was also here in the war.' He busies himself attaching a neat little briefcase to his bike. 'She worked for Goebbels. Looked after his kids. His housekeeper or something . . .'

Goebbels? Hitler's propaganda minister? Had I heard right? I look at Dieter. Judging by our synchronised jaw drop, yes I had.

'Her husband serviced cars down here. And not only cars, if you get my meaning.' He pauses to make sure we do. 'Frau Steinke and Frau Goebbels had the same husband troubles. Oh yes, she told me all about it.' And off he cycles.

That night I can't sleep for thinking of Frau Steinke, a tiny cog in the smooth running of the Nazi machine, passing Max and Mally on her way to work for Joseph, Magda and their perfect blond, blue-eyed children, destined to be poisoned, one by one, by their parents in Hitler's bunker.

In RAF bombing raids, Jews not allowed to shelter in a segregated part of the garage had to take pot luck in the hallway. 'This is fairly safe if a bomb hits the roof, since the chances are that it will not penetrate to the ground floor,' the American journalist William L. Shirer reported for *Life* magazine in October 1941. 'But experience has shown that it is the most dangerous place to be in the entire building if a bomb lands in the street outside. Here, where the Jews are hovering, the force of the explosion is felt most and the greatest number of bomb splinters strike.'

I imagine Frau Steinke hurrying home. She's late. Brushing all those blond heads takes time, but she prides herself on making the children's hair shine to please their father when he returns from another busy day promoting total war.

The deafening vibration of bombers drowns out the sirens as she lets herself in. The hallway is full of people struggling to be first out into the courtyard and down the steps to the garage. What are those Jews still doing here? High time the building was cleansed of the lot of them. She elbows Max and Mally to one side to reach safety. At least in an air raid she won't find that husband of hers at it with some woman in the back of a car.

Or did the Steinkes only move in after my grandparents were forced out?

I switch on the light and fetch Wolfgang's lists of inhabitants. Herr Steinke already rented the garage in 1939, the year the Insurers of Death 'bought' the building. Max is listed as resident till 1941. So, if Herr Steinke decided who could enter his kingdom during air raids, I don't rate my grandparents' chances of shelter.

It took twenty years after the end of the war for the Insurers of Death to restore the block of flats to the surviving heirs. Tenants came and went, but not Frau Steinke, still living there when Max and Marie's heirs sold the building, a sitting tenant when the new owner sold off individual flats. And on she stayed. On and on.

I picture her blond hair fading and body growing frailer. With failing eyesight and no one much to talk to, she pushes her chair up against the window and waits for the young man who lives opposite to come home from work. As he crosses the courtyard she'll wave and ask him in for a coffee. Normally she keeps quiet about those long-ago times which now seem oddly like yesterday. Most people wouldn't understand, but he's different. She'd like to tell him about the Führer dropping by and playing with the Goebbels children. Normal family life. Politics didn't come into it. She might even show him her letters from dear Frau Goebbels.

That day in 1975 when my parents and I stood uneasily on the other side of the street, Frau Steinke could well have passed us. Haven't I been searching for a link from Before to After? A bridge from Max and Mally to me?

Not this one.

TILTING

Ten thousand bronze discs are scattered over the floor as though discarded. Ten thousand faces, their mouths open in a silent scream. 'You can walk on them,' the guide says.

'I'll do no such thing.'

Only later do I learn that that is the point. The artist, Menashe Kadishman, wants visitors to make his installation *Fallen Leaves* screech.

I am in the Jewish Museum and, even with the guide, completely disorientated. The voids and zigzags of Daniel Libeskind's architecture are only partly to blame. My problem isn't alienation, it's recognition. I've walked slap bang into my cupboard and feel horribly at home. Closely written letters in that illegible *Sütterlin* handwriting, formal bride and groom photos, family groups on the beach and relaxing around café tables, passports stamped with a swastika and red 'J', Red Cross messages: 'goodbye goodbye goodbye, we were here, we existed, remember us . . .'

My hour's guiding over, I remain in front of a display I am unable to take in. What floor is this? Let me return to *Fallen Leaves*, where unsteadiness is the only normal response. That is what I need to explore. How else can I advance from the sidelines of the unknown and reach the centre . . . of what? Of feeling at home and not horribly so.

A man in a grey suit comes over. 'Are you a tourist?'

'Not exactly.'

'I thought not.'

I gabble something about following in my grandparents' footsteps.

'I last came here when the museum was still empty,' he says. 'It was somehow more impressive then.'

'I wish I'd seen it like that.'

'I'd like to talk to you . . .'

So do I. I want very much to talk to this solid, suited, grounded man, to sit down and explore connections between Before and After, between his experience and mine. 'We could have a cup of coffee,' I suggest.

'. . . only I've got to catch a flight to Frankfurt.'

Once again I am on my own, tilting.

A poster advertises a one-man show for that afternoon in the museum's main auditorium: a South African comic whose mother also escaped from Berlin. I reckon I could do with some light relief in English and buy a ticket. Then I go in search of lunch.

What a desolate area. There's nothing much open on a Sunday. All the cafés are shuttered. Eventually I settle on a gloomy Eastern European restaurant. On the table is a vase of misshapen red carnations. I look at them more closely; they are crocheted. Who the hell crochets carnations? Here's a skill you missed out on, Auntie Hedy. And so, thank goodness, did I.

Auntie Hedy tried really hard to teach me to sew, and I tried just as hard to get her to tell me stories. We both failed. But there was one story she did tell me, one that I never forgot.

I was six when Auntie Hedy gave me my first glimpse into In-Between. She had stayed the night, and in the morning I climbed into her bed with my book. She received me in her winceyette nightie and pink bedjacket with satin ribbons sewn on in perfect, tiny stitches – a far cry from Charlotte's silky shifts and dangling tortoiseshell earrings which she assured me she slept in. 'You want a story, do you?' Auntie Hedy's eyes were angry, and the book stayed shut. 'Then I'll tell you about my brother.'

Brother? I didn't know she had one. His name was Walter and he belonged to the shadow people who inhabited Before but not After. As she talked, his shadow came closer. In the late 1930s, with the Nazi net closing in, he had sought refuge in Belgium. By then Auntie Hedy cooked and cleaned in posh English houses and saved as much money as possible to send to him. Then the Germans invaded Belgium.

I see Walter's room in the attic of a tall, narrow house with brown lino on the floors. He's waiting for the postman. He needs money badly. He doesn't even have enough for a stamp to stick on his letters to her. I hear thunderous banging on the front door. That can't be the postman. Voices bellow in German. Feet stomp up the stairs. Walter stands at his attic window, trapped. Below him the roof slopes steeply, shiny in the rain. Voices and feet get closer. The door is wrenched open. Men in gleaming black boots trample Auntie Hedy's brother Walter underfoot. I watch him being dragged away. I watch his hand reach out to clutch the banisters, let go and disappear.

I sat very still when she had finished her story. Deep in my belly I knew I shouldn't have heard it and must never ever mention it because, if I did, my father would get cross with her. He might shout. Worst of all, the fragile boat in which my mother and I sailed through every day could capsize.

It was unpredictable. Some days my mother was fine. Other days would start fine, then suddenly change. I grew expert at watching out for the clouds, something no one else seemed to do. My friend Philippa certainly didn't. Our mothers had met before the war and were best friends, so Philippa and I spent a lot of time together.

One day my mother took us to Madame Tussauds. 'Show that man our tickets,' she said, pointing at an official in peaked cap and burgundy uniform swathed in gold braid. When he didn't budge, we looked at him more closely, then at my mother peering round a pillar, grinning.

I failed to see the point of waxworks. Once you'd looked, that was that. They didn't do anything. But I remember that day. I remember it really well. It had something to do with the Chamber of Horrors. We'd seen just about everything, and my mother was ready to leave. 'But we haven't been to the Chamber of Horrors yet,' Philippa said.

The thought both frightened and excited me. Would there be severed heads? Pools of gore?

'Can we see it now?' she asked.

We were on a staircase. That's when I noticed something was wrong. My mother had stopped moving.

'Auntie Hilda?' Philippa said.

Transfixed halfway up. People passing us.

'Please?'

Shut up, Philippa.

'Can we?'

Shut up shut up shut up! I was desperate to break the spell, for my mother to be all right again.

That moment in Madame Tussauds came back to me as I began to grapple with how the reality of Max and Mally's fates had slowly dawned on me. I suppose it was the very idea of horrors that my mother couldn't face. Goodness knows what horrors she herself had imagined and then made herself forget.

I wondered if Philippa also remembered that moment and emailed her to ask, although I wasn't too hopeful. To my surprise she replied: 'I remember Madame Tussauds. Nothing about the Chamber of Horrors, but of being on the landing.'

Immediately I pictured a turn in the wide staircase covered in a red carpet. I emailed her again: 'Tell me more.'

'All of a sudden we had to go back down and leave,' she replied. 'What I remember is seeing carpet.'

How extraordinary. I had not mentioned the carpet. Two little girls staring at their feet on the landing at Madame Tussauds while my mother struggled to control her panic, an image we had both retained for fifty years.

I pull myself back to the present, to the restaurant, to the vase with the crocheted carnations. It is plain white porcelain. Rosenthal. Very familiar. My mother had its twin, and now I use it.

What's going on? I feel my Britishness dissolving. When I get home, I shall take that vase straight to the charity shop. Then I think: no. Getting rid of a vase won't chase the shadows away. It's better to confront them. To do something different from what my parents did. Once, when we went blackberrying, we found a half-dead rabbit lying across our path. A gamekeeper arrived and grabbed it by the ears to finish it off, refusing to wait till we had passed. My father, furious, made me turn round, although he was the one who could not bear to look. I found not looking worse. All afternoon as I reached for berries, my fingers turning purple with juice, I kept seeing the rabbit palpitating on the ground and relived that long wait until the crack of its breaking neck.

The auditorium is buzzing. A young couple sit down next to me and begin to chat. The girl is relaxed and friendly, her boyfriend intense. He tells me his grandfather was an anti-Semite, yet made his young mother leave food outside the door of Jewish neighbours when they were no longer allowed to shop. A child was less likely to arouse suspicion if someone had a mind to report you to the Gestapo. The family lived near Sachsenhausen concentration camp and heard the trains. They knew what was going on but no one said. One day the neighbours' food stayed untouched.

He mentions someone 'looking Jewish'. What does he mean? Hooked noses? The *Stürmer* stereotype? He is in his thirties. Did he actually meet any Jews while growing up?

'They heard, they knew . . .' He is haunted by what the older generations saw and did not see, by what they told and did not tell him.

See no evil, hear no evil, speak no evil. We could do with a fourth wise monkey: imagine no evil. He conjured up the scenes his mother and grandfather had tried not to see, hear or speak about. And then he sits down next to me. We chat. And suddenly I am the embodiment for him of windows shut on the sound of trains, of the neighbours gone.

I begin to feel very peculiar. First I entered my cupboard via the museum's displays and now I am being sucked into this young man's head. Or is he invading mine? He is sitting too close, glasses glinting, insisting I fill his Jewish vacuum. 'They saw, they knew, they heard the trains . . .'

There's a hush, followed by clapping. The stand-up walks on. He bows and begins to speak but I can't make out a single word. All I hear is a rushing noise in my head. No longer am I English as well as British, born in London with a clean national slate, nothing to do with Before. To the man sitting next to me I have mutated into the disappeared and become everything to do with it, the stuff of his nightmares.

The performance has barely started when a cramping of the gut shoots me out into the freezing cold. The world seems to hold its breath. I stand shivering at the bus stop, willing the bus to arrive, and when it does I sit right by the window, nose to glass, staring at a clear-cut moon etched into the black sky. I don't let it out of my sight. I mustn't. I must absolutely *not* let it out of my sight. The moon has to hold me together until I reach the hotel.

'What did you eat?' Next morning the receptionist's sharp eyes scan me for foolishness.

Emotional upheaval had turned physical, and I had spent most of that night in the bathroom throwing up the day.

'Fish? Fish is the worst.' She shoos me back to bed and five minutes later arrives with a thermos of hot water and peppermint and camomile teabags. My flight is not till that evening, and no one has booked my room. I can stay all day.

At some point, through a haze of exchanged thermoses and sleep, I sense a long walk to the desk. Frau Lenck is on the phone. Or did I dream her?

Loud knocking rouses me. I was having such a good sleep, too, the sort where your limbs dissolve.

An anxious Frau Lenck stands in the doorway clutching a packet of rusks. 'Are you feeling any better? I thought I'd better take you to the airport.'

Pfefferminztee und Zwieback, my mother's remedy for childhood gut rot. I dare not risk the rusks. Not with the flight to come.

'You need to get up.'

My case is in the middle of the room, ready to go. I suppose I must have packed it.

Frau Lenck queues with me at check-in. I am fiddling with my case when she nudges me. 'He's beckoning you.' I continue fiddling and she nudges me again. Look here, I think. I don't have to jump to attention just because a man in uniform says so.

Jackboots marching through my mother's head are echoing in mine. A story she once told me of travelling from Berlin to Paris to visit her sister Charlotte, bringing tubes of oil paint for her sister's artist lover. The train stopped at the border, and two German guards entered the compartment. They ignored the French passengers and made a meal of her, rifling through underwear, tearing open packages. 'What's in here? Oil paints. Really?' Slowly squeezing each tube, checking the effect on the tight-lipped girl in their power.

A minor incident rendered major because of it being told at all.

Is this what my Britishness boils down to – crossing the road in defiance of the red man and a refusal to obey inoffensive orders?

Back home I sleep, wake, drink peppermint tea, eat a rusk and sleep some more. I surface properly as light is fading on the last day of January, the anniversary of Max's death. Somewhere I have a bag of nightlights. I put one in a glass dish by the living-room window.

'This is something Mum never did for you, Max. I never thought of it before, as it wasn't mine to do. Anyway, it's not as if I ever knew you. Childish fantasies, that's all I ever had. Only now I've seen where you and Mally lived, and stood by your *Stolpersteine*. You're remembered, and not just by me.'

I feel awkward. Never mind. I keep going.

'What will your letters tell me? Will they help me really get to know you at last? Let me light this candle for you and Mally.'

I watch the flame spurt and settle.

'It's from Mum, who couldn't. And it's from me.'

No longer reaching through the wallpaper. No expectation or hope. Simply a light sent out into the night.

PART 2:
HEARING THEIR VOICES

Ober-Schreiberhau, d 5. Aug. 33.

Lieber Ernst!

Mally's letter to Ernst, 5 August 1933

THE FIRST LETTERS

The package with Barbara Knoll's transcriptions of my grandparents' letters arrives a fortnight later. I carry it round and round the house and end up in the kitchen, where I fill the kettle, take the rubbish out, make coffee . . .

Will I be disappointed when my grandparents are no longer a mystery, when they turn out to be ordinary people who led ordinary lives until they were murdered? Suppose I don't even like them?

I take my coffee to the living room, sit in a patch of watery sun by the garden door, slit open the package and read Mally's first letter.

I find her in the gardens of a spa hotel surrounded by enormous trees. She is seated at a table in the shade, paper and pen at the ready, about to write to Ernst. It's peaceful here but she doesn't feel at peace.

'*Ober-Schreiberhau, 5th August 1933—*'

Where is Ober-Schreiberhau? I look it up. A resort in Silesia, still part of Germany before the war, surrounded by mountains and once famous for making glass. I check what's been happening both nationally and in the family as Mally starts her letter.

Hitler has been in power for six months. On 1 April he unleashes his first anti-Semitic action: a nationwide boycott of Jewish shops and businesses. Brownshirts roam the streets, defacing display windows and nameplates. They stand guard outside shops, brandishing placards: *GERMANS! DEFEND YOURSELVES! THE JEWS ARE OUR MISFORTUNE* and *DON'T BUY FROM JEWS.* Some shoppers take no notice and simply go round the back of stores to use the staff entrance.

The boycott is only for one day, yet it heralds what is to come. No longer can Jews rely on the police and justice system to protect and defend them. When a Munich lawyer complains about his treatment, the police force him to march barefoot and shaven-headed along the street with a placard around his neck declaring he will never complain again. One week later a law is passed barring Jews from working in the professions or for the state.

Charlotte, my aunt, immediately packed up and left for Paris. Aged twenty-five, she already ran her own business making and selling jewellery, and for that she had gained her parents' respect. However, they strongly disagreed about the need to leave Germany, and her frenetic love life appalled them.

A few months later twenty-eight-year-old Ernst – Mally's firstborn and favourite – went to the Netherlands. He was a graphic artist who designed advertising material and, as a Zionist, was attracted to Palestine. But it was in the Netherlands that he found work.

Max, Mally and my mother stayed put. But Max was so ill with the stress of it all that his doctor prescribed several weeks of treatment and a complete rest.

'*Dear Ernst,*' Mally writes, '*Your card reached us yesterday evening and I am pleased to know you arrived safely. Hopefully you have found a nice place to stay and have enough work. Write in more detail to Berlin and tell me what things are really like, warts and all. I'm going back tomorrow afternoon, Sunday, unless Father changes his mind yet again.*'

I imagine her glancing at Max, prone on his bed under a nearby pine tree, and inhaling the powerful scent of resin released by the summer heat. She takes several deep, invigorating breaths before continuing her letter.

'*He was very unsettled until we received word of your departure. His health is altogether very up and down, however I trust he will recover well.*

'*It is really very beautiful here. I am sitting in the park writing to you while Father does his rest cure in the open air. The week has also done me a lot of good. I wouldn't mind staying on, but I have so much to do. Anyway, Hilda is all alone.*'

Ah yes, Hilda. My mother. Eighteen and just left school. With further education now closed to her and Charlotte and Ernst gone, she feels trapped. If only they were all getting out of Germany, but Max throws a fit at the very suggestion. Hilda and her parents are in fact moving home – but only a few streets away to a smaller flat in their own block.

'*Write to us frequently,*' Mally rounds off her letter, '*you can imagine we want to hear how you are settling in. What are your flat and place of work like? Let me know what you have forgotten so that I can send things onto you.*'

Two more weeks go by until Max feels up to writing to Ernst himself.

'*Ober-Schreiberhau, 18th August 1933*

'*Dear Ernst,*

'*I have already received two letters from you, yet only today am able to reply. I should never have believed it would take me so long to feel stronger. At the root of the problem lies diabetes caused by the constant stress. Dr Schmidt had already detected it in Berlin.*

'*I am very pleased to see from your reports that you feel at home there and that the customs and lifestyle are to your liking. That is of course essential. Giving advice from here sadly lies beyond the realms of possibility . . .*'

Here Max seems to hesitate. The world of graphic art is hardly his field. The posters Ernst has designed are nice enough, but can he really make a living from that kind of work?

'. . . *nevertheless,*' he continues carefully, '*I have no doubt that you will make a success of things, be it initially only in a modest way.*

'*Mother is under a lot of strain. At the moment she bears all the responsibility as I am not strong enough to deal with things. I hope that she will stay the course as her nerves have also suffered. Had we had the slightest idea how things would turn out, we could have done things very differently – those are my limitations, which I have such difficulty overcoming.*

'*For now let me send you my best wishes for good health and commercial success; your parents are naturally very concerned about your future as well as about Lotte's.*

'*Fondest regards*

'*Father*'

I notice he steers clear of the tricky subject of Zionism, a movement he disapproves of as heartily as Ernst believes in it. As if German Jews need yet another homeland when, thanks to Max and his generation – he is a proud member of the Central Association of German Citizens of Jewish Faith – they have carved out a perfectly good one here. So I wonder what he wishes he had done differently as, during those early months of the Hitler regime, he would mainly have been concerned with keeping a low profile till the Nazi nonsense, as he saw it, blew over.

Come the autumn Ernst has moved to The Hague. Max, back in the office, is now ready to offer advice. On 3 November 1933 he writes:

'*Germans flooding into neighbouring countries looking for work will lead to fewer jobs being available for the resident population. This cannot fail to arouse unrest and is a major problem which is bound to grow more acute with every day that passes. In my opinion a backlash can only be avoided if every individual living in a foreign country behaves with extreme restraint and resists as far as possible making himself conspicuous. In this respect tact and prudence go hand in hand.*'

Be modest. Mind your behaviour. Don't arouse envy and resentment. Max's attitude reminds me of what my parents dubbed 'the good old anti-Semitism', the sort which excluded Jews from golf clubs but stopped short of murder. Prudence and tact, along with honesty and thrift, were his guiding principles. Max still did not realise – would he ever? – that he was already a foreigner in his own country.

I read the letters out loud to hear the rhythm of their voices. Mally is more straightforward than Max. She seems to write at the same speed as she thinks, missing out punctuation and using abbreviations to keep up with herself. His complex sentences I keep having to disentangle.

Subclauses within subclauses propel verbs half a mile from a subject that I cling onto until I reach the end, out of breath and none the wiser.

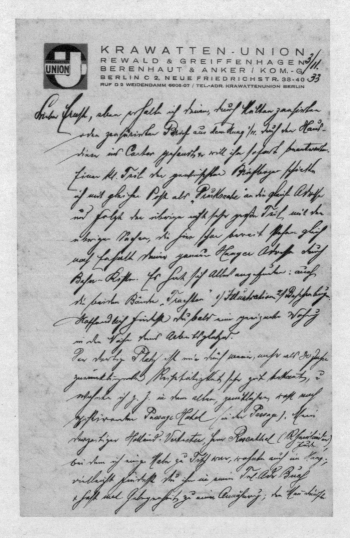

Max's letter to Ernst, 3 November 1933

'*With regard to your field of work, I am convinced that your area of activity is equally as wide as the opportunity it will afford you to gauge your skills and abilities, providing at the same time a source of satisfaction, both in financial terms and commensurate with your interests.*'

Blimey. Perhaps all he is trying to say is: 'do your best'.

I return to an earlier part of the letter and search for the spark I detected among his tortured clauses where he recalled visiting The Hague as a young man.

'*I know your new place of residence very well. More than thirty years ago I used to travel there on business and stay in the cosy old Passage Hotel, which must surely still exist. I have very fond memories of those times, of the inhabitants' quiet way of life and the importance they gave to eating well. Mind you, in the meantime the Dutch have probably also adjusted to the changing world.*

'*In those days my Dutch agent was Herr Rosenthal from the Rhineland. I had dinner at his home several times. He also lived in The Hague. You might still find him listed in the telephone directory and maybe have a chance to get to know him; he'd be slightly younger than me. We used to go on business trips together to small places such as Delft, Haarlem, Liuwarden, Groningen. Once we even crossed the Zuiderzee in a storm.*'

Five minutes later I am in the loft, scrabbling through an old suitcase of school exercise books. Geography – I open one buff-coloured cover. Cultivation of ground nuts . . . the Suez Canal . . . squirm-making notes on pygmies. I shut it quickly and open another one. Europe. Here it is, my neatly drawn map of the Netherlands, *Ijssel Meer* written in blue ink with two red lines across it and the word *Dam* transforming the Zuiderzee into green scallops of polderland.

That storm brings home to me the different worlds we inhabited, Max and I, his allowing him to sail across a sea drained dry and sealed off by my two firm lines on the map.

Suppose he and Mally had managed to escape Germany? If he took after his father, who lived into his nineties, I could have known him. I picture coming home from school to find him lost in his own world. I give him a kiss. For a moment he can't place me. Am I his daughter Hilda? 'Did you work hard today?' A remnant of the old strictness.

'We did the Netherlands in Geography today, Grandpa.' I open my exercise book. 'We learned how they made farmland from the sea.'

'I sailed across it once.'

'Across this land?'

'It blew a gale.'

His fingers trace my map, but his eyes look inward. I take his hand. Together we brace ourselves against the pitch and roll. We ride the storm he weathered then, and we ride the storm he could have weathered had he made a different choice, a choice that gave him a granddaughter and another life.

MONEY

In London the sun has disappeared. Still holding the letters, I stare unseeingly at plants on the other side of the glass door.

Suddenly I notice the hellebores are in flower. When did that happen? I've been so preoccupied that I've not noticed life going on around me. I shake myself. This won't do. The *iris reticulata* are at it, too. One has unfurled into a glory of sapphire blue with three tiny sunbursts. You can't stop life. Well, you can, but then it starts up again. Maybe that's why I like gardening. And cooking. Growth and food. Great antidotes to extinction, as money was for pre-war German Jews, provided they had both the means and the foresight to use it well.

In a hymn of praise to money, the emcee in *Cabaret* duets with Sally Bowles and slyly ridicules the Nazis while swastikas invade the nightclub and the menace grows. Sex and brutality, glamour and sleaze. 'They got the atmosphere to a tee,' my mother said.

The emcee was spot on about the Nazis' relationship to money. No sooner were they in power than they restricted the jobs Jews could do and imposed massive taxes on their assets, including the *Reichsfluchtsteuer*, a tax on those who emigrated. Sending money abroad was forbidden. As other countries required immigrants to support themselves financially, only the well-connected and those with a job offer were granted a visa to stay. Those holidaying abroad were restricted to 10 Reichsmark, and if they wanted to take more for emergencies they had to apply – 50 Reichsmark maximum – to stop them absconding with quantities of cash.

In the early days of the Third Reich, émigrés could still ship out the tools of their trade, their furniture, personal possessions and, with luck, some valuables. But between 1933 and 1939 the screws steadily tightened until, in the end, those who had delayed fleeing could take very little. That left anyone without a job or a guarantor – mainly children and the elderly – especially vulnerable. By the time war broke out, the flood of refugees was so great that many countries – notably the USA and UK – would enforce strict immigration quotas and refuse entry visas even to those with a financial guarantee.

I pick up Mally's next letter.

'Berlin, 25th March 1934

'My dear boy, Our lives have meanwhile returned to normal. Nice though the upheaval was . . .'

I scan it quickly. She, Max and my mother have returned to Berlin after meeting Charlotte and Ernst in The Hague to celebrate Max's seventieth birthday. Early spring. Tulip time. But something is missing. Mally doesn't mention another important and imminent family event. No one ever explained it, probably because only Charlotte knew the full story. And now, thanks to her papers, so do I. I rewind five months to the bombshell she dropped the previous autumn.

'*Well, well, well,*' my mother wrote to her on 25 October 1933, '*you can't begin to imagine the success your letter had here. I didn't want to read it to Mally – God, no! I just gave her the gist, and she discussed it with Max.*

'*I'm not at all happy about this wedding business and don't care if I put my foot in it. I think a marriage of convenience is all wrong. Not that I believe in love matches that last for ever either, and I think it's better for us (women) if the man's feelings are stronger. But at least you've got to be fond of one another. Just telling yourself he's a decent human being – no, come off it!*

'*Please don't be angry with me for writing this, and I won't mind if the next thing I hear from you is that the ceremony is taking place on such-and-such a date. I'll understand. I just feel sorry for him. You'll be unfaithful and, when you can't stand it any longer, divorce him and mess up his life. Still, what do I care about him? You're the important one.*'

My God, I think while reading this. Only eighteen and already with such a shrewd head on her shoulders, my searingly honest mother-to-be forecast exactly what was going to happen. And I feel envious, wishing I had seen more of that spirited side of her. In my world of After, between flashes of fun she became increasingly tentative.

With Charlotte now in Paris, my mother acted as her spy in the camp and the family go-between.

'*One thing Mally did ask me is what clothes you would need. I said a winter suit. That's something she likes doing. (I need a new coat, but Max reckons wool will do as fur's too expensive – it doesn't matter if I freeze . . .) Mind you, your*

*marriage would suit me. I could then do "Season in Cairo".
That's a film in case you don't know.'*

The following day Mally wrote to Ernst about their move
to the new flat and didn't mention Charlotte's proposed
marriage at all:

'Berlin, 26th October 1933

'My dear boy,

*'We're now more or less sorted out, although unfortunately
haven't yet managed to sell the grand piano or the living-room
furniture. I'm really looking forward to settling into the cosy
new flat and living there in peace.*

'Love and kisses,

'Mother

'P.S. Father's at the dentist.'

Living there in peace, Mally? Who are you trying to
convince?

Through autumn into winter my mother slogged away
at a secretarial course, anxious to work, anxious to get away
from her parents, unable to see that Max was doing his
cautious best to make sure his youngest could hold down
a job before allowing her to emigrate.

Meanwhile she planned a mini escape to Paris to see her
sister for the New Year.

'Berlin, 12th December 1933

*'God, I'm working hard', she wrote to Charlotte. 'I see
every single word as a shorthand outline and touch type it in
my head.*

*'Now then, Paris. Max has as good as agreed – yippee!
Keep your fingers crossed that I get a visa. I don't think it
should be a problem for only ten days. Just as long as I don't
have to be at home when Mally brings in the punch and*

invites Berta to join us and toast the New Year. I don't think I'd survive it. Max let loose another of his tirades about me staying out late. I'm not talking to him at the moment.'

I can just see Max and Mally blundering about, trying to stop my mother from going down the same shameless road as her sister.

'A few days ago Mally asked me who I'd kissed. I looked at her sadly. "Have a guess," I said. Then I asked her who, apart from Max, she had kissed. She went red and said her neighbour at some wedding dinner. Also Uncle Hermann's brother. (Men from the Rhineland are so jolly.) "See what you've missed," I said. Upon which she left the room. Ha!

'Just write and tell the parents that you've got somewhere for me to sleep, otherwise they won't let me come. I don't care where it is, I'd happily sleep standing up in the bathtub.

'Love H.'

The man Charlotte currently lived with, and the one she truly loved, was the artist Alfred Jan Weissembergh, known as Nepo, also a Jewish refugee. So why was she planning to marry someone else?

I believe it was a question of money. Extracting money from Max was on a par with getting it out of Germany. And Charlotte will have known that when she married she could depend on a financial settlement as her father was a stickler for tradition. Daughters got a dowry. The problem was how to send it to Paris? There was now only one country where you could officially transfer a substantial sum: Palestine.

Throughout the nineteenth century, Russian and Polish pogroms had provoked an increase in Jewish migration generally, as well as inspiring the rise of the Zionist movement. After the First World War, the newly established British Mandate for Palestine promised to put into effect the 1917 Balfour Declaration to found a Jewish homeland there.

In 1933 Hitler's spanking new Third Reich, in economic difficulties, made the Haavara (Transfer) Agreement with the Zionist Federation of Germany and the Anglo-Palestinian Bank. In order to lift a threatened boycott of German goods, as well as initially to get rid of its Jews, Germany allowed Jews emigrating to Palestine to transfer the equivalent of £1,000 sterling (approximately £60,000 today). The Haavara Agreement, a contentious issue at the time among both Nazis and Jewish groups, remains controversial to this day.*

All Charlotte had to do was find a man bound for Palestine, wed him there, wait a couple of months to 'realise' what a mistake she had made, ask her obliging husband for a divorce and return to France and Nepo clutching what remained of her £1,000. What could possibly go wrong?

A family introduction soon provided a suitable man in the shape of Walter Hurtig, about to emigrate to Palestine with his family.

In the New Year she wrote to her parents enclosing a photo of her fiancé, and my mother reported back:

'*Berlin, 19th January 1934*

'*Your letter arrived yesterday. Mally reckoned he looks, if not handsome, intelligent, lively and decent. Max had, as usual, left the letter on the bed and gone out without a word.*

---

* An article in *The Encyclopedia of the Holocaust* summarises the main points and signals more detailed studies that discuss its complexities (London: Macmillan, 1990, vol. 2, pp. 639–40).

'He returned from the office in a bad mood. When Mally asked for money, he exploded. She started crying and went to bed like a child. As it was Berta's day off, I had the joy of making supper for our dear parents. So far they haven't discussed your marriage business. Suddenly Max asked me if the Russian was in Paris.'

My mother had liked Charlotte's previous boyfriend – André Andreyev, the Russian film architect and set designer for *The Threepenny Opera*. Charlotte and André had taken her around the Babelsberg studios while the film was being made, and she was astonished to recognise the beggars, real ones, First World War veterans usually seen along the Kurfürstendamm, employed as extras. As soon as Hitler came to power André left the Berlin film world for Paris, and Charlotte followed. Twenty years older than Charlotte, married, and with a career that sent him to the studios of Rome, London, or wherever the next film was being made, his relationship with my aunt remained intermittent. Meanwhile she met Nepo.

I imagine Max doing a mental tally of Charlotte's past lovers – those he knew about – and trying to get his head around this marriage. Was it too much to hope that with a ring on her finger his wayward daughter might at last settle down?

Two months later, on 15 March 1934, Max turned seventy. Parents and children gathered in The Hague to celebrate.

What on earth did they all talk about? The marriage? Max and Mally's plans?

I can see Charlotte jumping in with both feet. 'Well? Have you thought any more about leaving Germany?'

'For heaven's sake!' Mally tight-lipped. 'We've only just

moved flats. Father's seventy, in case you've forgotten—'

'I know, I know! It's just that—'

'Easy for you to say "Why don't you do this?" and "Do that".'

'At least send valuables out of the country! Things that can be sold!'

Before returning to Paris, Charlotte visited Amsterdam and wrote to Nepo from there.

'*22 March 1934*

'*Dearest Arse,*

'*I shall be back later than planned. I've let my friend persuade me to stay in Amsterdam over the weekend. Her husband is away at the moment. On Monday morning I shall come from the station straight to your bed. Can you wait that long? If not, you'll just have to pleasure yourself.*

'*My dear little one, I can't tell you how relieved I am to have The Hague behind me. At last I can breathe again. This morning Hilda got woken up at 5.00 a.m. and we all said our goodbyes. (The Berlin train leaves incredibly early.) The farewell really affected me. Our family has never done any of that Jewish lovey-dovey stuff, one of us usually getting on the others' nerves – well, you have some idea of our family dynamics. But when it comes to saying goodbye in a comforting way – like how quickly the last year has passed and of course we'll meet again next year – then one can't help thinking perhaps this really will be the last time. I couldn't stop crying, Hilda too, my mother joined in, and a tear even rolled down my father's cheek into his beard. Those are the sorts of things that happen at 5.30 in the morning in ugly hotel bedrooms.*

'*My brother came with me to Amsterdam, and we've*

just been to the museum together. Lovely. I wish you could have been here too.

'*You're not angry, are you, that I'm staying for two more days? Even though Paris beckons, I'm not likely to get the chance to see Amsterdam again so soon. Or will you punish me by shutting the door on me?*

'*This morning, after they had all gone and I had cried myself to sleep again, I felt so sad. I missed Hilda when I got up and dressed. I made sure she got away on time. Mind you, she wasn't very nice to me and had made me angry. Oh well, I won't bother you with my trivial problems.*

'*Instead let me tell you where I am – in Amsterdam's answer to Café Dobrin. Sitting all around me are fat Jewish "bubbas" from Berlin's Bayerischer Platz, a sad chapter of the emigration saga. What's more, everyone here can tell I'm a foreigner. Tour guides keep pestering me, and all the Dutch lust after my fur beret.*

'*My sweet man, you can't know how much I'm looking forward to being with you. Do you remember when we recently held each other in Rodels and danced to "How much do you love me" – why do I say "we"? You were the one pressing yourself so hard against me. And if I cry "Ow!", I still like it . . . I love you very much.*'

Charlotte would eventually marry Nepo, then divorce him, but was to keep on good terms with his family. Decades later, when he died, they let her 'retrieve' items from their marriage. Perhaps that is when she got hold of her own letters.

I go back to the one Mally wrote to Ernst a few days after that tearful dawn farewell in The Hague:

'*Berlin, 25th March 1934*

'*My dear boy, Our lives have meanwhile returned to normal. Nice as the upheaval was, it is somewhat taxing when it goes on for a long time. Lotte shed floods of tears when we parted, yet, judging from her postcard from Amsterdam, what a quick recovery she made.*'

Ouch. Here's my first glimpse of her side of their battleground.

'*Father coped really well with the journey and was on good form upon our return, but the slightest difficulty with the business or the house knocks him for six.*

'*We did have to pay duty on the tulips. But the official was really nice and didn't charge at a rate of 1.50 Marks per half kilo <u>at all</u>. Anyway, here a bouquet that size would cost 5 Marks. And the main thing is that the flowers give us a lot of pleasure and look beautiful in the conservatory.*'

That makes me smile. My uncle and his tricky presents. On my first visit to Israel one sweltering August, a beaming Ernst had welcomed me with a bag of peaches that quickly turned to mush. At least Mally's enormous bunch of tulips, hoisted on and off trains, hadn't disintegrated.

'*The Board of the Institute for the Profoundly Deaf gave Father a leather bag and purse. The children presented him with a wooden menorah they had carved themselves.*

'*Auntie Findel had lunch with us today; Hildchen nobly collected her and took her home again. Auntie sends you her love, as does Berta, who thanks you for your good wishes.*

'*Frau Max Senger and Inge have also just visited us . . .*'

'Who cares?' I shout. I don't give a toss about these people I've never heard of and the minutiae of their lives. And at the same time I do, because every paragraph, no matter how dull, is a clue to what the grandmother the Nazis deprived me of was like.

'*On 5 April Inge is marrying her cousin Katz (a qualified engineer) and will join her parents in Florence where they have taken over a small hotel . . .*'

The Hague get-together presented Max and Mally with a breathing space, an opportunity to reflect, a window of escape. Outside Germany they could speak freely and discuss their options. The war lay a good five years in the future. They would still have had time to prepare. Yet that window stayed as closed as their minds.

Mally's relief to be home again is palpable. Back to charitable activities, entertaining family and friends, to normality. She remains stoic in the face of constantly changing regulations that are bewildering for everybody, but especially for someone as rigid, scrupulous and law-abiding as Max. As the rug is being pulled from under him, he clings onto the one thing he can still control – family money – unable to foresee the time when he won't be able to.

The regime may have been in power for a year now, but surely it can still only be an aberration. All Mally can do is keep her head down and soldier on.

TEN YEARS OF *STOLPERSTEINE*

The phone rings. It's Wolfgang to tell me about a conference to mark the tenth anniversary of the *Stolpersteine* project. 'There's a session on archives with the archivist from the Brandenburg Landeshauptarchiv.' He pauses, almost hesitates, although I doubt Wolfgang does much hesitating. 'I told them you've got your own private ones. Would you come and give a talk about the family?'

'When is it?'

'In May. There's a reception in the evening for Gunter Demnig. A few days before that he'll be placing more *Stolpersteine* and you could meet him then.'

Preparing for this talk is like being a kid again. Sitting on the floor, photos spread out around me. Those who escaped, the ones who didn't. Which stories shall I tell? Charlotte's Middle East adventure might go down well, especially with the pictures to go with it: pyramids, camels, robed men straight out of the Bible.

From Tel Aviv she wrote to Nepo in Paris:

'*26th July 1934*

'*My Darling,*

'*Now to your queries. Some things you won't like, my love, but I'm being honest with you.*

'*1. When am I getting married? The day before yesterday. The wedding took place on the 24th. What a farce it was, like a third-class burial, with the next weddings already queueing up behind us. All in Hebrew. Someone read a few words out loud and I was given a sip of wine.*

'*2. How long do I need to wait to have grounds for divorce? <u>Not at all</u>. That's the way things are here. According to Jewish law, if the husband wants shot of his wife, he can write her a "Get" (letter of divorce) and the marriage ends as swiftly as it began. The wife needs a reason which is more difficult, but he'll give me a letter, I'm sure. He won't hold onto me if I tell him I need to go to you (he said as much yesterday).*'

So that was all right, then. Charlotte had told her new husband about Nepo and, as far as she was concerned, they had come to a 'gentleman's agreement'.

'*3. How long does it take to get divorced? Only a few days.*

'*4. The earliest I can be in Marseille? Autumn. Because of my parents, I can't simply abandon my husband. I have to prepare the ground bit by bit: how I don't feel well, then depressed, finally how unhappy I am. I could only start doing that after the wedding. (I'm writing the first letter today.)*

'*5. Have we already lived as man and wife? Yes, my love, otherwise it would make things much more difficult . . .*'

After the ceremony the newly-weds will have dipped into Charlotte's £1,000 to travel through Palestine and Egypt. Charlotte wrote regularly to Nepo.

Charlotte and Nepo

'Jerusalem, Tuesday 31 July or maybe 1 August 1934

'Sweetheart, you don't realise how constantly you've been with me. I can't possibly be in Jerusalem without you, so you'll just have to put up with me dragging you around everywhere. While I'm busy taking photos, you're looking over my shoulder the whole time, laughing at the hordes of tiny children surrounding me wailing "baksheesh".

'Darling, don't you think Jerusalem is the most beautiful city in the Orient? Vibrant and decaying, modern and ancient, both international and uniquely itself, hot during the day and cold at night. None of the flatness of Tel Aviv – proper, solid houses, the authentic, beautiful Orient – here everything is just as it should be!

'Last night I bathed in the Dead Sea by moonlight. You

float on the surface like a leaf and everything smells of sulphur
and brimstone. Dearest Stinker, the mountains were magical
with the moon shining on them.

'*I've just inched my way through the bazaar and already*
have an impressive collection of bangles. It's wonderful to
watch skilled craftsmen at work, especially as I love such handi-
work. The Orient is not at all as sleepy as people say, but
busy and active.

'*Darling, here I'm completely self-contained. I speak only*
to you. I feel only you. I see you walking everywhere with that
slightly awkward gait I love, leaning forward, your eyes taking
everything in, swallowing everything on offer. You are with
me all the time, sleeping with me, waking up with me.

'*When our relationship began, I wanted to protect myself*
from "love" and never slept at your place. The fire only really
started when you returned from Switzerland, that's when I
was happy to say: tonight I'll stay with you. That meant
"I love you" – but I never said it.

'*I shall come back to you and be with you always . . .*'

A month later, now in Egypt, Charlotte took notepaper
from the hotel and sat in the shade to write.

'*Hotel-Pension Astor*

'*Cairo*

'*(Hot and Cold Running Water in All Rooms)*

'*31st August 1934*

'*Sweet, sweet one,*

'*Do you know the large tranquil park in the centre of Cairo?*
I'm sitting in the middle of it, beneath a tree with swollen
seed pods hanging over me and splinters of rolled-up cinnamon
bark lying on the ground. I've just been to the post office and
collected a letter from you and two cards from the family.

You've really emptied yourself out onto the page, my sweet darling, after I've treated you very badly and must make so much up to you. Meanwhile, I am not going back to Palestine. You can set your mind at rest.

'Today I wrote to my mother. It was very difficult. I told her that my illness is psychological, not physical, that the reason I feel dreadful is because I'm so unhappy and how completely different I'd imagined things would be. The ice is now broken, my love, and I'm marching onwards.

'Hard seed pods are continuously splitting and falling from the tree above my head, and a bird that looks like Maître Corbeau *is cracking them all open.*

'A lemonade seller has just gone on his way, and I am sitting here with a glass of "limmunnum", slurping and slurping in order that I can sweat it all out again.

'I can't tell you how relieved I am that Tel Aviv is a dim and distant memory, its overpowering family life far behind me. Here I feel perfectly happy and cheerful, even though ahead of me lie unpleasant discussions. But I shall get through them, my sweetheart, and creep back into your arms, into your bed, into your mouth, and I shall amble around you and explore the whole of you, and when I need to come up for air I'll emerge from under your arm to take a quick gasp, and I'll develop all your films while inside you because you are your very own darkroom.

'And we shall smile again and celebrate resuming our everyday lives. And you will rouse and arouse me, and I shall transform you once more into the man who laughs his way through life.

'Even when I'm your wife, I'll never slip into the rôle of "wifey". I'll always be your girlfriend, your lover.

'*My dear, sweet man, it won't be much longer until I send the telegram: come to Marseille on such-and-such a date. So, you arse, start packing your paintbrushes and sketchbooks.*

'*I'm going to caress you and tease you, kiss you and hold myself back until finally I let you do as you please and take me . . .*'

Perhaps not. How to explain the impact of Charlotte bursting into my hedgebound childhood, where trundling my orange tricycle up and down the street – don't annoy the neighbours! – was the acme of excitement? How her arrival from Paris, emptying her pockets of garlic and blood-red nail varnish, spelt mystery and danger. She brought with her an aura of sex well before I knew what sex was. It was she (she later reminded me) who got me to walk. Apparently, it hadn't occurred to me to try until then, nor to my mother, content to leave me safely crawling. Safe Charlotte wasn't. Honed by Berlin and Paris of the 1920s and 30s, in my place she would have gone full pelt into the Swinging Sixties, and I may have disappointed her after galumphing through puberty when I didn't.

Despite her parents' disapproval, or very likely because of it, she squeezed the juice out of every experience. Later I shall discover that, out of the three siblings, she faced the greatest dangers in the war and survived purely on her wits. But as the conference I am to speak at is built around those who didn't survive, focusing on Charlotte's story would be wrong precisely because she was such a life force. Max and Mally are the ones I need to concentrate on.

In Berlin my mother finished her course and replied to a small ad in the Jewish newspaper *Jüdische Rundschau* for a secretary/assistant to a dentist. When Dr Rosenkranz offered her the job, she accepted and took her first step on the road to escape.

Then, out of the blue, Ernst turned up.

He was not alone in making what now seems the nonsensical move of returning to Nazi Germany. There is anecdotal evidence that in 1934 and early 1935 others did the same. After the first flurry of anti-Semitic actions, the situation appeared less aggressive. Could Max and Mally be right after all? Were things returning to normal? The Nuremberg Race Laws – protecting 'German blood and honour' and excluding Jews as citizens – would not be passed until September 1935.

As he relaxed into home comforts, Ernst got the backwash of Charlotte's love life.

'*I picked Max up from the office and he regaled me with the sins of his youth as a warning*,' he wrote to Charlotte on 15 January 1935. '*As your older brother, I should have stopped your affair with André as, if I'd wanted to marry a decent girl at that time, the André situation would have scuppered it. Well, I told him in no uncertain terms what I thought about that!*'

It was all right for Max, then. Men sow wild oats, women are sluts – what's new? – and Charlotte, for all her bravado, minded her parents' disapproval. Her mad dash across the Middle East had provoked the only letters from Max and Mally she had kept. It would be a while until I learned what was in them – bewilderment at her behaviour and reference to an 'ugly letter' she had written to her parents, stung by their sympathy for the abandoned husband, Walter Hurtig, and little support for her. Max was shocked by the way she had hotfooted it back to Paris without sorting out her paperwork first. They broke off all contact, and the standoff lasted more than a year.

What's more, Charlotte's great scheme had backfired. The gentleman's agreement she thought she had made with her five-minute husband had come to nothing. '*I did what I could to appeal to his better nature*,' she would later write to Ernst, '*only to be told I'd never see one penny. It's nice of you to offer to help get the money back, but with nothing in writing and no good will, there's no point.*' She referred to '*the three-headed Hurtig monster*', Walter and his family, who were now, thanks to her, comfortably off in their new country. '*I was stupid. Some things you just have to write off.*' The £1,000 down the toilet she could shrug off more easily than Max and Mally's cold-shouldering. That would leave a lasting scar. When I visited Charlotte shortly before she died – by then she was in her late eighties – she would tell me flatly: 'Mother love? I never got that from Mally. I got that from our nanny.'

Meanwhile the clock kept ticking, the Nazi noose tightening. Charlotte guessed her brother would drag his feet once they were back under Mally's table and from the Paris sidelines nagged him to get himself to Palestine.

Ernst defended himself. '*I am making progress, if only slowly,*' he wrote. '*I enjoyed New Year's Eve, and it did me good to put to one side the constant worry about tomorrow. Unfortunately I am constantly worn out as I get home late, then every morning Berta appears with a torch and clatter of spoons. Still, she is a good cook. I haven't lost sight of my end goal; I just find it very hard to know what to do first but am now really getting on with it!*

'*I especially enjoy seeing Hildchen again, even at the dentist. He drilled and drilled. God knows what my bill will come to . . .*'

* * *

The May conference coincides with a ceasefire between me and my teeth, and I arrive in Berlin with nothing worse than a temporary filling in a rickety molar. Wolfgang picks me up at the airport. He and Barbara have invited me to stay with them, and as he wheels my case up to his house three flags flutter a welcome: to Berlin, to Germany, plus the Union Jack to make me feel at home. Up the stairs, past his office where bookcases overflow with works on Hitler and the Holocaust. Up another flight of stairs to my room.

It is lunchtime. Would I like a *Brot mit Wurst, Käse*?

I most certainly would. The choice of bread is as great as that of sausage and cheese. *Landbrot,* bread with poppy seeds, sunflower seeds, rye, wheat . . . I take a bite out of a piece of pumpernickel and chew . . . and chew . . . My molar feels horribly empty, then full of a soggy mass. The temporary filling has trekked to the other side of my mouth and stuck in the indentation once occupied by the wisdom tooth. I try to release it with my tongue.

Bread and dentistry. Can there be a connection between our differing traditions in both? My mother was shocked when a young couple turned up at the Willesden Green surgery demanding the extraction of perfect upper and lower sets 'so we don't have any bother after we're married'. If pre-war Brits viewed their teeth as a liability, causing only pain and disease, Germans expected theirs to be filled, crowned and bridged, with dentures a last resort. On they went, chomping wholegrain crusts and risking fillings raining onto plates, while the British sank false gnashers into soft white sliced.

'Are you all right?' asks Wolfgang.

'Fine.' I liberate the temporary filling and slide it under some pumpernickel crumbs.

Early next morning Wolfgang and I go to meet Gunter Demnig. First stop: Pariser Strasse. We park next to a little red van, its doors open.

The artist in boots and knee pads is busy with buckets, chisels, mallets and heavy-duty gloves. He inspects the pavement in front of a restaurant. 'I'll need to drill,' he says. 'How many?'

'Two.' Wolfgang picks them out of the shiny row of new ones in the boot of his car and disappears into the building with an extension lead.

Two middle-aged men in baseball caps are watching. The previous year they attended a dedication ceremony for fourteen Jews deported from one large house in their street. All the current residents had contributed to the cost and the men felt so moved that they wanted to make a gesture of their own. 'We asked if we could sponsor *Stolpersteine* for people with no living relatives to do it for them,' they tell me. 'These are ours.'

HIER WOHNTE ERNESTINE PLAUT GEB. LÖWENTHAL, I read on one, *JG. 1864.* Born the same year as Max, also in her late seventies when deported to Theresienstadt, where she died a few months later. *HIER WOHNTE HANNA PLAUT, JG. 1896.* The dates suggest that Hanna was Ernestine's unmarried daughter. She would survive two years in Theresienstadt before being murdered in Auschwitz.

Wolfgang ferries buckets of water and helps to mix cement. Gunter Demnig lowers the little blocks into two waiting holes, Ernestine above Hanna, mother above daughter. Max and Mally's *Stolpersteine* sit side by side – a spatial way, perhaps, of indicating relationship.

I wonder what passers-by make of it all. Most shoot a sideways glance but do not slow their pace. Some stop to ask and listen before moving on. One man mutters: 'I only look down to avoid dog shit.'

The artist, hidden under his wide-brimmed hat, smooths and brushes the surface until the inscriptions are clean and flush with the pavement where the two women once walked. He stops for a breather and says how especially pleasing he finds it when schools sponsor stumble stones. 'If it affects only a few children in a class, that's a result.'

I tell him how his project helped open my long-closed cupboard of loss.

There is a moment's silence. Abruptly he gets up and turns to Wolfgang. 'Right, what's next?'

Now I feel foolish and wonder if people like me, who come After, are irrelevant? Or am I having a rush of child-hood sensitivity, the effect of decades tiptoeing around the forbidden subject? Or is it simply that the most important words are etched in brass ten centimetres square? So let's not waste time spouting unnecessary ones, let's go on answering the silent call of the dead.

My touchiness sets me thinking about the long-term effect on my mother of her last two years in Berlin. With Ernst in Palestine, she was once again alone with her parents and, as Charlotte was *persona non grata*, felt even more isolated. She had provided a different address for her sister to write to, but Charlotte got it wrong.

'*At last your letter reached me*,' my mother replied on 18 November 1935. '*Children*' – for this is how my mother addressed Charlotte and her lover – '*you've no idea how grateful I am for the time you've spent agonising over what's to become of me. I really mean it, these truly are not empty words.*

'*Actually, it was no bad thing your letter was delivered at home and probably best it happened that way. Mally finally said she needed to write to you, and I said: "Now listen: if you do write, then you must answer in the friendliest way possible." She then spoke to Max, and suddenly it's OK.*

'*I know that Palestine really is my only possibility. Of course I'd prefer to be with you in Paris, but not as a burden, and I believe our parents would also prefer Palestine, despite the distance, because job prospects are better there.*

'*Whether things can move as quickly as you – and I – want, I really don't know, given that Ernst's situation is up in the air. If, God forbid, he has to leave, then I won't stand a chance.*'

The Government of Palestine had rejected Ernst's application to remain permanently as an immigrant, and he was waiting for a reply to his appeal.

'*When you wrote that I should come to Paris for Rosh Hashana* [Jewish New Year], *that was totally impossible. Max lost it completely, exploding like in the old days. Still, since then I've let hardly a day go by without mentioning visiting you for Christmas. They've now got used to the idea, even though you're no more married now than you were three months ago – that was the reason.*

'Children, you've really no idea the battles I've had to fight. You probably think I'm letting myself be pushed around, but I'm not. My days of being compliant are over.

'Oh, you stinkers, I've got no one here I can really talk to. Everyone only thinks of themselves. Write soon . . .'

* * *

These days Gunter Demnig has his work cut out keeping up with the demand for *Stolpersteine* and leaves most dedication ceremonies to local organisers. The following afternoon I accompany Wolfgang and Barbara to two of them.

I am surprised when we stop by a familiar front door: the entrance to my January B&B, where I was so sick. Side by side in the pavement outside are two stumble stones for the parents of the woman who commissioned them. Unable to come herself, her cousin reads out her message:

Dear Mummy, dear Daddy, I find it hard to believe that I left this house in 1938. Even now, more than sixty years later, I think of you every day and every night. I think of you before I go to sleep and ask: who will forgive me for not having saved you because I cannot forgive myself. Today two *Stolpersteine* have been placed in your memory in front of the house where you spent so many happy years with us, your children.

Every night for all those decades a daughter has kept her parents and her own guilt alive. To remember or 'forget'? Her way or my mother's way? What a choice.

The second rendezvous is in a quiet residential street. When we arrive, the family who commissioned the *Stolpersteine* are nowhere to be seen. A few people are standing around chatting. I read the three inscriptions. One commemorates a baby born in 1942. He had barely glimpsed life before it was snuffed out.

The front door of the house bursts open and four people rush out. 'Sorry, sorry, but I knew which flat it was!' the older woman explains excitedly. 'I'd already been here twenty years ago with my mother, so this time I could show my husband, son and daughter.'

The memorials are for her aunt, uncle and their baby son. She addresses her aunt's stumble stone: 'My parents told me you had blond hair and blue eyes. No one else in our family did. Nor in my husband's. So who knows? Maybe my children's colouring comes from you.'

They lay a few flowers, and we take photos. The ceremony is over, yet everyone seems reluctant to move. It is as though we all want to keep that little family in the forefront of our thoughts before our own lives take over again.

As people finally disperse, I hang back and look up at the windows. To have walked around the actual rooms the family had lived in – I envy the woman her knowledge and a mother able to share it.

* * *

By April 1936 Charlotte had finally managed to gather together the paperwork ending her first marriage, and she married Nepo in the *mairie* of Montparnasse. My mother was the only family member present, still too young to act as a witness, so a passer-by obliged. She then played gooseberry on their honeymoon to the châteaux of the Loire before returning reluctantly to Max, Mally and Berlin.

Meanwhile Ernst was still waiting for a reply to his appeal to remain in Palestine. A month later, in May 1936, the Commissioner for Migration in Jerusalem finally granted him immigrant status.

By then my mother had ruled out Palestine and was bound for London, where her dentist boss was soon to emigrate. He had offered her a job with his family, an escape route that Max finally agreed to. Once there, she would have to hang up her typewriter – officially at least – and pick up her scrubbing brush. Pretty much the only way women found refuge in the UK was on a domestic work permit.

Hilda practises for life in London

'*Berlin, 8th August 1936*

'*Dear Stinkers*

'*I'm sitting here on my own in charge of the practice and spitting tacks. We've already got an English typewriter, that's why I've got to type "ae", "oe" and "ue". And what on earth is the "@" for? None of us has the faintest idea.*

'*My boss left the surgery suddenly last Saturday to go to London. He wrote that my permit will be valid for a year, but that I will need to start working over there no more than two months after it's been issued, otherwise it will lapse. But when exactly he can start there, no one knows. I might also need to go over in preparation.*

'*It's like the fairy tale where the whole family goes down to the cellar one after another, first the father to fetch wine, then the rest of them go, each one to fetch the last one, until they're all down in the cellar.*

'*Well, whether I go to London now or in a few weeks' time, I want to travel via Paris – that's allowed.*

'*Meanwhile Mally and I went to see a lawyer, but we haven't been able to drag Max there yet, and without him we can't get anywhere. When I tell him what the lawyer said, he says that's nonsense. At least he's now agreed to ask the one who handled Ernst's affairs to come over. Such unbelievable pigheadedness is enough to drive anyone mad. I can't tell you how angry I am, and the weather's not helping . . .*

'*Write soon, please, you're my only consolation.*'

The meeting with the lawyer was about money. 'There were two types of visa for Palestine,' my mother had explained in our taped interviews. 'Either you could go on a "capitalist visa" and take £1,000 [the Haavara Agreement], or you could go without money, provided you had a job. So my father's adviser said: "I've another client whose son is going to Palestine on the other visa, but we could work it that he goes as a capitalist. With your younger daughter emigrating to England, I guarantee the money would be safe and transferred to her there." But my father said that was against the law, and my father was a law-abiding man.' I can still hear the edge to my mother's voice. Once she was in London she could have offered that £1,000 as a guarantee to bring her parents to the UK. Max had effectively denied her the means to save their lives.

Respect for the law was branded through my grandfather as through a stick of Blackpool rock. In his youth that had been the law of Moses and Israel as enshrined in Bible and Talmud, and now he obeyed the law of the land, no matter how perverted.

Sitting in my room in Wolfgang and Barbara's house, I highlight letter extracts to quote and think if only Max had listened to his children, I might not be doing this at all. But he was the parent, and in Max's world parents always called the shots. 'Honour thy father and thy mother that thy days may be long upon the land which the Lord thy God giveth thee.'

As well as respect for the law, at Max's core lay his sense of family responsibility – head of his own family, unswervingly loyal to the wider one. While he still held the purse strings, he remained doggedly in control. So he ignored the fragmentation already taking place and arranged another family get-together, this time in Switzerland, paying for everyone's travel and hotel vouchers in Reichsmark. But would my mother, poised to leave for London, be able to join them?

'*15th September 1936*

'*My dear Stinkers*

'*I'd have liked to have written to you sooner but, believe me, I'm only a shadow of my former self. The practice is buzzing, 35–40 patients per day, as well as the daily arguments at home, and in my free time (what free time?) there's the shopping.*

'*Despite what Max told you, it's not at all certain that I can come along, although I'd love to.*

'*At the moment I'm having two suits made and having to fight over every little thing. Mally insists on an evening dress, my boss and his wife agree, and it's pointless me saying: instead of an evening dress, how about something more practical? But you know what Mally's like, one's powerless. So tell me what material and colour, something that hopefully won't go out of fashion too quickly.*'

I visualise another Cinderella moment. My mother puts away her mop, tucks her boss's boys up in bed and wriggles into a slinky number for a night on the town.

'*Should I get a velvet dress to go with the fur (not ordered yet because Max still hasn't uttered the magic word "yes")? Oh, if I only had you here to help me choose.*

'*It does now look as if the trip will go ahead, but possibly without me.*'

The Swiss trip did go ahead, and the photos show my mother went, too. '*Lugano, October 1936*' is written on the back of them.

Everyone poses awkwardly on a balcony, except for Charlotte who flicks cigarette ash.

Max sits at a table calmly writing postcards.

Max

Mally and Ernst smile a little too eagerly.

Max reads the newspaper while Mally stares into space.

A tense Mally clutches her handbag while Charlotte holds forth and my mother gazes pointedly in the opposite direction.

Mally, Charlotte, Hilda

The unseen photographer was Max and Mally's new son-in-law, now welcomed – just about – into the family. Hardly the man they would have chosen for their daughter. Nepo was a portrait painter and restorer of old paintings who earned very little and scorned the conventional life. But at least they were now married.

Mally, Nepo, Max and Ernst

Once again, I wonder what they all talked about. Charlotte had only recently made peace with her parents, Ernst was still finding his feet in his new country and my mother about to leave for hers. Everybody's nerves must have been at screaming point. I imagine they kept to safe subjects: the weather . . . Auntie So-and-So's health . . . let's meet again next year . . . Having faced so much resistance, I bet this time none of the children said to their parents: 'Well? What about you getting out of Germany, too?'

It was the last time the whole family would be together. Ernst returned to Tel Aviv, Charlotte and Nepo to Paris, my grandparents and mother to Berlin.

Two months later, in December 1936, my mother finally left for England.

I try to imagine their farewell as she boarded the train in Berlin. Did tears flow, as they had done in The Hague, or were they held back because, if let out, there would be no stemming them? Did Max and Mally settle my mother in her compartment, or did she do it herself, avoiding looking at her parents, wanting the moment to end and willing the train to move?

Hilda – ID photo stamped on arrival in the UK

Other scenes I can conjure up with no difficulty. The train chugging through northern Germany. Stopping in Hamburg, where Mally's brother Fritz – my mother's favourite uncle – came to the station with his daughter Ursula to say goodbye. My mother leaning out of the window. Fritz and Ursula waving. Ursula running alongside as the train pulls away, blowing kisses. But Max and Mally's farewell to my mother I can't see at all. It's as if the shutter she pulled down over her own mind has extended to mine, and that moment remains a complete blank.

The train took her to the Hook of Holland, and from there she crossed the North Sea to Harwich. Several decades were to pass before she set foot again in Germany.

* * *

Next morning members of the public join pupils, parents and teachers in a school in Berlin's Kreuzberg district, together with volunteers on the *Stolpersteine* project who have come from all over Germany. Several workshops are being held simultaneously in different classrooms, and I make for the one on archives. My session is not until this afternoon; for now I want to find out all I can from the Brandenburg archivist.

She projects document after document onto the classroom wall, illustrating the Third Reich's mania for keeping records. Forms, lists, declarations, questionnaires. *Are you Aryan or Non-Aryan? Warum wollen Sie auswandern?* (*Why do you want to emigrate?*) *Aus Existenzgrunden.* '*To make a new life*' is probably the right translation, but more truthful is the literal one: '*in order to exist*'.

A regional card index system contains 150,000 names. 150,000 fates. A drop in the ocean compared with 6,000,000, but even so, how do we grasp such numbers? This afternoon it will be just two. My two. I shall show my grandparents' last Red Cross message, their final twenty-five words written carefully and clearly by Max. He signed his name *Max Isr. Rychwalski. Isr.* is short for *Israel.* Male Jews were forced to take the name *Israel*, and women *Sara.* Another dehumanising step along the road to anonymity, disappearance, nothingness. Max, obedient to the end. How I wish he'd left out the *Isr.*, that he'd shown one tiny sign of resistance to the regime about to vaporise him and Mally. But he resisted the wrong people. He resisted his own children. Ernst, Charlotte and my mother carried that with them, and I have lived in the aftermath.

'In Potsdam, in the Brandenburg Landeshauptarchiv, we hold proof to counter those who would deny the Holocaust,' the archivist tells us. 'The Gestapo destroyed their files when they saw the war was lost, but the Finance Ministry kept theirs.' Jews had to complete a Declaration of Assets before deportation. Once packed into cattle cars and sent east, the Gestapo sent a copy of the transport list to the Finance Ministry, together with the go-ahead to seize the assets of those on it. 'These lists are evidence of the Nazis' systematic annihilation of the Jews,' she says, '"The Final Solution of the Jewish Problem".'

Six years passed between my mother's goodbye to her parents and their deaths, and during that time they somehow managed to go on living. However grim, there was still living to do, and if anyone can help me investigate it, this archivist can. Precise, suited, correct and thorough, she makes me feel safe.

Onto the wall she projects a grainy white-on-black negative of a transport list. 'We have thousands of these,' she says. 'Every single deportee is recorded on a list like this one.'

We are looking at numbers 1 to 20 of 763 Jews packed into Transport XIV/1 that left Tilsit, East Prussia, on 27 August 1942 bound for Theresienstadt. The information on each person is detailed: name, address, date of birth, state of health, any useful work skills.

Yes, I shall find out everything I can, right up to the moment my grandparents were sucked into that nothingness. Every detail of their final years, months and—

Suddenly I home in on a word on the right-hand side. A place name: *Betsche.* I recognise it. There was a Betsche (now called Pszczew in Poland) in the old German province of Posen. My mother had told me that Alfred lived there, the older cousin who was wounded in the First World War. A gentle soul, he had married a girl from Betsche, and they had had three? four? children – she couldn't remember how many. At this point her story grew vague, almost dismissive – country cousins out in the sticks . . . far from her sophisticated home in Berlin . . . none survived – and I imagined a gaggle of children rushing barefoot along unpaved roads, kicking up clouds of dust that hung in the air long after they had disappeared.

Maybe these poor people knew Alfred. There can't have been many Jews living in a little place like that—

Good God. It's them. Numbers 3, 4, 5, 6 and 7. Alfred (aged 48), his wife Ruth (42), mother-in-law Henriette (78) and two daughters – only two – Helga (17), '*a factory worker*', and Emmi (7), both girls considered fit for work. I even learn where in Betsche they lived: *74 Markt.* Of all the lists the archivist could have picked . . .

'Excuse me,' I exclaim to the room, 'that's my mother's family. Alfred – at the top, look – he was her cousin. Fought in the First World War. Lost an eye. She remembered him bouncing her up and down. She would try to peep under his eye patch. He gave her the first orange she had ever seen and helped her eat it.'

For several seconds there is silence. Together we picture the injured soldier peel the fruit, break off a segment, hand it to the curious toddler who hesitates between tasting it and touching his face. Cousin Alfred emerges from fragments of memories that are not even mine, steps out of the list and into the room. Still no one moves. Then a woman at the front swivels round and gazes at me intently.

The moment is broken, the session over. People stretch and get up. Out of the corner of my eye I see the woman bear down on me, all spiky hair and big jewellery. Her fervour makes me uneasy. I need someone calm. Dependable. I need the rock-solid archivist in her suit, only she's surrounded by a group of questioners.

The woman touches my arm and whispers: 'It's as if they've been waiting.'

Here we go.

'Calling to you . . .'

Auras and ley lines. Cobblers and piffle.

At last, the archivist is coming over. Thank goodness.

'Accept it. Just accept it.' The woman smiles and backs away.

But what's my rock up to? She stares at me oddly, then crumples into her seat. 'That gave me such a shiver down my spine.'

Et tu, Brute! I feel seasick, my edges fraying, pushed backwards by the whole murdered family coming at me at once. Yes, I want to bring my grandparents out of the fog. Yes, I need help. But I simply can't manage all the others at the same time. Frau Dr Archivist? Please will you sit up and straighten your pinstripes.

We break for lunch. People flow out of neighbouring classrooms, and I am relieved to be swept up in a sea of them, to be amongst living, breathing, chatting humanity as we clatter down the stairs to the canteen.

The lists are the worst. The thousands, hundreds of thousands, the millions . . . I must put them out of my mind and concentrate on two. My two.

It's hotter down here. Whiffs of curry. Fish. I join the queue and edge closer to the steaming vats. Another woman from the morning session comes up to me. 'We had a Jewish neighbour when I was a child. She had lovely clothes with matching shoes and used to let us dress up in them. I was the youngest of four, and we had six ration cards. When she no longer had a card, we brought her food.'

I draw level with a mountain of rice and curried chicken.

'Suddenly she was gone.'

The clinking of plates and cutlery becomes deafening. My throat closes up.

'*Wir haben nichts gewusst* (we had no idea what happened).'

And you didn't dare ask.

Back in the classroom, I start my own talk with a letter Max and Mally wrote to Ernst after they had been on their own for almost two years.

'*27th August 1938*

'*Dear Ernst,*' Mally began, '*We are really delighted that you are now writing to us more often. We are interested in everything, your dog as well as your flowers.*

'*The summer heat is now well and truly over here, and it has become misty and autumnal – which again makes one feel rather sad. Hopefully the worst of it will soon be over for you, too. I can imagine how much people must be suffering from the heat.*

'*Hilda wrote to us from her holiday in Bréhat (Brittany) and is already back in London.*

'*We are well, doing our best to withstand the difficult times . . .*'

That reference to 'difficult times' is the closest they come to mentioning their plight.

'. . . *and hope that we will also live to see*—' Mally broke off in mid-sentence.

'*What?*' Max inserted. '*She must of course mean "to see the children again". That is what I also wish with all my heart.*'

Mally explained in a footnote: '*I had to open the door, then forgot to continue the letter. Love and kisses, Mother*'

Why did I choose this letter? It's not as if it says anything much. The doorbell rings. Mally drops her pen, dashes to answer it. Max finds the letter, finishes Mally's sentence for her and says what is in both their hearts. Unremarkable.

Yet I've kept going back to it, continually surprised by its warmth – as if the grandparents of my imagination had absorbed elements of the monstrosity that eventually claimed them – then surprised by my surprise. Whereas many people are excited to discover a larger-than-life ancestor – hero, swashbuckler or rogue – I've been delighted to unearth the ordinary. That's what I want to convey to everyone.

I project photos of the last family meeting in Switzerland, the one my mother thought she might not make. Charlotte's husband specialised in candid shots – an expanse of thigh here, a glimpse of knickers there – and in a boat with the two sisters his camera was ready for action:

My mother prepares to row. She takes off her ring, and a moment later—

Click. It's in the lake. She can't believe what she's just done.

Click. Hands over face.

Click. Smiling and wiping tears.

Click. The confession. Back on shore Mally raises her hands to her face in shock.

'But they look so . . . ordinary,' someone says.

Exactly. They communicated neither victimhood nor signs of being Jewish. No side curls or skullcap. No *sheitel* (wig). In fact, along with many assimilated German Jews, Max and Mally distanced themselves from the orthodox of Eastern Europe. Although they gave to Jewish charities and attended synagogue, they also revered the God of the great outdoors, swimming in German lakes, hiking through German forests, climbing up and skiing down German mountains. They went to concerts to hear the music of Mozart, Beethoven and Schubert. Hadn't one of Max's nephews been killed and three injured fighting for the Fatherland? He himself had given generously to the Kaiser's cause. Surely the Nazis didn't mean to target Jews like them?

I produce Mally's locket. It is a plain black enamel-covered oval with one tiny pearl in the centre of gold petals. Open it, and behind protective slivers of glass are her parents. Moritz Meseritz, dark-eyed and dapper, looks at Hulda, who gazes straight at us, her magnificent fair hair plaited and coiled around her head. My grandparents named my mother after her. Little did they realise when they changed the 'u' to an 'i' that they had equipped Hilda for her future life in England.

'My mother's ring may still be lying at the bottom of Lake Lugano, but here's my grandmother's locket, smuggled out of Berlin to my aunt in Paris. She escaped across the Pyrenees, onto a ship to New York and eventually gave it to me in London. Seventy years after it left Berlin, here it is, back again.'

One girl puts up her hand. 'Please could I hold it?'

I hand it to her.

She clasps it between both palms as if to grasp the history that it represents. One object that had escaped confiscation, theft and loss; one object that crossed continents, war and generations and, unlike its original owner, survived.

The talk is over, and I gather up my papers. Chairs scrape as people prepare to leave, but the girl hasn't moved. She remains sitting quietly holding Mally's locket, reluctant to let go.

Hulda and Moritz Meseritz

CRACKING THE CODE

Late that evening, back at Wolfgang and Barbara's, we dissect the day. I'm too revved up to go to bed. Wolfgang wanders off to fetch a bottle of wine.

Barbara tells me how, like Gunter Demnig, she is particularly moved when schoolchildren are involved in the project. 'It's so distant for them. Even during my own childhood, I never really grasped what had gone on. I don't know to what extent my parents kept quiet in front of us.' She helps Wolfgang with his research, but at times feels overwhelmed by his shelves full of horrors. 'Such books are not for me.'

I should think Barbara looked forward to a very different retirement. Travelling, maybe. Spending more time with their children and grandchildren. Instead, she finds herself immersed in the Holocaust and meeting the likes of me.

'Did you find it upsetting dealing with my grandparents' letters?' I ask her.

'On the contrary, they drew me in because they're personal and tell an individual story.'

Here is my opportunity to ask if she will transcribe some more, but I don't. What's stopping me? Is it because Barbara's already done a lot, so that would be pushing it?

No, it's not that. While I'm dithering, Wolfgang returns with a bottle of red, three glasses and a message.

'A woman phoned earlier. Julia Schumann. She lives in your grandparents' block of flats and wants to know more about their *Stolpersteine*. Would you like to meet her?'

You bet.

I say hello to Max and Mally's *Stolpersteine*, step over them, ring the bell, then Julia buzzes me in. I cross the courtyard, past the steps leading down to the creepy garage, and enter the garden wing. The decor here is simpler – no intricate carving on the banisters – and the lift a modern one. This part of the block would have been downmarket in the old days, whereas now its attraction lies in being set back from the street and much quieter.

Julia's flat is unmodernised, with large, airy rooms. She has prepared coffee and snacks in the kitchen, 'but maybe you'd like to look around first? Although I think your grandparents will probably have lived in the front wing.' She flings open every door so that I can snap ceilings and parquet floors, brass door handles and plaster mouldings. Plain cream tiles decorate the kitchen walls, with a few Dutch figures dotted amongst them. The bathroom, similarly tiled, has a lavatory chain attached to a high-up cistern. Its ceramic handle is set inside an old wall-holder to stop it swinging and hitting you on the head. Relating to my grandparents via a lavatory chain strikes me as ridiculous, but I point and click anyway.

There is an understatedness about Julia and lack of clutter in the rooms. She has lived here a long time, she tells me. She bought her flat from the man who had acquired the whole building. He then sold off each flat individually and made a packet.

Over coffee, I show her some shoebox photos that I have brought along. Like Wolfgang, she wants to put faces to the names in the pavement.

'When did your family buy the block?'

'I don't know.'

'That we can find out.' As an owner, she has access to the *Grundbuch* containing details of the building's every transaction. She hands me a large envelope. Inside is a fine photo of the two *Stolpersteine*, each ten centimetres square, their actual size.

A feeling of warmth washes over me, much as it did when Frau Lenck gave me the book of poems. People reaching out. Going the extra mile. I could get used to it.

As we sit in Julia's kitchen, in the very building confiscated by the Nazis and clawed back by the surviving heirs who then disagreed about selling it – Marie's descendants wanting to keep it, my mother, Ernst and Charlotte wanting shot of it – the very building where my grandparents wrote most of their letters, I get an inkling of the reason I held back from asking Barbara to transcribe more. Yet I still can't quite put my finger on it. Only later, lying in bed looking at the photo of their *Stolpersteine*, do I realise what it is. A good fifty letters and postcards wait to be deciphered, but not by Barbara. By me.

I have dealt with impossible handwriting before. As a postgraduate student, I reconstructed an eighteenth-century French Jewish community that had completely disappeared except for written records. With only signatures to help me distinguish between individuals with the same name, the quickest way to identify them was to copy each one by hand. As my forging improved, personalities began to shine through the pen strokes. Flourishes, wobbles and blots revealed the confidence of one signatory, the hesitation of another, and one meticulous individual who dotted every 'i' – much, I imagine, as Max did.

In those days I had no idea what drove me, although now it seems obvious. You don't have to be Sigmund Freud to see why I should have wanted to reconstruct a community from nothing and bring into the light ordinary people who had lived, worked, fought, loved and been forgotten. It was a safe way to learn about Judaism and anti-Semitism. One that would not frighten the horses or my mother.

Different country, different century, different language, but surely the principles of unscrambling will be the same?

It's heady stuff, breaking through a barrier to reach people you had thought unknowable, and what's more who are your own flesh and blood. Max and Mally's letters lay undisturbed for decades waiting for me to find them, and now I want no intermediary. Deciphering them will deepen our one-way relationship. It will bring me closer to grandparents who could never hold me. I shall tackle them as soon as I get home.

* * *

Back in London I open Ernst's folder and stare at two letters, one written by Max and the other by Mally, on the flimsy headed notepaper that Max's business once used for carbon copies.

Mally . . . Max . . . back and forth I go, skimming lines, picking out punctuation to get a sense of an openness in her writing, a tightness in his, a faster flow of Mally's looser, greyer lettering versus Max's exact characters in very black ink. He allows enough space between lines for massive capitals with long tails and insertion marks to squeeze in extra words.

Mally's '*Lieber Ernst!*' is in modern script. Then she switches to *Sütterlin*. I run my eye over the page, and a few more words leap out: '*Paris + Hilda*' and her signature '*Mutter*'. The convention must have been to write proper names and foreign words in modern script to separate them from, and not sully, pure German. I home in on another word: '*Patience*'.

My mother used to play patience at the kitchen table. Or is the term 'lay a patience'? While she waited for a bubbling saucepan of fruit and sugar to set into jam, out came the pack of slightly sticky cards.

The next word seems to start with a 'g', then a squiggle, and then . . . is that an 'l'? I get out the key to the *Sütterlin* alphabet. It looks like an 'l'. Then a squiggle, another 'g' and a final 't'. *Gelegt*. 'I laid a patience'. The same phrase in German and English brings me one word closer to my grandmother.

I can't make out Max's '*Lieber Ernst*', but what else could those first two words be? A great hook tops the initial 'L', a tail coils beneath the 'E' of Ernst. Another mammoth capital starts way below the line, soars up, round and round, revealing itself as a 'B'. The last character of that word resembles an 'f', and a dot hovering over the middle suggests an 'i'. Increasingly convinced that Max would never have left an 'i' undotted, or put one in where it didn't belong, '*B-i-f*' must be '*Brief*' (letter), so the phrase reads '*Brief v. 28/8*'; '([your] letter of 28th August'). Max and Mally's replies, dated 1/9/38, were written a mere four days after Ernst had put pen to paper in Tel Aviv. Happy times for the postal service if for nothing else.

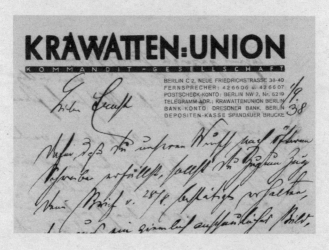

I turn the page – Max wrote unhelpfully on both sides of the onion-skin paper – and another word hits me: 'Paris'. With words surfacing randomly I shall treat them like a jigsaw puzzle and gradually join the pieces up.

No sooner do I think that than I judder to a halt, faced with an expanse of black lettering that flows to the very edge of the paper and, for all I know, beyond it. The *Sütterlin* key is no longer any help, and Max remains tantalisingly out of reach.

An invitation comes my way. Friends have asked me over for tea to meet Edith. 'She's very intrigued by what you've found out in Berlin,' they say.

I don't need asking twice. What's more, tea will be accompanied by home-made *Sachertorte*. Edith grew up in Vienna, where the ultra-chocolate cake is a speciality.

In March 1938, shortly after ecstatic Austrians had welcomed Hitler and embraced the *Anschluss*, eighteen-year-old Edith prepared her escape. She arrived in England on a domestic work permit, like many women refugees, but having never so much as boiled an egg in her life she laid waste to several kitchens before finally being allowed to do office work.

'I just don't understand it. Your grandparents had money. Why didn't they leave?' she asks.

'I wish I knew. Maybe their letters will tell me, if only I could read them.'

'Are they in the old writing? We learned that at school,' she says. 'I could help you, if you like.'

And so our deciphering sessions begin. Sitting side by side on the sofa in her study, we tackle that letter from Mally. I keep my voice recorder at the ready as Edith unveils each sentence.

'*Dear Ernst!*

'*I laid a patience today with you in mind and it came out wonderfully well – may that prove to be a good omen for you and your future!*

'*We were pleased, as always, to get your good news. I feel reassured to know that you're being careful and avoiding unnecessary journeys and dangers, as you promised me you would.*'

What dangers? When home again, I check what had been happening in Palestine. After an influx of Jewish immigrants, many scrambling to leave Hitler's Germany, the Government faced an Arab revolt and quashed it. Arab groups then started bombing Jewish areas, and now Jewish groups were retaliating.

I imagine Mally sighing as she continues writing, wondering if Jews are safe anywhere these days.

'*The children in Paris + Hilda are keeping up a satisfactory correspondence. We live a simple, quiet life and are in good health which is the main thing. Many people around us are getting ready to emigrate – or have already gone – but for most the preparations are very lengthy and difficult because the pressure on all the authorities from so many is too strong – plus very few options.*'

While listening to the recording, I follow the text. Mally uses a lot of dashes and abbreviations to keep up with the flow of her thoughts. She is gradually opening up to me, petals unfurling, letting me buzz about and drink her in.

'*Most older people are now trying for the USA – provided they fulfil the conditions and can get an affidavit.*

'*Thank you very much for Jumbo's good wishes. I reciprocate by sending mine to him. For want of any other offspring I'll just have to make do with being a dog's grandmother!*

'*Keep your letters coming. With love and kisses,*
'*Mother*'

She had entrusted some of Ernst's belongings to friends and family heading for Palestine. '*Hopefully you've been reunited with your things . . .*' But uppermost in her mind must be those bomb attacks and Ernst's safety. So get the gist down and send the letter off; never mind if the odd word is missing. Her sentences are straightforward and easy to understand.

Max's are the opposite. At the start of our next session even Edith is stumped. She points at words, shakes her head, mutters and tries somewhere else. '*Bomben!*' she says suddenly. (Bombs) Then '*Juden!*' (Jews) Like me, she seems to be homing in on random words before trying to join them up. But where I failed, she gradually succeeds. Max may tie himself into linguistic knots, but his handwriting is consistent. The 'u' always has a tiny circle above it which helps to distinguish it from an 'n', and one particularly troublesome squiggle turns out to be either a 'w' or an 'e' – the context will eventually reveal which it is.

'*1/9/38*
'*Dear Ernst*

'*In return for fulfilling our wish for more frequent corre-spondence I am replying point by point to your letter of 28/8 which gives us a fairly graphic picture, particularly regarding the mystery of the bombs which exploded in specifically Arab areas. This probably forms part of the terrorists' vital armoury, irrespective of their motives and final objective.*

'*What really gives me hope in all this madness is the confi-dence, toughness and courage shown by young Jews from the start of the disturbances and their willingness to shed their blood uncomplainingly for their ideals.*

'It seems to me that, once again, there will be no winners or losers. But I believe that for us Jews their sacrifices and privations have not been in vain and that finally, despite the times, the English are working on behalf of the Jews, otherwise they would hardly be able to hold on to this essentially strategic position . . .'

How Max's stance has changed. Gone are the days when he had little time for Zionists, secure in his belief that Germany was his home. Now, stripped of his citizenship and lumped together with stateless Eastern European Jews who know all about pogroms, he pins his hopes on those young fighters and on Britain.

At our next deciphering session it is tempting to have an easier time of it with another letter from Mally. But Max writes far more often, so Edith and I take a deep breath and plunge in.

What a surprise. Expecting to be caught up in another thicket of clauses, it comes as a relief to find him simply describing what is going on around him.

'Dear Ernst

'Today, on a gloomy autumn Sunday afternoon, we want to acknowledge your last letter of 25/10. Mother and Hedy are listening to the radio – Hedy is staying with us while making final preparations for her departure to Holland. This morning Herr Ginsberg and another acquaintance from the Lodge came over for a game of skat; our Lodge is closed for the time being. After supper we're going over to the Charleses' who are on the point of relocating to Melbourne; their son has invited them. At the moment departures to all destinations are mired in terrible difficulties. Many of our close friends have been waiting so long that some have had to unpack their

belongings again in order to air them – as is the case with the Charleses.

'*The liquidation of our business is taking its inevitable course; we think we'll have completed it by the end of the year. Being forced to participate in every stage of such a demolition process while still continuing to function must belong to one of the saddest chapters in the history of our company. Manfred, who went to Holland on business a long time ago, is not coming back.*

'*The reports we receive from you, Paris and London come, thank God, as a welcome relief. Hilda's 4th anniversary . . .*'

Edith's voice tails off, and she sits motionless. Suddenly I am worried this is all too much for her. She is naturally so open and curious that I forget she was born only a few years after my mother and has to cope with her own ghosts – the stepmother whose fate she could never bring herself to investigate because of the guilt she felt at being unable to save her.

'Would you like to stop?' I ask.

'Why?' She looks up, surprised. 'It's fascinating. Only I can't make this out.'

I peer at the text. *4th anniversary . . . something-R . . .* It's an abbreviation. Of course! 'That must be "Dr R",' I say. 'Short for Dr Rosenkranz. My mother's boss. She left school in 1933 and started working for him in 1934. Now it's 1938. Four years.'

This is the first time I have decoded something before Edith. But then I know the context, and she doesn't. Perhaps it's a fluke. Then again, perhaps it isn't. It feels like a big moment, and I sense a shift.

Edith continues: '*Hilda's 4th anniversary working for*

Dr R. was marked with a small celebratory dinner. In Paris, the economic outlook is so gloomy that the two of them [Charlotte and Nepo, I explain] *are considering other countries; unfortunately, it is no longer possible for me to pay their passage as we did previously (foreign currency situation). I went to no end of trouble to make a request (France–New York return) to no avail. Now I want to try once more via the benevolent society.'*

A decision is forming. The time has come to grapple with their writing on my own. No doubt there will be gaps, and Edith can help me fill them in. But from now on I want to be the very first person to read their letters since Ernst received them. Just Mally, Max and me. Finally.

'*What particularly pleases us, despite the difficult circumstances over there, is the positive tone of your letters; Jumbo would certainly seem to have something to do with that.*

'*Write and give us news about all our acquaintances and friends over there.'*

All over Germany trunks and suitcases are packed and ready to go. Yet Max continues to treat regulations as if they are temporary; his Lodge is closed '*for the time being*'. He observes the upheaval of emigration as a bystander, more concerned with obeying the order to close down his business. As for Mally – one nudge from Max would, I bet, make her drop her pen and rush to join their son, bombs or no bombs – she puts her faith in the outcome of a game of patience and remains loyal to the old husband who once weathered a storm on a sea that no longer exists.

'*Surely a solution to the crisis will be found soon. We must now put our trust in the decency of England's statesmen.*

'*Fondest greetings for now,*

'*Father*'

I glance again at the date of the letter. *6th November 1938*. Three days before *Kristallnacht*.

THE DAM BURSTS

9 November 1938. *Kristallnacht* – 'The Night of Broken Glass' – so-called because of the shards and splinters that littered Jewish homes, businesses and surrounding streets after the orgy of destruction unleashed by the Nazis. Burnt-out synagogues, Torah scrolls desecrated and 30,000 Jewish men rounded up. Amongst them were Max's nephews Kurt and Horst – sons of his youngest brother still living in Tirschtiegel, the small town where the whole family grew up. Dragged off to Sachsenhausen concentration camp, where they got a taste of worse brutalities to come.

On 18 November 1938 my mother wrote to Ernst: '*What the hell can we do about Max and Mally? Anyone with parents still in Germany is now trying to get them out, and I feel like an unnatural child not to be doing anything, but what should we be doing? None of us has any money, nor can we wait for some oil magnate to carry me off. When one thinks how easily they could have been out by now if only they had listened to us. If they tried to leave now (and who knows if they even want to?) they wouldn't be able to take so much as one penny with them; everything is being taken away from them. Yet surely it's better to have nothing abroad than in Germany. What do you think?*

I know what I'm thinking: of the £1,000 Max didn't send my mother; of Charlotte's £1,000 snaffled by her first husband, Mr Hurtig; and of the one person who got his £1,000 and, as far as I know, held on to it – Ernst. How much did he have left? Did my mother's desperate letter push him to act, or would he have done so anyway?

Ten days later the dam burst.

'*Berlin, 29th November 1938*

'*Dear Ernst . . .*'

I spend two days on Max's letter, roaming from study to kitchen, making tea I forget to drink, going for a walk in the wet, hoping rain will wash the fog off his words and make them sparkle. And most of it I manage alone.

'*. . . The main content of your letter really energised us. Only two days earlier we had begun to have the same thoughts as you without being aware that you were in a position to offer us the means of realising them. You are shining a real ray of light into our darkness, which with God's help will open another window of opportunity even if only a small one; in so doing, you have renewed our hope. It would appear that what all of you suspected all along can no longer be avoided. Therefore, we want to let you know that we would like you to take the necessary steps and put in a request for our immigration as quickly as possible. Not a single moment should be lost that could result in the slightest chance slipping through our fingers. The pressure from all sides is so strong. Even under normal circumstances procedures take a long time, so we urge you to act immediately and keep us constantly informed.*

'*Our business ought to be wound up shortly after the end of the year.*

'*The rest of your letter brought us great comfort inasmuch as it also convinced us of your deep feelings and sense of purpose.*

'*Fondest regards,*

'*Father*'

Oh Max! I see a rabbit caught in the car headlights. The *pater familias* who used to brook no argument was in control no longer. And look at his priorities. Still winding up the business rather than letting it go to hell and concentrating on how he and Mally were going to escape. All the while forming his convoluted sentences instructing Ernst to '*act immediately*'. It can't have been easy for him to admit that his children had been right all along, and my guess is he did so only to his son.

Mally added:

'*My dear boy,*

'*While spending an hour at the Vosses' on Saturday evening and learning that they had an affidavit for the USA, Father at long last came round to the idea that we should also consider our options.*'

I see. The Vosses (whoever they are) were the trigger. Not Max's children. Not his own wife. The Vosses – Herr Voss probably. If *he* had finally come round to not only thinking about escaping but actually doing something about it . . .

'*We thought then that Palestine was the only possible route for us. We would ask you to invite us so that everything may be expedited as quickly as possible, but purely on the understanding that we support ourselves. We shall seek an advisor here and let you know what we find out. In any event, your true and loving offer has given us great pleasure, but I still hope that we can emigrate under more favourable conditions so that we are not a burden.*'

For Mally, too, it was against the natural order of things for parents to be dependent on their children, so she quickly returned to her maternal comfort zone:

'*Last week we sent you some chocolates as samples. Enjoy them and tell us which you like best, then we'll send you some more. We'll write again for your birthday.*

'*Love and kisses*

'*Mother*'

Parcel-sending, like hope, was infectious. My mother also posted a birthday present to Ernst:

'*London, 1 Dec. 1938*

'*Dear Brother Ernst,*

'*First of all, many happy returns of the day, 'ealth and 'appiness (as the Cockneys say) and here's hoping for better times. Yesterday I sent you as a small token a Dundee cake from Lyons. You'll like it, it keeps well, and anyway it's in a tin. With luck you won't have to pay any duty. I could have paid it here, only that would have cost more than both cake and postage and the girl at Lyons said it might get through because of all the Christmas parcels.*

'*As it's not done to swear at people in birthday letters, I won't tell you that you're an old arsehole and that "I would like to kick you in the pans [sic]". Instead, I shall say that it would give me the greatest pleasure to hear from you, if you could possibly spare ten minutes to write to your little sister. You last wrote to her about six months ago.*'

She did not have to wait long. Max and Mally's decision released a bout of letters between their children. Of the sibling trio, Ernst had always been the odd one out, sharing little of his sisters' sense of humour or interests. They used to mock his mania for collecting anything and everything, alive or dead, historical and actual, his Berlin bedroom a chaos of insects, fish, mice, fossils, posters, piles of advertisements and albums overflowing with stamps and photos.

Charlotte particularly resented Ernst for having sucked up all Mally's love, leaving none for her. My mother's feelings were more of irritation with an absent-minded brother who would eat a banana and drape the peel over a chair, or forget her birthday. Now all three tried to help their parents.

On 13 December 1938 my mother wrote to Charlotte:

'Yesterday I got a letter from Max and Mally and at last one from Ernst. I think it's really fantastic of Ernst, and there truly is no other way than to invite them to Palestine. It's pointless trying for England. Here – as I heard yesterday from a very reliable source – 40,000 immigration requests are currently stuck in the Home Office, and the amount of money needed for the guarantee is much greater than for Palestine; also here one's money would run out in half the time as it's cheaper to live over there. Ernst writes that "capitalist" visas are available, although they cost £60. All I could do is sell my jewellery. However, conditions continue to get worse, and now that they have at last got the message, we must simply get them out; it doesn't help knowing how wrongly they've acted all along. Have you written to Ernst yet? What do you think? God knows how things will turn out with Max as a beggar, but at least they've now understood it's better to be a beggar abroad than in Germany, if only we can still get them out.'

On 12 December 1938 a less appreciative Charlotte wrote to Ernst:

'Now to the nitty gritty: Mallymax. Like you, I agree they have to get out, and what's more, as quickly as possible. It is nice of you to put your savings at their disposal, and Hilda and I would do the same if we could. You should, however, have made it clear what those savings consist of and if they're happy to leave under those conditions. They have already misunderstood twice.

'*Of course it's good that the matter is now being discussed, as in any case I believe the situation is going to develop as it did in Russia. Enormous ransoms will have to be paid to free people the Nazis are currently letting out without a penny, true enough, but later on will only "sell" for unimaginable amounts. Besides, the earlier they come, the younger they will be. I am sure that Mother will be able to busy herself, be it just by helping someone with the cooking or some such activity. I shall of course suggest no such thing as it is bound to be taken the wrong way. People only make changes when they're ready to do so; I don't believe in theoretical transformations.*

'*Yesterday evening I received a letter full of reproach from Max and Mally: "Ernst is the only one who is keeping track of the situation and inviting us." First of all, you haven't invited them yet, secondly other people are also keeping track of the situation. Perhaps I'll still have enough energy to reply to them tonight and clear up the misunderstandings.*'

Four days after firing off that letter, Charlotte reloaded her typewriter, took aim at their parents and made a copy for Ernst.

'*16th December 1938*

'*Dear Parents,*

'*I have been expecting your letter for several weeks now. You may remember, I often used to ask what your plans were.*

'*We share your opinion that Palestine is the only possibility. First of all, Ernst is the only one in a position to invite you; secondly, it would be irresponsible to emigrate within Europe (we also have plans to move elsewhere in order to keep one step ahead of events); thirdly, the cost of living is lower there, you will be able to speak German and meet old acquaintances.*

'*Necessity is always the mother of invention, so now that*

the penny's finally dropped I beg you not to compound past mistakes by making any more. Please pay attention to your children's advice in pushing ahead with your emigration.

'*Dear Father, you must stop championing causes like the Institute for the Profoundly Deaf as you're only fighting losing battles. I know it's a life's work that's close to your heart but, sad as it is for you, you must now at last really concentrate purely on yourselves and your own future. Much time has been lost, but it still isn't too late.*

'*Your unspoken reproach that Ernst is the only one keeping an eye on the situation tells me that you have completely misunderstood our letter asking for small items and reme- dies. Perhaps you will now realise that I've been keeping an eye on the situation for several years and am continuing to do so and that my letters, which I dare say you find crude, are well meant. I confirm receipt, with thanks, of the following medicines: Felamin, Amphotropin, Frontesil and Zupako tablets.*'

The pills may have cured Charlotte's gall bladder, but not her frustration with Max and Mally.

Some Jewish lawyers, no longer permitted to practise, had set up as advisors to those fleeing Germany. In the face of constantly changing regulations, the choice of advisor was crucial, all the more so after *Kristallnacht*, when soaring numbers of the desperate began to clog up the administra- tive works. Ernst asked around, and on 18 December 1938 immediately informed his parents:

'*I have been told that ASCHNER and GOTTLIEB are very reliable Berlin advisors.*'

Max had yet to follow his own advice that '*not a single moment should be lost*', but Mally leaped into action. She made straight for the Jewish Agency's Palestine Office, where she avoided a certain Fräulein Holder whom Max had offended the previous year because of his anti-Zionist views and who *'had immediately thrown Father's attitude back in my face and said that we could perhaps have difficulties if it came to emigration.'* Instead, she made a beeline for the chairman, Benno Cohen, whom Ernst knew.* She reported to Ernst on 23 December 1938: *'He was very nice and dismissed any doubts we might have regarding those earlier issues as completely unfounded. They are there to help. He recommended as advisor Dr Rich. Marcuse and asked if you have already put in a request* [to the Immigration Department in Jerusalem] *for us to come and for what date. Given the demand, it is unlikely to be successful. However, upon refusal you should immediately sign us up for the next list. I am to read him your letters over the phone regarding which authorities to approach here, and I can contact him personally any time I need to.'*

Ernst followed Charlotte's instruction to put the record straight and on 1 January 1939 typed an encouraging letter to Berlin, keeping a copy.

'First of all, I get the impression that you regard me, quite undeservedly, as the only "good child" who is helping you. The three of us have been racking our brains for quite some time now, sending letters back and forth, and this is the only logical solution, given that neither Lotte nor Hilda can do anything from where they live. I reside in a country where, as a citizen, I have the right to invite you, and furthermore have modest savings at my disposal. Let me stress once more that my sisters and I are in complete agreement with one another, and that

---

* Benno Cohen would later become a Liberal Member of Parliament in the new state of Israel.

I am only doing what they would naturally also be doing if they were in a similar position.

'*It is pointless to try and think too far into the future. Your children are in any case three well-rounded individuals, each proficient in his or her own way, all striving to do what they can for you. Personally, I am convinced that in the years ahead Lotte and Hilda will offer whatever practical help they can. As for me, I believe that the responsibility I bear now will serve as an incentive.*

'*Let me add a few words on the subject "Why Palestine?". As older people in any other country you would find yourselves isolated, treated as foreigners, barely tolerated, whereas here you will belong from the word go. A Palestinian who only speaks to youngsters in his own language will take the trouble to treat older people with consideration – something I have observed time and time again. Here you will have few language difficulties. You can, if you wish, meet enough like-minded people of your own age who will be only too pleased to socialise. Only theatre and politics will remain partially closed to you because of the language barrier.*'

In reply to Max and Mally's unease at not being Zionists, Ernst added:

'*I am convinced that will not be held against you. In my opinion, long-term Zionists should only receive preferential treatment if certificates are in short supply.*'

When Max finally chose an advisor, he ignored both Ernst's and Benno Cohen's recommendations and played by the only rules he understood and trusted, the rules that had governed his life: choose someone with family connections and an eye for detail. On 6 January 1939 he wrote:

'*Dr Aschner and Dr Gottlieb, the two gentlemen you mentioned, are currently overloaded with work and are therefore unlikely to be able to offer us as thorough a service as this gentleman apparently can; by the way, Dr Jacobi is in the same Lodge as Uncle . . .*'

Dr Jacobi took his time, and this Max interpreted as thoroughness. If Mally understood the need for speed, she gave no sign of it. On 19 January 1939, when she realised his first letter to Ernst had gone surface mail, she commented mildly: '*In future I shall ask him to send you everything airmail*'.

My mother already had doubts that their parents would make it. On 9 January 1939 she wrote to Ernst:

'*I had a letter from Max and Mally. Max writes in a helpless, distracted way, and I have the feeling that they are no longer able to cope. Write and let me know if anything has happened yet. Are you buying the capitalist visas you mentioned, which cost £60? Do you think they can salvage as much as one penny? When one thinks how different things might have been, it's enough to make one bite a chunk out of one's own arse. Well, it's just too late now, and we all simply have to do what we can.*'

My mother, working from dawn to dusk in the small flat in Willesden Green, made up her bed in the dining room for a few hours' sleep before turning it once more into the patients' waiting room. Each new tide of refugees swelled the number with grumbling teeth. They brought fresh stories of harassment, changed regulations, ways round them and the best advisor to push through applications. These she forwarded to Berlin and on 4 February 1939 reported to Ernst:

'*My dear little brother,*

'*Write and tell me what's happening with Max and Mally. I hear little from them, and they don't seem to be doing much other than rely on you. Recently, for example, I heard about an advisor in Berlin who's supposed to work fantastically well and quickly (tax affairs and liquidations); admittedly he charges ridiculously high prices because he can, there's such a demand for his services. But so what? The trouble is that, even now, I don't think Max has grasped the fact that the time to save money is over. Anyway, I sent them the gentleman's name and address, and they wrote back saying they already had Mr X, who is very good.*'

On 19 January 1939 Charlotte gave Ernst a graphic description of their parents' inability to speed up:

'*They now truly want to make changes, insofar as they are modernising the beds in which they have always slept by turning them into couches. And the fact that they are prepared to abandon their desks and make do with a cupboard with a pull-down flap is both touching and shocking. But the simple truth is that they won't be able to take any of that stuff with them – something they don't understand and won't let themselves be told. They would be better off shipping out [smaller] items they want to keep. When we wrote to them a few days ago, saying that other people, e.g. my in-laws, were sending abroad cases full of clothes, bed and table linen, etc., and what they thought about that, Max replied – and you can really hear his tone of voice: "There is a certain amount of unclarity surrounding that particular state of affairs, so that I am unable, dear Lotte, to answer your question precisely. What we can do we are doing; we are not privy to the activities of others."*'

'Over the past few weeks there's been a wholesale shipping-out of suitcases to Paris, something that won't be happening to the same extent with Palestine. The situation smacks of the tragi-comic; I've witnessed scenes that you simply can't imagine. For example, we receive from an émigré in one foreign country a key to a suitcase, and a few days later from someone else in another country a luggage receipt. No one dares post them in Germany and, what's more, the cases are registered under a false name. We then go to the station and give a porter the receipt. At least, that's what we try to do, but 20–30 émigrés are already there, all fiddling with luggage receipts which say 'Berlin-Zoo – Paris-Nord'. By now the porter has cottoned on and says: "Ah, les valises de ma mère." Eventually we hand over the receipt, and the porter brings us a case and asks: "Is this yours?" We walk around it and say yes, I think so . . . With no name on the luggage receipt and the relatives never having seen the cases before, it doesn't occur to anyone to check the number, and some keys fit more than one case. In the end, it's only by the initials on the linen that the émigrés can tell whose is whose. Then the customs officer asks if there is any duty to be paid on anything. In Germany everyone is in such a state of confusion and panic that their only thought is to get rid of everything that would otherwise be taxed or simply confiscated. They have forgotten that customs and excise also exist abroad, and the shoes are brand new, the underwear still has its price tag attached, etc. The customs officers behave decently. (Mine just said: "Do you think I enjoy raking through other people's belongings? Ça me dégoûte.") He allowed through some brand-new fabric, suits, bed and table linen, and only kept back a camera that had not been very well hidden. He gave me the choice either to pay the duty or have it sealed and *sent on. As the in-laws are going to America, we let the Rolleiflex go and they can sell it there.*

'*Our studio is full of everyone's enormous cases, and I am only sorry that Mallymax continue to cling on to their possessions so obstinately.*'

Charlotte and Nepo's studio – 1938 Christmas card

The Dundee cake from Lyons had meanwhile arrived duty free in Tel Aviv. A delighted Ernst quickly demolished it and immediately thanked my mother. On 4 February 1939 she replied:

'*My dear little brother,*

'*Well, I must say, over the last few months we have been having a decidedly lively exchange of letters. Credit where credit's due, long may it continue.*

'*Let me now turn to your offer of a blouse. If possible, I would prefer linen to wool. I had such a pretty one from*

Berlin, only now it's falling apart. Polo-shirt style, quite plain, to be worn either open or fastened. Take a butcher's and see if anything like that exists. I run around mainly in skirt and blouse under my white coat, so that would be very useful.'

As for their parents:

'Do you think they'll be able to take out so much as one penny? Buying new stuff is also very difficult as their own money is now being doled out to them. Max never let on to us what his assets were. I would just be delighted if they got out, even without any money or furniture – unfortunately you'll be the one faced with the greatest difficulties, at least to begin with. One day I hope to earn more than £1 a week. My permit runs out in December, and I very much hope to get a permanent one, then I'll be able to do any job. I'm already learning English shorthand.'

With my grandparents more in focus, I am surprised to feel as connected as I do to the Victorian patriarch whose sentences tie me in knots. Pedantic, penny-pinching and unable to adapt, no doubt, but he also appreciated Mally and respected working women. Controlling, yet at the same time loyal and warm-hearted. Virtues that didn't figure in the picture I constructed from the clues I was given.

Something else. One of Max's characteristics reminds me uncomfortably of myself. At primary school I would spend ages producing intricate drawings which earned gold stars. Later, poring over ancient documents, I used to wonder where my zeal for detail came from; not from either of my parents, that's for sure. My father slapdashed his way through a job 'to get it over with' and my more careful mother quickly ran out of steam. The downside of thoroughness is that with big decisions you can spend so long weighing up the pros and cons that either you've left it too late or you're falling over yourself in a panic. '*Not a moment must be lost.*' For Max the long period of dragging his heels had ended, replaced by seething mental activity but little action.

When I think back to my father telling me about his narrow escape as we walked across Hampstead Heath, I could easily imagine surviving too because wasn't I my father's daughter? Surely his luck had rubbed off on me. Yet suppose I am more like Max? I might have got lost in detail and left it too late.

Then again, why was it too late? Other elderly people managed to flee at the last minute, especially those with adult children on the outside to reel them in.

I begin to get a dreadful sinking feeling. Could the strained relations between the two sisters and their brother have had more sinister origins than just sibling resentment? Maybe the remaining letters would explain why Max and Mally failed to escape and, more troublingly, reveal a connection between that failure and the rift that later seemed to grow ever wider between their children.

CRUCIAL MONTHS

It had taken Max a good two weeks to reply to Ernst's letter pointing out Palestine's many advantages.

'Berlin, 19th January 1939

'Dear Ernst

'We have been thinking of you constantly. We especially want to thank you for your very detailed letter of 1st January. It exuded so much warmth, comfort, encouragement and confidence that in one fell swoop all qualms and inhibitions that are bound to accompany such an emigration project were removed. We were already convinced that there was no point trying for any other country, and this belief was reinforced by your descriptions of the conditions of life over there, the social environment, absence of language difficulties and, last but not least, the country's natural wonders.'

I sit motionless, picturing a feverish Max tumbling over his pen nib to get it all down, the endings of some words almost blurring, but never quite.

'The main point, as you yourself say, is to take what appears to us to be the right action now, once you and we have examined matters thoroughly.'

For goodness' sake. How much more thoroughly do matters still have to be examined?

I turn to Mally, also writing on 19 January, a week after her birthday:

'*I didn't really want to do much, but then thought, God willing, next year we and many others will no longer be here on my birthday, so in the evening we invited Uncle Louis and Lina, the Reichs, Hartwig and Regi Voss, also Alfred Rychw., who happened to be in town.*

'*We are doing our best to stay young and flexible and to face the future with courage. As Father has already written, even <u>before</u> your kind offer we had <u>only ever</u> considered Palestine, insofar as we had thought about emigrating at all. However, without your encouragement we would probably have waited until things became more urgent before approaching you for an invitation.*'

Ye gods, how much more urgent does it have to get? As for 'young and flexible . . .'

'*Your loving suggestion has made it easier for us to reach our decision – not that we want to offload the responsibility onto you – that thought had <u>never</u> occurred to us, and you must have misunderstood. I believe and hope that the other children would be equally willing to step in and help – but I also hope that will not prove necessary. Hilda always writes loving and good-hearted letters; the Parisians probably also mean well, however you know their tone, dredging up all manner of old issues, which upset and depressed us quite unnecessarily; circumstances are already difficult enough. Lotte has never shown us much affection – yet of course I believe that in an emergency she would also be there for us. I think to begin with we should be able to muddle through with your help and without being too much of a burden. When we know if and when, we can discuss living arrangements. Would a fridge and/or an old cooker be a good idea?*

'*Love and kisses,*
'*Mother*'

A fridge and a cooker? Just go. Pack a bag and go.

By February Dr Jacobi had put them onto the Jewish Agency's priority list; Max's age and Mally's charitable activities ought to count in their favour. Should they be doing anything further in Berlin or was it up to the British authorities in Palestine? Max continued to go to the office but missed his business. Two former employees were still dealing with its liquidation. He and Mally felt very tired.

By March their world was emptying. Friends visited them en route to Palestine but were no longer able to take along a little something for Ernst as '*now everything, even hand luggage, is controlled*'.

Felix Reich, Director of the Institute for the Profoundly Deaf, dropped in before accompanying a group of pupils to England. Max had been on the board for more than thirty years, and they were old friends. Hedy, whose Dutch job had come to nothing, finally left for England. At this point even Max urged Dr Jacobi to hurry up.

By mid April they had not heard from Ernst for weeks. A rabbi, Dr Nussbaum, came round collecting for the Keren Hayesod charity. He implied that a sizeable donation could help the Jewish Agency in Berlin speed things up. Max gave him 3,000 Marks. Should he send Ernst the receipt? They were doing what they could to prepare. However, without hearing from him, they could not make arrangements such as dispersing the household. The Jewish Agency said it could do nothing until his invitation had been received.

The newspapers reported that the Government of Palestine had begun to issue immigration certificates again.

May arrived; still no word from Ernst.

'*Dear Ernst,*

'*I beg you to reply to us immediately upon receipt of this letter, as Mother and I would like to go away from 18 May for about ten days (over Whitsun) for a relaxing holiday near Hamburg and, if possible, take preparatory steps re our emigration before we go.*'

A relaxing holiday? Now? What a time to choose. Then again, perhaps they needed a breather before the last push. Mally's brother Fritz and sister-in-law Olga were in Hamburg. They will have wanted to say goodbye.

Mally added: '*You congratulated Hilda one month too soon. Her birthday is on 27th* <u>*May.*</u> *We know you can't perform miracles, yet want to know soon if you are in a position to invite us yet. That lies at the basis of all our endeavours and is the* <u>*first*</u> *question posed by every official and advisor.*'

On 11 June 1939 Ernst finally wrote to his parents. He had moved flats and was affected by the extreme heat.

'You idiot!' I explode. 'You choose this time to move?' Lazy . . . Procrastinator . . . The sisters' criticisms of their brother rise like bile. 'And you're still getting Mum's birthday wrong. Pull your finger out!' If only Charlotte had been the one in Palestine. She would have bulldozed through bureaucracy, slept with the Immigration Officer, reached across Mediterranean and Alps to seize Max and Mally in her blood-red talons and yank them into edgy safety. Here was everything I had begun to suspect and fear.

A forlorn Max described how they were helping the next wave of refugees leave Germany. Alfred from Betsche, my mother's cousin with the eye patch, was staying with them, having recently sent his eldest daughter to England on a *Kindertransport*.

On 22 June 1939 Max wrote: *'What do you really think of our chances of getting to Palestine? At the moment it seems impossible to achieve anything from this end as the Pal. Office is only able to process the most urgent cases, and the British Consulate's activities seem to have ground to a halt due to illegal immigration and political manoeuvrings.'*

I plough through letter after letter as more weeks passed and Ernst remained silent, willing them to abandon flat, furniture and change the end of the story.

Then, suddenly, there *is* a change.

'Berlin, 5th July 1939

'Dear Ernst

'By the same post you should have received a letter from my new lawyer Dr Marcuse (dynamite in his field). I pestered the Palestine Office months ago, but to no avail.'

Richard Marcuse, the new stick of dynamite, was the very advisor recommended to Mally six months earlier by Benno Cohen of the Palestine Office and ignored by Max. Retained at last, he immediately got cracking. The Government of Palestine had to give the green light before the British Consulate in Berlin could issue visas; but the consulate, unchallenged by both the Palestine Office and previous damp squib of an advisor, still hadn't forwarded Max and Mally's application to immigrate. Now Richard Marcuse made sure it did. At the same time, he wrote to Ernst: *'Please could you speed things up by pleading your parents' case in person at the Immigration Department in Jerusalem?'* As Max explained to Ernst on 5 July 1939: *'Our emigration business had ground to a halt at this end.'* Mally, full of hope, added: *'At last things really seem to be moving forwards!'*

So Ernst had remained silent because, until Dynamite Man took over, there was no further action he could have taken. Had his two sisters ever known that? Probably not. Communication wasn't Ernst's strong point – written communication, that is. Get him talking and he wouldn't stop, whether about his collection of ceramics, or the flora and fauna of the desert. Charlotte and my mother would roll their eyes and switch off.

I feel for him, my reticent uncle, used to being led by Mally and told what to do by Charlotte, suddenly in charge of a desperate situation that he had no control over. Even so, as war marched closer I can't help wondering: could he have done more? Fought harder? The trouble is, he wasn't the kind of man to bang on closed doors and demand his parents be let in.

As I continue to stare at these desperate last letters, I realise that my seething suspicions were mine alone. Charlotte's and my mother's criticisms of their brother centred around his indecisiveness and reluctance to part with money, his secretiveness and closeness to Mally. They wondered if he might be gay – not that they would have minded, but why not be open about it? – recalling how his girlfriends had all married someone else rather than wait for a proposal that never came. I now think the post-war rift simply opened up a pre-war faultline – with one extra element. I was only twelve when Ernst first visited us, yet got the strange sensation that I was older than he was. He was like a little boy as he sat at the kitchen table talking, talking, talking, before launching into the next apple or cheesecake straight from the oven. My own mother, silently working around him, had morphed into ersatz-Mally. No wonder she felt uncomfortable. Still, it is unlikely the sisters blamed Ernst for their parents' failure to escape any more than they blamed themselves.

Upon Ernst's death nearly thirty years later, I discovered three of his girlfriends had remained in touch – one in Austria, one in Germany, one in Sweden – and continued to visit him. By now all were widows and had a hotline to one another. They kept an eye on him, and neither sister had a clue.

Maybe that crucial spring and summer of 1939 was the one and only time the three siblings felt truly connected, sending each other news, recommendations, updates and suggestions as to how to help their parents. And all the while Max and Mally's situation grew increasingly grim.

July passed.

Half of August.

From her summer break on the Côte d'Azur Charlotte wrote to Ernst.

'*At the moment I think the parents are quite happy that things aren't progressing all that quickly and they can stay in Germany as things have gone "quiet" again. I don't know whether you know, indeed if there is any way you could have heard, that Max remarked: "Oh, if only we could stay in Germany, even if it means moving to the Grenadierstrasse." You'll be well aware of Max's distaste for ghettos and Eastern European Jews, so now you can see how reluctantly they are "striving" to reach Palestine.*'

My mother's correspondence with Ernst had dried up. She eventually wrote to him at the end of her own summer holiday.

'*21st August 1939*

'*My dear little brother*

'*We're as bad as one another, that is to say you are worse. You never answered my last letter and I never acknowledged the blue blouse. It arrived, and I didn't have to pay any duty. I ironed it and am wearing it here with white shorts, many thanks.*

'*I am on holiday in Juan-les-Pins and have another week here before returning to shit London; I really can't stand it there any more. If I find the slightest opportunity to work in France, I'll go.*

'*Listen, you old stinker, why don't you ever write? They don't have to be long epistles, but I should at least like to keep up some sort of regular correspondence.*

'*Re Mallymax I suppose you know as much or as little as I do. They always write confidently but I simply don't see how they're going to get out.*'

The last letter from my grandparents to Ernst before war broke out is dated 16 August 1939. Max wrote:

'*Dear Ernst*

'*This time we are the ones who owe you a letter; we would have written long ago, had I not felt continually inhibited by having nothing concrete to say about our emigration given your report on the subject. One can only suspect that our application will remain stewing in the Immigration Dep. for all eternity as long as there is no way of approaching the authorities over there. If only one knew that the great efforts being made this end were bearing fruit over there, then one would worry less about a precise date . . .*'

I find myself holding my breath because I know it was already too late, and they didn't. It is the same feeling I once had in a two-man canoe during La Descente des Gorges de l'Ardèche, a spectacular stretch of the river Ardèche where it narrows and the banks rise to cliffs on either side. Your job at the front is to paddle. Steadily. Rhythmically. Steering happens at the back. As you enter the gorge, the surface of the water becomes smooth as silk. Gone are the ripples and eddies. All appears calm, yet you have picked up speed. You are so low in the water, you only see the rapid a second before you're in it. 'Now, now, now!' the voice at the back yells as you plunge over the edge. All is foam and spray. You paddle like hell, a bucking bronco paddling paddling to stay upright, paddling paddling to beat the current, paddling paddling to emerge into stillness.

'How we spend our time? I find it hard to cope without a regular, ordered activity, whereas Mother is busy with the household; she is running the kitchen single-handedly. I pass the time by writing a lot of letters, visiting the sick, some social work in the Jewish community, much reading – and playing cards with Mother. As for going out, we only go to the Kulturbund theatre. We get hardly any fresh air.'

I think of Mally busy with her household. A fraction of it came to light after Ernst's funeral. In one cupboard of his flat I found piles of linen which had once been white. As I flattened yellow creases in a fine damask tablecloth, I saw in one corner an embroidered letter 'R' and shivered, convinced I was the first person to unfold it in its new home. Mally had packed the linen and sent it on to Tel Aviv. Ernst had saved it for her arrival and, when she didn't come, kept on keeping it.

In that letter of 16 August 1939 Mally made one last effort to picture life in Palestine:

'We regret, that is to say I regret, not having gone earlier, but hope with your help and that of others to be taking the right measures now. Do you actually want to live with us or just eat with us? In any case, I imagine a slightly larger flat won't be much dearer than a small one, then one could let one or two rooms. Can you live anywhere, or does your job restrict you to one district? I'm bringing a very good cupboard from the business with a flexible sliding door for your drawings. Many parents here are waiting to emigrate, and we must also be patient.

'My main worry at the moment is Uncle Fritz. Father is footing the bill for the operation and hospital expenses. All the family emigrants are turning to him for help, so it is good that we have always lived thriftily and have enough left over for others.'

The last photo I have of Max and Mally was taken two years earlier. It is dated 1937 and shows them at a train station with Ernst. Max's letters that year proposed another Swiss get-together, and the photo looks as if it were taken when they parted.

Max is smiling genially at Ernst, who smiles back, both doing their best to obey the photographer's call. Mally is standing between them. Although she seems to gaze at the camera, her eyes are blank with deep shadows under them, her mouth stretched into what could be mistaken for a smile were it not for her expression. She is looking inward at a place normally sealed off even from herself. It is as if she senses, the moment the shutter clicks, that she will never see her son again.

Last photo of Max and Mally with Ernst

CHANCING IT

By the end of August 1939 a curtain begins to descend, screening those left behind from the ones who got away. Without a guarantee or visa to enter another country, escape routes are blocked. Max's nephews Kurt and Horst, sons of his youngest brother Eugen, arrested on *Kristallnacht* and held for months in Sachsenhausen concentration camp, have exhausted all legitimate possibilities.

I first became aware of them when they and their wives came to tea on the few occasions other surviving cousins, who now lived in South America and Israel, visited London. These were pretty stilted get-togethers, with no one speaking the same language other than German. At some point my father would go to the piano and launch into Neapolitan songs to lighten the atmosphere. Otherwise we rarely saw Kurt and Horst, even though they didn't live far from us, because 'their wives are such hard work', or so my mother said.

Really? Kurt's wife Selma didn't strike me as hard work at all. She seemed gentle and must have been very pretty when young, with dark curly hair – greying now – innocent eyes and rosy cheeks. I reckon the real reason for my mother's reluctance was the brothers' close encounter with what she wanted to forget. Horst died relatively young, and we continued not seeing Kurt until the day Selma made my father a mouthwatering Stollen, a sure way to his heart. From then on, Stollen-handover became an annual Christmas event and gave me the opportunity to ask questions.

Kurt described Max's arrival at the old family homestead in Tirschtiegel. Sitting down at the kitchen table, dry and dusty after the journey, Max would turn to his young nephew: 'Go on, lad, run and fetch me a glass of fresh water from the well.' It was the same well he had drunk from as a boy. That was the moment he knew he'd come home. And, like my thirsty grandfather, I lapped up every drop of information.

The brothers worked the land. They were farmers. Tough young men with sturdy boots which helped them endure imprisonment in Sachsenhausen. Through the freezing winter of 1938/39 they had fared much better than their fellow inmates in thin city shoes that leaked.

Release was as arbitrary as capture and incarceration. Horst was let out first. He went straight to Berlin and stayed with Max and Mally, tramping from one consulate to the next, seeking five visas for Kurt, himself, their parents and young brother Heinz.

Max reported on their progress to Ernst. '*Horst is still trying to free his brother,*' he wrote on 23 January 1939. '*Sadly people are wearing themselves to a frazzle knocking on consular doors that are continually slammed in their faces.*'

By then South America was their best option. The USA was pointless because, even if they found an American willing to provide affidavits guaranteeing financial support – difficult enough for one refugee let alone five – visas could take years to be granted because of the strict immigration quota.

By February 1939 Kurt had been released and took over the search. One incident remained seared in his memory. As he toured the consulates, shivering with cold, he suddenly glimpsed a familiar figure across the street: Louis, his other Berlin uncle. What a stroke of luck. Louis was well off. They said he'd obediently (stupidly) closed a Swiss bank account when ordered to and brought the funds back to Germany. Surely he would lend his nephew some cash to buy a coat.

'Everything I have is tied up in investments,' came the reply.

'Much good did it do him,' said Kurt, his anger still raw. 'He also perished.'

Through that spring and summer, the brothers continued their search for an escape route for all five of them. But it was useless. Finally, they decided to chance it alone.

In late August 1939 they parted from their parents and young brother – Kurt told this matter-of-factly, as if it was an ordinary goodbye – and took the train once again to Berlin. Depositing suitcases with Max and Mally, they headed for International Departures, carrying in their knapsacks nothing more than a change of clothes, a few family photos, bread, sausage and cash for immediate needs: nothing to draw attention to themselves other than passports emblazoned with the fat red 'J' for Jew.

The train came to a halt at the border and the passengers alighted. A few feet away, on the other side of the barrier, lay Belgium. Kurt sized up the two officers on the German side, one young and sharp, the other older. 'I don't know why,' he said, 'but I knew I had to go for the older man.'

The officer opened both passports at the pages displaying the red 'J' for Jew. 'Rychwalski?' he queried. 'I stayed with an Eugen Rychwalski once.'

'That's our father.'

At that moment, the younger officer looked in their direction. 'Open your bags!' barked the older one, adding softly, 'Please.' He made a show of rummaging around before chalking them. Then he turned away, and Kurt heard two click-thumps as he stamped the passports. 'Good luck,' he whispered as he handed them back.

The brothers grabbed their passports and bags and stepped into Belgium.

Kurt, a rare smiler, smiled as he finished his story. 'We landed in England on 1st September 1939.'

On 3 September Britain declared war on Germany.

WAR

With the postal service immediately suspended between all British territories and Germany, Max's niece Lisa became the family's go-between. Lisa had married an officer in the Dutch Navy, and the couple lived in Wassenaar. She forwarded letters between Berlin, London and Tel Aviv until German occupation of the Netherlands put a stop to it. '*Hallo Ernst. How are things?*' she scribbled on a letter from my grandparents dated 26 September 1939. '*I've been a grass widow since 11th April and now I'm a post office, but we won't let anything get us down.*'

Max wrote:

'*Dear Ernst*

'*Since your letter of 31st August we have heard nothing from you and are as worried about you as you must be about us. We are well and would of course be happy if we heard more often from you and the girls. You will be interested to learn that Kurt and Horst have arrived at Richborough Camp.*'

The old Kitchener Camp in Richborough, Kent, had been used as a holding centre for German and Austrian refugees considered young enough to begin new lives overseas. Then the war intervened.

'*I am forwarding the luggage they were unable to take with them,*' Max added.

How, I wonder, did he intend sending suitcases into enemy territory when letters were already difficult enough? Maybe his ever-helpful niece Lisa in the Netherlands was to perform that miracle.

Kurt and Horst were two amongst many refugees who would join the Pioneer Corps, later dubbed 'the King's most loyal Enemy Aliens', where finally they could exchange their worn-out boots for British Army issue.

To those trapped in Germany, letters became more nourishing than food.

'*We keep up a regular correspondence with Uncle Eugen and Alfred. Things are slowly shutting down there, and of course they feel very alone.*'

Mally added a hurried greeting:

'*Dear Lisa, dear Ernst,*

'*I'm about to do my shift in the charity kitchen. Before that I prepared supper and washed up as I don't have any help at the moment. So I'll make it short and send you, my dears in Wassenaar, and you, dear Ernst, my fondest greetings and best wishes. I hope you're all well, as we are.*

'*Love and kisses*

'*Aunt Mother Mally*'

Two months later the strain was more obvious. On 24 November 1939 Max wrote:

'*Dear Ernst,*

'*In the midst of all the distress and turmoil we are going through, what we miss most are the more or less regular reports we used to get from our children. Even if the circumstances are mainly to blame, you would greatly reduce our suffering if you would only send us now and then a few lines on a postcard.*

'*Uncle Louis had to go to hospital. We visit him constantly.*'

Max's brother Louis, a widower, lived nearby with his unmarried daughter Lina, who was in her forties. They had sometimes dropped by while Max and Mally were writing to Ernst and added a greeting. '*Dear Ernst, We're about to play rummy. Usually they ply me with drink first, but this time I've resisted*', Lina had scribbled on 6 February 1939, adding sadly: '*Shall we meet again on Capri? Love and kisses, Lina*'

Now, three months into the war, Louis was dying.

Max continued: '*Your forthcoming birthday is the main reason for this letter. We wish you many happy returns and good luck from the bottom of our hearts. May you achieve that inner equilibrium which these days is so hard to find; let us hope that an early peace will once again make that possible.*'

Their next letter to Ernst, dated 7 December 1939, shows my mother as the last link in its delivery chain. Across the top she has added: '*I got this letter today (via Lisa) and remain, with love and kisses . . .*'

Did she read between her father's carefully crafted lines? '*For the last few weeks the widow of our friend Voss has been staying with us*', Max wrote. '*Her husband suddenly departed this life, and for the time being we have taken her under our wing.*' It was Voss's American affidavit that had triggered Max's decision to emigrate. But, as Charlotte explained to Ernst while waiting for her and Nepo's own green light to the USA: '*Only the best affidavit wins.*' Nepo's family in the USA had already provided them with the necessary guarantee (the affidavit), but the USA had imposed strict immigration quotas for Jewish refugees, and visas were in short supply. Voss, still waiting for his, had taken his own life.

These letters show Max and Mally opening home and heart to the dwindling family as well as to their stranded friends. All are desperate to see their children again, for the war to end quickly, for normal life to resume. Surely, surely . . .

Mally did her best to focus on practicalities.

'*My dear boy,*

'*We miss your news terribly and urge you to try via the Red Cross, Geneva, rue de Lausanne 22, or Universala Esperanto-Asocio, Palais Wilson, Geneva (Switzerland). Enclose postage or a reply-paid token, and send an open letter or a card.*'

At the end of the year Jacob, Max's eldest brother – 'the tallest and best-looking uncle' according to my mother – took over from Lisa as family postman. He had moved from the old family home in Tirschtiegel to be with his daughter in the Netherlands.

The letters Max wrote to his brother were more candid than those to his son, and these Jacob also forwarded to Ernst.

'*Berlin, 7th December 1939*

'*Dear Jacob*

'*Hard as the current conditions of life are, they have their advantages: namely, they keep us in closer contact with one another; thank you so much for all your efforts. We were delighted to learn that, despite the hardships of our time, you are keeping well and coping with life. What else is left to us?*

'*Last week Alfred* [Jacob's son] *spent a few days with us. They are having a hard time of it in Betsche at this time of year but their dear little Emmchen brings them a lot of joy.*'

I first met Emmchen, or Little Emmi, on the deportation list which the archivist projected onto the classroom wall.

On 12 February 1940, Max reported to Jacob: *'They have been freezing in Betsche for weeks now. Helga* [Emmi's older sister] *even managed to get a frostbitten leg while spending a few days there on leave. She is still recuperating and stays alternately with us and Lina, who is naturally glad to have family about her. Our circle has really shrunk.'*

'Marie has been meaning to write to you for ages, but never quite manages it,' Max continued. *'She is constantly occupied with her tenants; some with furnished rooms, some with full board. She is well but never stops, as was always her way.'*

Red-haired Marie, Max's sister and business partner (when they still had a business), tended her stream of Jewish tenants, who would keep on coming. Coming and going. Passing ever more speedily through her house on their way to 'resettlement'.

'Sadly the appetite for writing family letters, which used to be so strong, is fading,' concluded Max. *'Nevertheless! We must not give up hope for a return to normal, civilized life.'*

You who have gone, don't forget us. Feed us news. Nourish us with details. Remind us of who we used to be.

Jacob turned eighty on 10 May 1940, the very day the Nazis invaded the Netherlands. *'I may be 80,'* he said to Lisa – a remark relayed to my mother, who reported it to Ernst – *'but a miracle, I feel young.'*

Lisa moved her father into hiding. There he stayed until, at some point during the Occupation, he died a natural death. Helped by her blond hair, blue eyes and quick wits, not only did Lisa herself survive, she even managed to give Jacob a Jewish burial under the noses of the Nazis. 'A brilliant woman,' commented my mother, pleased to have one uplifting story to tell me.

WAR

Those letters of February 1940 were the last ones from Max and Mally to reach Ernst and took several months to arrive. On an accompanying note Jacob had written:

'*The Hague, 17th February 1940*

'*My dear Ernst,*

'*Your letter of 17th January is in my possession. After conveying its contents to your dear parents, I received the enclosed reply. All things considered, the situation in Berlin is still somewhat better than everywhere else; the big city enjoys certain advantages. Everyone must simply do what he can to keep his head above water, for after this era another age will dawn, a better one.*

'*With love*

'*Uncle Jacob*'

By the time Ernst received the letters, the Netherlands had been occupied. An official notice was attached:

TEL-AVIV/JAFFA POSTAL CENSORSHIP

This incoming letter from enemy occupied territory is now being released. But in future no correspondence from enemy occupied territory will be permitted except through the officially recognised channel.

FORM PCT/37

TEL-AVIV/JAFFA POSTAL CENSORSHIP

This incoming letter from enemy occupied territory is now being released, but in future no correspondence from enemy occupied territory will be permitted except through the officially recognised channel, all incoming letters from enemy occupied territory not passing through the proper channel will be detained.

For further information you should consult Post Office Public Notice No.10, dated 12th February, 1940.

From now on, the only way Max and Mally could communicate with their children was via Red Cross messages, twenty-five words maximum.

* * *

As soon as war broke out, correspondence between my mother and Ernst was also subject to censorship. Obliged to write to one another in English, they were unable to express themselves as fluently as in German and, with the censor looking over their shoulders, their letters and postcards appear stilted.

'*7th November 1939*

'*My beloved brother Ernest,* *

'*I know that you are waiting for news. Well, up till now we are all well and my boss is still very busy, we only don't work late at night any more as we used to because of the blackout. I think one has to be fatalistic these days, it is no good to worry about the future, what has got to happen will happen and I am doing my best to keep my spirits up and not to get depressed.*

'*I am getting news from Mallymax occasionally, of course they cannot say much. I was wondering whether there is still a chance for them. I heard of people who had their certificates that they were able to get to a neutral country and from there to Palestine quite recently.*

'*By the way, I think your english* [sic] *is very good indeed.*'

On 13 December 1939 Ernst sent a last appeal to the Director of Migration in Jerusalem. His letter ended:

'*So,* [my parents] *are in Germany without any relatives and*

---

* Now she is writing in English, Hilda addresses her brother as 'Ernest'. Her messages are reproduced exactly as she wrote them.

means. People in neutral countries have communicated with me and have assured [me] that immediate help is required.

'Clearly, it is a most pitiful situation living in freedom in Palestine, but knowing that my parents will go to ruin in Germany.

'I was not yet able to submit the formal application to bring my parents into Palestine as the immigration offices are closed for the submission of such applications.'

The reply was bald and final:

'23rd December 1939

'Sir, I refer to your letter of the 13th December regarding Mr Max Israel RYCHWALSKI and regret to inform you that I shall be unable to take any further action in this case during the continuation of the war.

'I am, Sir, your obedient servant,

'Commissioner for Migration and Statistics,

'Acting Director, Department of Immigration'

* * *

I want to lay blame. All along my grandparents had dragged their heels, engaged the wrong advisor, found the right one too late, not heeded their children, hung on to money and valuables, contributed to their own tragedy. Charlotte and her spendthrift husband, my mother earning £1 a week, could they have made a greater effort to find sponsors for their parents? Ernst moving flats in the heat of the Tel Aviv summer, did he do enough to chivvy the immigration authorities before the door slammed shut? At what point did it become too late?

Officials of other countries kept escape routes open. Two years into the war Hiram Bingham, the American Vice

Consul in Marseille, and Varian Fry, a loose cannon of a journalist, were to defy their own Government and cobble together visas for Jews on the run – like Charlotte – to escape across the Pyrenees and make it to the USA. So should I blame the Government of Palestine? It takes brave, awkward buggers who will risk careers and even their lives to strike out and save others. Sadly, the anonymous, pen-pushing Acting Director, Department of Immigration in Jerusalem, was not one of them. On the other hand, Frank Foley, Head of British Passport Control in Berlin – in reality a spy – issued visas for Jews to go to Palestine and forged passports left, right and centre to save them, even finding pretexts to pluck them out of concentration camps and spirit them away.

But someone is missing. While pointing the finger at Max and Mally, Charlotte, my mother, Ernst, Dr Jacobi, the British Government, even Rabbi Nussbaum, to whose charity Max had paid a vast sum of money, I have lost sight of the actual culprit. However futile Max and Mally's actions, ineffective the urgings of their children, useless their advisor, empty the rabbi's assurances of a Palestine entry certificate and obdurate the British Government, the main door at which to lay the blame for my grandparents' fate is the one sporting a swastika.

* * *

News from Max and Mally tailed away at the same time as their children's problems multiplied. At the outbreak of war the French had immediately interned Charlotte's husband Nepo, along with other German men, whether or not they were refugees. '*She is not very happy, being all alone and not knowing how long for,*' my mother wrote to Ernst on 7 November 1939. '*But he has been made head cook for 300 people, so has at least got a job that suits him.*'

Charlotte's permit to visit Nepo in internment camp

Nepo was an artist in the kitchen as well as on canvas and whipped up 'sinful sauces' to accompany dishes to feed the eye as well as the palate, a skill hardly needed in prison camp. After being held for six months, he was released. Charlotte waited for him to tuck into his first meal. Thin and gaunt, he sat for a long time staring at his plate. '*Endlich . . .*' he said. ('At last . . .') Charlotte thought he was going to say: 'At last something decent to eat!' But no. '*Endlich mal eine andere Farbe!*' ('At last, a different colour!')

In the UK all German and Austrian refugees were immediately classed as 'Enemy Aliens', and a tribunal determined whether they should be interned (Category A), have their movements restricted (Category B), or posed no threat (Category C). For the first year of the war most Jews, classed as Category C, were left alone.

On 15 April 1940 my mother wrote to Ernst: '*We are very busy, but at least I got a rise for Easter, 25sh a week now, which is very useful, as you can imagine. We got used to the blackout and go out at night to pictures or dances or parties, just as we did before the war. I often think we were born at the wrong time, it would be much nicer to learn about Hitler and his war in history books at school, wouldn't it? Anyhow, I am quite confident that we are not too old yet to live and see his end.*

'*I had a letter from Mallymax a few days ago, it sounded very depressed. They have not heard from you for a long time.*' That will have been the last letter she received via the Dutch letter route. Shortly afterwards the Netherlands were occupied.

'*I get regular news* [from Charlotte]*,*' my mother continued. '*He is busy painting, and they are leading a very quiet life. They are waiting to go to America but will be in Paris for a few more months to come.*'

How wrong she was. With the German invasion of France in May 1940, Charlotte and Nepo were on the run.

In the UK, once the phony war had ended and bombs started raining down, the British policy towards refugees changed. 'Collar the lot!' Churchill commanded, prompted by fears of a fifth column, and Categories B and C were now also rounded up. But not all of them. The treatment of women appeared to be arbitrary. Amongst my parents' refugee friends, married women were interned along with their husbands, whereas single women like my mother weren't. Some men, such as my father's GP brother and my mother's dentist boss, were also exempt if their work was considered necessary. But not my thirty-seven-year-old father. After three years in various sales jobs, including as an unlikely agent for Maidenform bras, he was interned.

Length of imprisonment varied. The Isle of Man, my father explained, was bad news as, once there, they might be held for years. So he considered himself relatively lucky to be sent to a series of provisional camps set up on race courses. After short spells at Kempton Park and Lingfield, in the late summer of 1940 he was transferred to York.

The weather was boiling hot. While queuing up outside the race track waiting to be processed, he noticed an ice cream seller. Fishing a sixpenny bit out of his pocket, he beckoned a bystander. 'Could you get two cornets, please, for me and my friend?' The man took the coin and disappeared. At that moment the column advanced, and my father waved goodbye to both ice cream and money. Then he heard a shout. The man, beetroot-red, raced towards him and thrust two cornets plus the sixpence back into his hands. 'Good luck to you,' he panted, sealing my father's lifelong affection for the country that would later adopt him.

On York racecourse the wind blew and tents collapsed. Disorientated men struggled to put them up again under the watchful eye of the British Army. Confined by barbed wire, they were all sitting ducks, trussed and oven-ready, should Hitler invade.

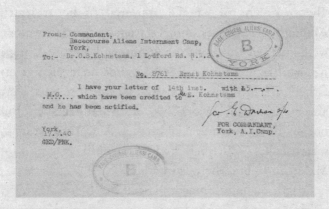

From:- Commandant,
       Racecourse Aliens Internment Camp,
       York,
To:- Dr.O.S.Kohnstamm, 1 Lydford Rd. N.W.2

No. 8761   Ernst Kohnstamm

I have your letter of 14th inst. with £5.—.—.
M.O.... which have been credited to M.E. Kohnstamm
and he has been notified.

York,
17.7.40
GED/PNK.

FOR COMMANDANT,
York, A.I.Camp.

Transfer of £5 to Ernst Kohnstamm in internment camp

My parents had met two years earlier in Dr Rosenkranz's dental surgery. My father – whose name, confusingly, was also Ernst – had been in urgent need of treatment. How quickly romance blossomed after my mother had peered at his teeth isn't clear. She wrote to him at 'Race Course Aliens' Camp B, York' – in German, I am surprised to see. Didn't the army censor letters?

'*17th September 1940*

'*Dearest Erni,*

'*We are now living a communal life in the shelter. Daddy* [her boss] *is reading, Margot* [his wife] *is darning, and I am writing.*

'*As you mention in every letter how good the sausage was,*

I've sent you another chunk today and hope it will taste as good as the last one. Enjoy.

'Herr Joachim visited us yesterday, just released from York. He told us that, as well as playing football, you are also busy singing. Keep practising the piano, my dear, and try not to bellow too much, even if that's what you prefer doing. I can just picture you, old busybody, constantly on the go. You're not missing anything in London. Our practice is very up and down, only half the patients turn up to their appointments. Having said that, the air raids are really only horrible and noisy at night. We all sleep in the dining room where we've attached shutters to the windows and, as it's a well-known fact that one can get used to everything, I'm now able to sleep both through Daddy's snoring and the explosions. As for going out at night, I've forgotten what that's like. My days off have shrunk to afternoons off, and shopping I do on the High Road. I read and knit a lot, and when the days get shorter and evenings longer, I shall read and knit more.

'Darling, my eyes keep closing, I'm so tired. I've never needed so much sleep. "Nerves," Mrs Coulson says. So let me press you to my heart and embrace you.

'Write to me again soon and stay just as cheerful.

'Love Hilda'

My mother's contact with Ernst and Charlotte had meanwhile dried up. For several months after France's capitulation in May 1940, she didn't know what had happened to her sister, and many letters to and from Ernst in Tel Aviv never arrived.

By the autumn communications had improved, and she finally heard from her brother.

'*7th November 1940*

'*Dear Ernest,*

'*At last I had a letter from you, the first since May, so the rest must have got lost, just like my letters to you. About a month ago I heard from Lotte. They are together in the unoccupied part of France, waiting to go to America.*

'*I had a letter from Mallymax via Red Cross from July, just to say that they were alright.*

'*I shall send you postcards like this regularly now. You, too, could write more frequently. All the very best and don't worry about me . . .*'

With the Luftwaffe pounding London, my mother's boss joined the mass exodus to the country. She stayed behind to deal with patients' queries and wait for news from her sister, who was hiding in the woods of southwest France.

'*28th January 1941*

'*My dear brother Ernest*

'*A few days ago I heard from Lotte and husband, a letter dated October, of course not what you would call fresh news. They were living in a tiny cottage, very primitive, in contact with his people in America and had (thank God) received some money from them and were waiting patiently to get to America.*'

But when would the USA issue more visas? Possibly in spring. Or maybe next summer. The rumours kept changing. The longer Charlotte and Nepo remained in hiding, the more precarious their lives became.

'*I have not heard from Mallymax for ages.*'

* * *

I go out into the garden and potter about. Everything looks straggly. It is late summer, August, and there are weeds galore. The golden hop is strangling a clematis and needs cutting back. The roses could do with deadheading. I see everything but do nothing.

So that's it. I've done it. Read all the letters. To tell the truth, the postal disruption has come as a relief. I no longer have to look because there's no more to see.

What now? I shall return to normal life. Except I'm no longer sure what normal is. After years of unknowns, I know everything, or as much as I ever can know. With each new letter there came a quickening: what might I find out this time? Not any more. That's over.

Having achieved nothing in the garden, I come back in the house and put Max and Mally's letters into their folder, the three siblings' letters into theirs. Receiving, writing and sending letters by whatever means possible. That's what kept my grandparents going.

I keep imagining Max at his desk, preparing to write. Filling his Pelikan fountain pen with the blackest ink. About to use words I've never heard of – throwbacks to the nineteenth century, his century – in labyrinthine clauses enclosed by commas forming sentences that, however agitated he may be, are always complete. That's how he holds me, my grandfather, firmly between his commas.

And Mally, doing her best to put on a brave face for three children spinning away in their separate worlds, torn between staying and going, between riding out the Nazi regime or being catapulted into a country of heat, dust and bomb blasts, dependent on the son who has always depended on her. At least in Berlin she can shut her own front door for a few hours and forget what lies on the other side.

I return the letters to the cupboard and close the door.

That night police sirens wail out urgency. I sleep intermittently and dream I am on a cross-Channel ferry unable to dock, battered by screaming wind and rain. For the sake of a month, of a week, how different my childhood landscape might have been. I used to enjoy friends' noisy homes with much teasing and bickering, their families a patchwork quilt to be drawn up around their shoulders in tough times. But my family quilt is torn, and a whispery draught has been left behind, a coldness between shoulder blades, the imprint of a hand taken away.

Luck, foresight, a willingness to shell out, to dive into the unknown, all played a part in survival, but sadly those were not Max and Mally's strong points. Instead, stubbornness and denial, followed by a muddle of hope and feverish action. All too late.

PART 3:
INTO THE FOG OF IN-BETWEEN

'WHAT ARE JEWS?'

The post brings a large envelope from Julia with the *Grundbuch* copies. They show Max and Marie bought the building in 1927 while their business was buzzing. 'I'm going away for a month this autumn,' Julia wrote. 'Would you like to use my flat as a base? You could find out more in the archives.'

I recoil. Live in their building amongst the ghosts of all this anguish? Surely I already know all there is to know. Her package follows the letters straight into the cupboard.

A few days later I take it out. Who am I kidding? There's always more to discover when you look, and if you close your eyes to it you only end up imagining awfulness. It's like when the sick rabbit lay quivering on the ground and the gamekeeper grabbed it by the ears to finish it off. My father made me turn away, and that was worse.

If I stop here, I shall have left my grandparents stranded and won't know what happened next.

I need to know what happened next.

* * *

For the third time that year I fly to Berlin. Julia meets me at the airport and whisks me off in a taxi.

It is late October. As we speed along an avenue of yellowing lime trees, leaves float down and hit the windscreen. I don't recognise any of the districts we are passing through. For the first few days, while Julia prepares for her trip, I am to stay at her friend Gisela's flat. One woman barely knows me, and the other, currently out of town, doesn't know me at all, yet both are giving me the run of their homes. Would I meet such trust anywhere else?

'This could interest you,' Julia says, handing me a flyer. 'A guided walk on Saturday.'

Printed across the top: *In the footsteps of former Jewish Mitbürger*. The prefix *Mit* gives to *bürger* a special significance, embracing Jews as '*fellow*' citizens. Meeting point: Spiegelwand (Mirror Wall).

'The Mirror Wall's near Gisela's flat. It's a memorial to the murdered Jews of Steglitz.'

Oh God, no thank you – that's my immediate reaction. Two kinds of fog swirl round the world of In-Between, and I still struggle to tell them apart. The first envelops the nameless millions, and if I get too close to that peasouper, it may suck me right in. I need to focus on the specific patch hanging over my grandparents.

As war intensified and anti-Semitic laws multiplied, sealing them off from the world, how did they cope with increasing isolation?

Could they still write and travel to relatives in Germany?

What notice were they given before deportation?

From which train station did they leave?

And what happened to their remaining possessions after they had gone? Mally used to paint and draw. My mother had described her landscapes and drawings of Hamburg fishermen. Did anyone take a fancy to them? Might her pictures still hang on someone's walls?

Then I see the local historian leading the walk has spent half a century researching his neighbourhood under the Nazis. He will know the archives inside out and be able to point the way.

Saturday is not a day for strolling. Head lowered against wind and stinging rain, I push my way through Steglitz's large market square, past stalls of books, DVDs, pastries, pullovers, hats, knickers, a van with hot dogs and sauerkraut, another with coffee. I scan gaps between trees edging the square, between red-and-white striped awnings covering blocks of cheese and an expanse of eggs. This is crazy. When new, the Mirror Wall caused controversy because of its size. So where is it?

Sometimes, when I try too hard, I can't find something right under my nose, so I stand still. A trestle table opposite displays trays of apples. Underneath are buckets of roses and pots of chrysanthemums. I turn around and see the same chrysanthemums, roses and apples in reverse. Columns of names gradually come into focus: *Lewinski, Max. Lewinski, Margarethe. Stern, Paul . . .* Reflections of flowers mingle with the names of people who have no graves on which to put them. A total of 1,723. At the foot of the wall lies one dried-up bouquet.

So who is coming on this walk? The shoppers filling bags, dipping into purses, trailing children, seem unlikely candidates. The carefully worded flyer is all very well, but how can there be an understanding of Jews as *fellow* citizens when none have played a part in local life for seventy years?

Two men arrive, one with a clipboard. A young woman joins them; she pulls off a sodden hat and opens an umbrella. A family of four drifts to a halt. I notice a middle-aged couple, arm in arm, studying names on the Mirror Wall. Finally, an older woman with wild grey hair and piercing blue eyes rushes up. I seem to be the only non-local. I wonder what made the others turn out on a raw Saturday afternoon to walk in the footsteps of their former Jewish *Mitbürger* rather than stay in the warm.

We start with the synagogue, spared during *Kristallnacht* because a fire might have damaged adjoining Aryan houses, then set off through spread-out suburbia with big, turn-of-the-century houses, generous gardens, wide pavements and the odd stumble stone. Our guide pauses here and there to tell us of lives that flowered before being cut short.

Names, names, ever more names. I'm not interested in any of them. Come on, I want to say, hurry up.

'Who cares anyway?' a familiar voice keeps whispering in my ear. 'What difference will it make? They've been dead for decades. You never knew them, can never know them. Give it a rest. Go home.' The voice is my mother's.

No, it isn't. The voice is mine, imagining what my mother would have said had she ever said it.

Our guide tells us that many Third Reich files, taken from the GDR to Moscow, have been dribbling back since the fall of the Wall.

I whip out notebook and pen. Max and Marie's tie factory was in former East Berlin. Where might I find details? And what about family members who died before they could be deported? He says the Jewish cemetery at Weissensee holds an index card for each person buried there.

I notice people glance at me then look away. I feel a barrier rise up. Us and them. Victim and perpetrator. As I drag my shroud of relatives along these suburban streets, I wonder if memorials to the murdered are more palatable than an alive-and-kicking descendant.

We turn a corner and the pavement narrows, forcing us to walk two abreast as in a school crocodile. The woman with the wild hair falls into step with me. 'I think it's wonderful what you're doing, searching out your mother's past, here where she grew up.'

But my mother did not grow up in this part of Berlin. I only came along because I'm staying nearby, because I saw the walk advertised, because it's Saturday afternoon, all archives are shut, and I want information . . . I have sunk into my otherness and her attention feels like an invasion. Just leave me alone in this strange place. The ghosts we are walking amongst are yours. I've enough of my own to contend with.

Our guide is talking about points of deportation. Something about a memorial at Grunewald station – I yank out my notebook – yet most Berlin Jews were deported from the goods-train depot at Putlitzstrasse.

Where is Putlitzstrasse? I need to go there. And Grunewald.

'Why?' It's my mother again.

'Because I've had enough of being on the edge of the fog. It's time for that fog to clear. I want to pinpoint their exact spots. Right up to deportation.'

We continue to walk, pause, move on, our guide giving us aural snapshots of human beings with no one else to remember them. For fifty years he has been unearthing his district's wiped-out Jews. No big fanfare. No headline-grabbing revelations. Just quiet, dogged research, bringing them back into the light. Walk, pause, another life sketched out, move on.

His voice is gentle, the act of walking and naming soothing. My shroud unfastens. If he and the rest of the group feel the same absence from their collective history as I do from my personal one, then we all want to grasp hold of what is missing.

How flat Berlin is, exposed to wind, heat and cold. My mother was just twenty-one when she exchanged this city of extremes, swimming in and skating on its lakes, for the temperate climate of England, for rain and smog, stiff upper lips and 'I didn't like to ask'.

The tour is almost over. The guide turns to me. 'The Jewish Library, that's a good place to start.'

'Where is it?'

'Fasanenstrasse. Off the Kurfürstendamm.'

We return to the market square. Stalls and awnings have gone. No more eggs, hats or buckets of flowers. The food trailer, hitched to an estate car, drives off. Audible now is the swish of traffic from a nearby flyover. A few paper cups whirl and bounce in the wind. Everyone begins to peel away.

I go up to my earlier walking companion. 'Did you like the tour?'

'I always learn something.'

'What's your interest?'

She turns bright red, and there are tears in her eyes.

'My grandfather was an anti-Semite. He forbade my

father from sitting next to a Jewish boy at school. It couldn't have happened without people like him.'

She explains that her grandfather's anti-Semitism existed way before the rise of Hitler, that he and his kind prepared the ground for the Third Reich to come into being in the first place. She fears that passivity and ignorance will allow those who deny the Holocaust now to triumph. 'It's in the Prussian nature,' she says, stressing the link between fascism, order and a type of manic cleanliness – a sense of always being alert for the dark forces of filth.

Her remark reminds me of an incident that morning at the local supermarket. A carton of fruit juice had leaked over the conveyor belt, and the checkout girl switched it off. She and the customer removed and wiped every item, then the belt, but the man next in line wasn't satisfied. He scoured invisible smears with tissues. Traffic was held up for several minutes, and no one objected. Imagine that scene on a crowded Saturday in London, the girl behind the till giving a quick wipe with an old J-cloth, an impatient queue doing nothing to help. Three cheers for a messy nation, then, if it shuns ethnic cleansing, too.

So here we both are, descendants of perpetrator and victim, feeling our way towards understanding, if understanding is possible, and, if not, at least towards knowledge. Today's walk, the *Stolpersteine* project and my quest all stem from a common urge: to pull individuals out of the anonymous millions and restore them to their place in the world.

She despairs of getting the message through to her grandchildren, who did not want to accompany her today, preferring to stay indoors and play computer games. The youngest asked, mystified, 'What are Jews?'

The Mirror Wall, reflecting the grey expanse of paving stones, is barely visible now. Only the top glows pink in the dying sun. At its base lies a fresh bunch of flowers.

THE FAMILY IN PUBLIC

I follow the guide's advice and start my search in the Jewish Library.

'Did your grandparents belong to any Jewish associations?'

'Their synagogue was the Friedenstempel. The rabbi was a family friend.' I don't mention he was also Charlotte's lover – in the late 1920s some of her lovers overlapped. I had tried to read his letters but soon gave up, irritated by his use of ten words where two would do. They aren't a patch on André Andreyev's, written in chaotic, Russian-accented German, bursting with energy and peppered with illustrations. Beneath a ship of love named *LOTTE* powered by a billowing red heart-shaped sail, he proclaims: '*Meine beste Hertz, ich begrusse dich und wünsche dier gluck, sonne, freide und geld.*' ('*My dearest heart, greetings! I wish you luck, sun, joy and money.*') His signature – an 'A' on a chamber pot holding a flower – bobs on the waves. No sooner had he left the Berlin film world for Paris than Charlotte jumped in the sea and swam after him.

'Any other organisations?' asks the librarian.

'The Jewish Institute for the Profoundly Deaf in Weissensee. My grandfather was on the board.'

'I'll check. You could also look at these.' She plonks two enormous tomes on the counter. 'Only . . . are you here on your own?'

What an odd question. 'Yes. Why?'

'These are the memorial books. Everyone whose transport went from or through Berlin is listed here.' She taps one volume. 'Name, address, age. Where they were taken. Also their fate, if known.'

Hell's bells. All the ones who didn't get away. Had Charlotte not blazed the escape trail for her brother and sister, then their names might also be here, and I wouldn't exist to find them.

'Seeing the names can be distressing.' She seems to be sizing me up behind her glasses. 'A father and son came once, and the father collapsed. Maybe you'd like to have someone with you?'

Would I? Well, yes, I suppose I would, although no one has ever offered to come with me, and it has never occurred to me to ask. Until now I have always done my Max and Mally foraging alone and quietly – even secretly while my mother was alive so as not to upset her – and I reckoned no one else wanted it rammed down their throat. This must be a leftover from the reaction I used to get when someone asked about my mother's family, then clearly wished they hadn't – a sliding away of eyes and quick change of subject, as if mentioning their murder was in bad taste.

'What's in the other book?' I ask.

'A few years ago another register was discovered in Theresienstadt, and now it's been published. It lists all the transports from there to the extermination camps.'

No no no. Don't get sucked into that fog. Steer clear. Stick to my grandparents. They weren't sent on anywhere. Max and Mally stayed in Theresienstadt. They died in Theresienstadt. *Not the worst camp*.

And I shan't look at the first volume either. Because right now I want to know how they *lived*. Because, after their letters dried up, they did go on living somehow or other. And it's that somehow-or-other I'm after.

'Take a seat,' the librarian says. 'I'll bring you anything we have on their synagogue and the institute.'

I choose an empty table but can't seem to coordinate taking off my coat and sitting at it. I feel all at sea. Like in the Jewish Museum when I sensed I'd walked slap bang into my cupboard. I should have someone with me, should I? That was a gentle warning. What might I unleash? The trouble is, there's no way of knowing until I unleash it.

The librarian returns with a slim volume. 'We've nothing on your grandparents' synagogue, but I found this.'

> '*Öffne deine Hand für die Stummen*'
> *Die Geschichte der Israelitischen Taubstummen-
> Anstalt*
> *Berlin-Weissensee 1873 bis 1942*
>
> ('*Give a Helping Hand . . .*'
> *A History of the Jewish Institute for the Profoundly
> Deaf*
> *in Berlin-Weissensee 1873–1942*)

My mother used to accompany Max and Mally to the institute for the festival of Chanukka. The appearance of the director's wife, who had converted to Judaism, fascinated her. 'Erna Reich had long, blond plaits, which she wore wound around her head like any true Bavarian,' she said. 'Her appearance would have brought joy to any Nazi, yet there she stood singing "Maoz Tzur", the Chanukka song.'

Here's a grainy photo of children and a few adults sitting around a long table laden with gifts and a cake. The caption reads: *Chanukka in the Jewish Institute for the Profoundly Deaf, pre-1938*. I home in on a figure at the back. Although blurred, the wide forehead, half-profile and stance as she turns to the girl on her right are unmistakable. It's my mother.

I skim the rest of the photos and stop at a head-and-shoulders shot of a young Max and fellow board members opposite a letter dated 1938 to the Berlin Chief of Police. The *Herr* before each trustee's name is crossed out and the letter stamped with a large 'J' for Jew. Dehumanisation under way. The beginning of the end.

The following morning Wolfgang picks me up and we drive southwest out of Berlin across a vast plain surrounded by thick, dark trees. This is the forest where Frederick the Great hunted and built the Palace of Sans-Souci. I'm trying to remember a rude verse my mother recited when I once asked for help with my German history homework – I should have known better.

The road is perfectly straight. No hill, no valley, no up, no down. Not so much as a wiggle. On and on and on. We are heading for Potsdam and the Brandenburg Landeshauptarchiv. Here, deep in the forest, is where the starkest information is held. Wolfgang needs details for a new batch of stumble stones, and I have an appointment with the archivist I met at the conference. I hope she can give me an idea of Max and Mally's lives right up to their deportation.

The first line of the verse comes back to me. 'Frederick the Great shits his pants . . .' I say it out loud. 'Remind me how it goes on.'

Friedrich der Große macht sich in die Hose
Friedrich der Kleine macht sie wieder reine
Friedrich der ganz Kleine hängt sie an die Wäscheleine!

After Frederick the Great shits his pants and Little Frederick washes them, Tiny Frederick hangs them on the washing line. Cleanliness vanquishing filth. An indication of the Prussian character, according to my Mirror Wall acquaintance.

We reach the outskirts of Potsdam. A line of drab buildings fringes the road, then they peter out and trees take over again. It would have been a job to get here by public transport – train and bus, but the bus stop is miles away. I see it as we turn down a side road and drive through yet more trees. It's as if they don't want anyone to find them.

I am shown into a room. Five minutes later the archivist arrives, beaming. Behind her an assistant carries a pile of photocopies and puts them on the table. When deportations started, the archivist explains, people were given notice. They had time to fill in the sixteen-page questionnaires at home giving details of their assets. 'You may remember me saying how the Gestapo destroyed their records when they saw the war was lost, but the Finance

Ministry kept theirs.' She indicates the papers. 'Here are your family's documents.'

I'm gobsmacked. I had expected to look up everything myself, and she's done it for me. Not only that, she's made me photocopies.

Jews weren't deported immediately after being picked up. They would spend several days, perhaps a week or more, in an assembly camp. As time went on, people got wise and, when notified, might take evasive action. Some went into hiding. Others took their own lives. Didn't the Nazis welcome suicide if it saved them fuel for transport and a portion of gas? Apparently not. To avoid general unrest, a delicate balance had to be maintained between terror and compliance. In any case, suppose the suicidal didn't bother to complete their questionnaires first? What a nightmare in man hours and paperwork until the Reich could get its hands on their property. Far better to round them up without warning and make them complete the forms at the assembly camp. Don't allow fountain pens, mind. Some have tried to stab themselves with those. Take all pens off all Jews and give them an indelible pencil instead.

Immediately after deportation, houses and flats were sealed by the Gestapo, then assigned to an Aryan family and the contents auctioned.

'Which of these are my grandparents' papers?'

The archivist shakes her head. 'Theirs are the only ones we don't have.'

'What?'

'Some files were destroyed in air raids.'

'You mean you've got nothing of theirs at all?'

'I'm afraid not.'

Oh no. She's unearthed my mother's uncles, aunts and cousins. Everyone I've been doing my best to avoid for fear of being overwhelmed.

I trail along the corridor behind the assistant. She takes me into the reading room. The deportation lists are on microfilm, she explains, and shows me where to ask for them. Here I can also request the original files if I want to, as not everything has been photocopied. Then she leaves me to it.

Now what do I do? I am marooned in the forest until Wolfgang is ready to leave. Then I think: given the chaos of war, is there a chance that something of Max and Mally's got put in the wrong file? You never know . . .

An hour later, in the quiet rustle of the reading room, I am still standing up. I pulled out a chair ages ago but there is no way I am going to sit on it. On the table in front of me lies my murdered Rychwalski clan. I need to be on my feet, ready for every official bastard who leaps out of the pages.

On the binding of one file, property of the *Oberfinanzpräsident Devisenstelle* (*Superintendent of Finances, Foreign Currency Division*), a civil servant had carefully written the names inside the designated box:

<u>Rychwalski</u>
Jacob & Alfred
currently in <u>Wassenaar</u>
<u>Holland</u>

Good for you, Uncle Jacob. You found refuge with your daughter Lisa, went into hiding and died before they could kill you, unlike your son Alfred, half blinded fighting for the Fatherland, who was made to see much and suffer plenty.

Flick, flick, flick. Here is a letter headed *Geheime Staatspolizei*. I am touching a page that has been touched by a member of the Gestapo. However much you know in theory, it's being nose to nose with this stuff that makes it real. Why is everyone around me so calm?

Alfred travelled back and forth from his home in Betsche to keep an eye on Jacob's property in Tirschtiegel. He wrote evasive letters to the authorities: his father fully intended to return home after visiting Lisa, but regrettably age and infirmity had intervened . . .

What open, flowing handwriting, fairly buzzing with energy. As Alfred's pen flies over the page, I read between the lines and cheer him on – *you'll never catch my father, you bastards, he's out of your stinking reach*. Good for you, Alfred. Good for you, Lisa. Result!

A man in the next seat looks at me. I didn't actually cheer, did I? I move away, prowl around the reading room's edges and stop at the request desk. Before I know it, I've ordered the deportation list I first saw projected onto the classroom wall, the one with Alfred on it. Now I've seen the way he wrote, he's become a *Mensch* again. A human being. A presence. Not just a number. I could do that with the others, too. Get to know them through their handwriting.

I return to my place and the files. Let's get a sense of who Cousin Lina was before she was no more. Uncle Louis's unmarried daughter who longed to travel again. '*Shall we meet again on Capri?*' she had written to Ernst. Little did she guess her next journey would be in January 1942 on Transport Number 8 to Riga. In her final Declaration of

Assets she listed a grand piano and 200 books amongst an abundance of fine furniture, plus a whopping deposit of RM 73,617.42 in the Deutsche Bank (worth approximately half a million US dollars today). The Gestapo and Finance Ministry will have been itching to get their hands on that.

A boy's signature makes me catch my breath. Fourteen-year-old Heinz, whose big brothers had squeaked into England at the very last moment, declared a small inheritance. I can just see him bent over the table as he dipped his pen in the ink, determined not to make a blot, and painstakingly wrote his name. That spiky signature is all that remains of his brief life.

Heinz Israel Rychwalski
(Unterschrift)

Further lists of assets, more modest than Lina's, allow me to peep into living rooms, bedrooms, kitchens, cellars, attics and the day-to-day lives of other family members: 3 beds, 4 mattresses, 1 sofa, 1 armchair; 2 jackets, 2 silk dresses, 8 sheets, 3 blankets, 8 pillows; 1 table and sewing machine; cooking pots and baking tins; an old iron and laundry basket; 1 sack of coal. Everything had a value, from 300 Marks down to 50 Pfennig. In the end, what the Senator für Finanzen really wanted were the bank details and shareholdings. Account number? Balance? No sooner had their transport gone than the Gestapo gave the Finance Ministry the go-ahead to help itself.

By now I've completely forgotten I was only looking for signs of Max and Mally. I'm hooked.

I return to Alfred and his father Jacob's files, thick with several years of correspondence, and skim through them, as if waiting for something special to claim my attention.

Flick, flick, flick.

Suddenly I see what I've been waiting for. The same name has been cropping up again and again. A doctor. What a dear little oval rubber stamp he applied to his communications. Curving around the top *Dr. K. Mathwig*, around the bottom *Tirschtiegel*, and in the middle *Arzt*. A doctor you wouldn't want to consult. Shortly after *Kristallnacht* he began his tireless correspondence with the authorities.

Dr Mathwig was a tenant of Jacob's. The house he rented at 112 Adolf Hitler Platz needed repairing. The roof leaked. But the Jew Rychwalski had remained in the Netherlands, was anyway no longer a German citizen and had no right to own property. His Jew son was failing in his duties as manager. When would an Aryan be appointed? And another thing: Dr Mathwig wanted to buy the house, but apparently the Gestapo had also shown an interest in it. So would they kindly clarify:

'*Who is currently considered to be the owner, the Jew or the State?*

'*Heil Hitler!*

'*Mathwig*

'*Tirschtiegel.*'

Tremendous heat welds my feet to the floor. A wave rushes up the back of my legs. I am so hot that if you plugged me into the mains I would fuse the whole of Brandenburg.

This was not a question of faceless officials following orders. Dr Mathwig knew Jacob. The two men would have signed the tenancy agreement, perched on chairs drinking coffee from cups, which, now he comes to think of it, would fit very nicely into his own home . . .

I spend several minutes at the washbasin scrubbing off traces of Dr Mathwig.

Wolfgang and I drive back along the flat, straight road in silence.

When travelling with my parents as a child we used to sing canons on tedious journeys, a trilingual repertoire: 'London's Burning', 'Frère Jacques', 'Oley Voley'. In the days when German was still the language of parental secrets, '*O wie wohl ist mir am Abend*' was more than I could get my tongue around. 'Let's sing "Oley Voley"', I would say, and the name stuck.

We pull up next to a wooden wheelbarrow displaying pumpkins, squash and flowers. Wolfgang returns with a bunch of dahlias for Barbara, welcome relief after a day steeped in the grim.

As we speed off, I sing to myself:
'*Oley voley mir am Abend, mir am Abend,*
'*Wenn zur Ruh' die Glocken läuten, Glocken läuten,*
'*Bim bam, bim bam*
'*Bim bam, bim bam.*'
('Oh how lovely is the evening, is the evening,
'When the bells are sweetly ringing, sweetly ringing,
'Ding dong, ding dong,
'Ding dong, ding dong.')

* * *

Back at Gisela's I prop the heavy package of photocopies against the wall and flop on the bed. All day long other members of the shadow family have eclipsed Max and Mally. I hadn't bargained with them but now can no longer push them away. Their handwriting has seen to that, those last traces of personality before, reduced to numbers, they stepped onto the rolling microfilm of transports and disappeared. How the indefensible became acceptable had been beyond my understanding until today. Now I can't escape the image of Dr Mathwig erupting from the centre of his anodyne rubber stamp, one tiny component driving the whole machine. Millions of Dr Mathwigs swarm behind my closed eyes, they divide and multiply like cancer cells, they scurry out of corners to join the marching hordes . . .

I must have dozed off. Footsteps rouse me, very quiet ones, more like a gentle padding. I sit up. Gisela is back.

Ten minutes later, after introductions – did you find everything? how was your journey? – we sit at the kitchen table drinking tea. She is tired and relieved to be home after visiting her father. He is now in his late nineties. Caring from afar isn't easy. She tells me about his war activities, not that I asked but the reason I am here probably impelled her. She explains that, as a deeply religious man, he had avoided fighting. I am surprised. Was it possible to be a conscientious objector under the Nazis? Apparently they could use his skills in other ways. He was a master builder.

I salute him, sip my tea and relax into the moment. The grim day is fading, the world takes on colour and balance. I remember there were decent people, too.

So they sent him to Riga.

One word, that's all it takes. Off go the sirens in my head, and I am back in the reading room with the deportation lists. Lina wasn't the only family member sent to Riga. On my last visit to Charlotte before she died, she had talked scathingly of Mally calling all her menfolk Fritz – that was the name of her beloved brother. 'Max, Ernst, they were all "Fritz" to her,' she said, adding: 'Of course, Fritz and Olga were shot in Riga.' Of course? I had thought, shocked. Then: yes, of course, that's our family's normality.

With Riga's ghetto still full of its own Jews, early transports had nowhere to discharge their cargo. Trains were halted on the edge of town. Everyone herded into the woods. Gunned down.

So Riga needed a master builder, did it? To do what exactly? Expand the ghetto? Demolish it and clear the way for something else?

'Do you mind if I have a cigarette?' Gisela defies her own house rules, lights up and blows smoke out of the window. 'I don't feel guilty,' she says as if reading my mind, 'I simply can't grasp all that happened.'

My own thoughts repel me. They feel like a betrayal of her hospitality. I try to rationalise them, then give up. Fritz, Olga and Lina may have left no trace amongst the forests and marshes of Latvia, but their fate gouged three scars across my family landscape. That's just the way it is.

We sit for a while saying nothing. Gradually this turns into a good nothing, the awkwardness of our different legacies acknowledged in the silence. Tomorrow I am moving to Julia's flat.

'How have you got on?' Gisela asks.

I tell her of my frustration at discovering little about Max and Mally, yet a bagful on the rest of the murdered. 'Many didn't live in Berlin but in small towns that were German until 1945 and are now in Poland: Tirschtiegel, Betsche—'

'Betsche?' she says. 'My father grew up in Betsche.'

'No!'

I mumble something about needing to pack, go back to my room and sit on the floor, stunned. I will my suitcase to open and my belongings to jump in and pack themselves. Betsche, for goodness' sake. Betsche was a far cry from Berlin. Betsche was tiny. In 1939 its population numbered 1,749. Gisela's father would have been a schoolboy by the time Cousin Alfred married and moved there. Their paths cannot fail to have crossed.

'Can't you give it a rest?' I call out to the bag of photocopies propped against the wall.

Alfred's thick-nibbed scrawl pulsates across the room. He and his girls will be remembered. They bloody well will be remembered.

A gentle knock on the door brings Gisela with a pre-war picture of the town. The caption reads *Betsche – Market Square* and shows a statue in the middle of an open space ringed by houses, and in the background a church tower topped by an onion dome.

Their address on the deportation list was *74 Markt*, so they must have lived in one of the houses pictured; either single-storey with a steep pitched roof, or two storeys with bigger windows. Five out of a total of twenty Jews, here one minute, gone the next, house sealed up, possessions auctioned. I can just imagine the neighbours queueing up to bid.

'Gisela, could you ask your father if he remembers a First World War veteran, blinded in one eye, wore a patch? Alfred Rychwalski. Lived right here on Market Square.'

At the end of the war, when the province of Posen (Poznan) became part of Poland, it was her family's turn to be dispossessed. They left Betsche and fled west. Gisela asks her father. He does not remember Alfred.

THRESHOLDS

I show the clouds my keys, jingle them over Max and Mally's stumble stones – 'look what I've got!' – and let myself in. Through the hall and out into the courtyard, I cross into the garden wing and take the lift up to Julia's flat. Shoes off, slippers on, I pad around the gleaming parquet and go into the kitchen. A cuppa, that's what I need. After all, I'm English.

Julia has prepared my bed in the large living room. I sit on it and look around at bookshelves, two armchairs and a lot of space. It feels odd to be here on my own. I go over to the window, and suddenly it no longer feels odd at all. Suddenly it feels absolutely right.

Across from me are the rear windows of the front flats where Julia reckons Max and Mally will have lived. Not the ground floor, as that belongs to a shop and a gallery. Probably not the attics either. That leaves four storeys. One set of those windows must be Hans and Dieter's, the first people to invite me into the building and show me around. I phone them. 'Guess where I am.'

'No! Where? Give us a wave.'

A light goes on in a lower window. I can see a silhouette through the branches of a tree in the middle of the court-yard. 'Here I am,' I wave.

The silhouette waves back. 'Only me,' says Hans, 'Dieter says he isn't decent.'

'Tell him I can't really see. The tree's in the way.'

They invite me over to watch a film on TV, *Nicht alle waren Mörder* (*Not All Were Murderers*). Their neighbourliness is heartening, yet I'd like them to know that there are other sides to me than just being a descendant of Nazi victims. Only that's the reason I'm in Berlin – what's more, in my grandparents' block of flats – so who am I actually trying to persuade? Underneath my urge to find out lurks the constant fear that I'll remain stuck in the shit: a fear that battles with the hope – the fantasy – that the seesaw between wanting to know, and being overwhelmed by knowing, will stop once all the unknowns that can be known are known. At that point I shall walk into the sunrise of a new day.

Meanwhile there is nothing spooky about being in my grandparents' building, and I sleep soundly under their sky.

The following morning I go into Julia's office on the other side of the flat. She has cleared the top of her desk for me. I sit at it and look across a wide open space to the backs of the buildings in the next street. Through a gap I glimpse traffic lights suspended over its junction with Lietzenburger Strasse, the main road, and hear the distant swish of cars.

I unpack my notebooks and papers, then notice a sheet of paper held in place by a pebble. *EX-NEIGHBOURS WHO MIGHT HELP YOU.* Julia has left a contact list of people who had moved into the block well before she did. First on the list is Alex.

*   *   *

'1951 to 1983! To think I lived here for more than thirty years.' Alex and her daughter Steffi are sitting at the kitchen table in Julia's flat while I make coffee. 'So how can we help? What is it you want to know about the building?'

It is a question I struggle to answer as I am still feeling my way. I really want to pinpoint my grandparents' flat, something I realise Alex and Steffi can't tell me. But after a lifetime of silence and absence, I am doing the next best thing: getting to know my grandparents via their geography – the streets they trod, the thresholds they crossed. As Alex and Steffi moved into the block soon after the war, they will have lived alongside the same neighbours who had dodged the same bombs as Max and Mally. What was it like, living here at that time?

'Well, the kitchen used to be the centre of our lives, too,' says Steffi, looking around. 'This is where I grew up. We had the same flat two floors down with exactly those tiles. That cupboard under the window was the *Eisschrank*. A truck used to come round and deliver blocks of ice. As it melted, it dripped through to keep things cool.'

Alex, although in her nineties and almost blind, has needle-sharp memories. 'Astonishing to think my flat was still empty in 1951. Probably because the damage had been so severe, the front ripped open and ceilings down. A fire-bomb had gone right through it, destroying the hall. We stole stones from the street to rebuild the walls. My mother's room had a stove, but it was still terribly cold. Hardly any gas, just for a couple of hours a day.'

'That's odd,' says Steffi. 'I've no memory of the flat in that state. But I have recurring dreams of living somewhere with trailing bits of straw—'

'Yes, the old ceilings, plaster packed with straw, were left hanging. Refugees kept on arriving and everyone sublet. Frau Peters, one floor below us, hung a curtain across one room and let the space behind it. A Jewish man rented it. I once had a disagreement with Rabbi Galinski – he was head of the Jewish community by then. He said parents must prepare their children for the meetings he organised between Christians and Jews so they understood exactly what had gone on. I thought he was being too severe.'

'He was right, Mummy!' protests Steffi. She explains: 'When I was fifteen I gave a talk at school about what had happened to the Jews in Germany and was attacked. Because the other children's parents had told them nothing. That's how it was in the 1950s. But my mother had a lot of Jewish friends, and we tried to find out what had happened to them.'

'Yes, I eventually agreed with Galinski.' Alex sips her coffee. 'Can we tell you anything else?'

I show them the wartime lists of residents. 'Do you recognise anyone? These people would have lived alongside my grandparents.'

'Lulu Michels!' cries Alex. 'She was a singer at the opera in the eastern sector and lived below us. When the Wall went up, she was no longer allowed to go across and gave singing lessons every evening. From 8 p.m. it was non-stop scales – "mi-mi-mi-mi-MI-mi-mi-mi-mi". Then at 4 a.m. the dreadful pigeons got going. I begged her: "Lulu, the singing I can understand, but can you at least stop feeding the pigeons?" Directly beneath us was a dance school with a record player. That also carried on till 11.00 p.m. "And repeat once more . . ." Then at 6 a.m. it was time to get up, and everything started all over again. Strange times.'

'There were about six of us children in the block and a disabled child in one of the flats at the front,' said Steffi. 'The front flats were the classiest. They were the only ones with a lift. The porter was always drunk and complained about us playing in the ruins, making too much noise.'

'For years there was no hot water,' Alex recalls. 'And they said: "There's nothing we can do. The heirs disagree with one another."'

Oh really? It is true that Max and his sister Marie's heirs disagreed about what to do with the building once they finally regained ownership, but the Insurers of Death had hung on to it until the 1960s. I sense a managing agent unwilling to break old habits, preferring to pin the blame for lack of repairs on Jews scattered over continents.

We return to the wartime lists of residents.

'Steinke!' exclaims Steffi. 'Remember Herr Steinke? The garage?'

'Always stank.'

I ask if they remember Frau Steinke. Is it true that she worked for the Goebbels household?

There is a long silence.

'I heard she looked after his children.'

'Possibly,' says Alex at last.

Steffi can't remember her at all, whereupon Alex bursts out: 'Frau Steinke is the only one I really remember.'

What kind of a person was she?

'I always had the feeling . . . hard . . .' She hesitates. 'I can't really be more explicit because . . . I can't . . .'

And I'm left with an all-too-familiar feeling of frustration at a truth about to be revealed crumbling into nothing. It's like being with my mother all over again when the shutters came down.

In those early post-war years, as Alex fought to feed her family, as she rubbed shoulders with ex-Nazis while making contact with her Jewish friends, she tried to absorb the unspeakable and agonised over what more she could have done. Later, despite having grandchildren in Israel, she never set foot in the country herself. 'Someone of my generation. What would people think?'

They put their coats on in the hall once wrecked by a fire-bomb. 'Was the lift put in while we still lived here?' asks Alex.

'Yes, but too late for Granny. She still had to climb the stairs.'

I remind them of the moment Alex seemed about to say something important about Frau Steinke, then stopped.

'Time and again I've asked my mother to write things down, but she won't even talk about it,' says Steffi.

'The trouble is, whenever I start to write, or even to think about it, I can't go any further. I always seem to reach that threshold . . .' Alex's voice tails away once more, and that is where her resemblance to my mother ends, my mother unaware of the thresholds she avoided crossing.

They get into the lift.

'I came along today as I hoped to find out things my mother never told me,' says Steffi as the doors close.

Me too, Steffi. Me too.

And thanks to them, I have found things out. Between air raids my grandparents will have heard Lulu the singer trilling her scales across the courtyard and done their best to avoid the Steinkes. I imagine them hunkering down in their own flat when the siren went off, locking and bolting the front door and keeping away from the windows.

Which brings me back to the one question no one can answer: which flat was Max and Mally's?

I recap what I have learned about the building. A bulge in the middle of the stonework in each side wing contains a narrow flight of stairs, but no lift. Alex and Steffi have confirmed that the garden wing had no lift until well after the war and that the front flats were the classiest. That settles it. Max and Mally must have lived at the front. There are two flats on each level, one to the right and one to the left of the main staircase.

Armed with Julia's letter of authorisation, I go to the Bauamt, the office which handles planning applications. A grey-faced official, tense as a wire coathanger and reeking of smoke, brings me the pre-war folders. They contain a clutch of requests made between 1933 and 1936 to split front flats into two 'as it is proving impossible to find tenants for the large ones'.

The architects who worked on the early conversions signed their letters to the Bauamt with the standard *Hochachtungsvoll!* (*Yours faithfully*), but by 1936 that had changed to *Heil Hitler!*.

In his memoir *My German Question: Growing Up in Nazi Berlin*, Peter Gay explains the significance of the way you closed a letter: '"*Heil Hitler!*" showed enthusiasm for the Third Reich, whereas '"best regards" was about as explicit a sign as a letter writer could give of his politically unreliable opinions.' Max submitted some later applications himself and signed his letters *mit deutschem Gruß* (*with German greetings*), which, according to Peter Gay, was 'still within the circle of respectability'.

The plans show a large entrance hall with bathroom near the front door, then the typical Berlin layout of a series of rooms opening one into the next. Three have windows overlooking the street. A fourth large room goes round the corner and leads to a conservatory on the courtyard side – the *Wintergarten* once festooned with Ernst's tulips. Then comes another small room and finally the kitchen. The side-wing staircases provide the only access to the new small flats and serve as a tradesman's entrance to the ones at the front.

My mother had mentioned their move in a letter to Ernst: '*The new flat's really nice. My room is far from terrible, Mr Merrybell. I've a direct route into it for gentlemen callers*' – the tradesman's entrance in the side wing – '*and shall presently be extending an invitation to Mr Persistent, who's still phoning and pestering me several times a week.*' Her letter was dated 26 October 1933. Only three flats had been converted by then: first floor left, third floor right and fourth floor left. But which one was theirs? Maybe another archive will reveal it. But for now I'm archived out. I need to move, to walk. I need fresh air.

Grunewald – Green Wood – lies at the far end of Kurfürstendamm and I catch the M19 bus all the way to its terminus there. The station gives off an air of *Gemütlichkeit*, with its beer garden tucked away amongst greenery. Pleasant on a warm summer's day, I imagine, but deserted now. Empty paths disappear amongst dripping trees, and I don't fancy going down any of them. Then I see a sign – *Platform 17 Memorial* – and remember Grunewald is one of the deportation stations mentioned by the guide.

A cobbled ramp leads up to platform level, where a scattering of stones, candles and flowers surrounds a plaque:

*ZUM GEDENKEN AN ZEHNTAUSENDE
JÜDISCHER
BÜRGER BERLINS, DIE AB OKTOBER 1941
BIS FEBRUAR 1945 VON HIER AUS DURCH
DIE NAZI-HENKER IN DIE TODESLAGER
DEPORTIERT UND ERMORDET WURDEN**

(IN MEMORY OF THE TENS OF
THOUSANDS OF BERLIN'S JEWISH
CITIZENS, WHO BETWEEN OCTOBER 1941
AND FEBRUARY 1945 WERE DEPORTED
FROM HERE TO THE DEATH CAMPS AND
MURDERED BY THEIR NAZI
EXECUTIONERS)

Rusty rails disappear amongst weeds and I follow them as far as I can, noticing a row of trees thinly screening the backs of old houses. Anyone looking out of those windows would have seen and heard the deportees herded onto the trains.

It has started to rain. I return to Platform 17, where an iron grid along its edge gives details of the transports: date, destination and how many people in each one. I find Max

---

* Since my visit to Grunewald Station, an additional memorial has been placed there. The plaque I refer to is set in the brickwork next to Platform 17.

and Mally's – a small transport of one hundred Jews to Theresienstadt – and wonder if they really left from here. The memorial seems to be for all Berlin Jews, whatever their station of deportation.

'Oh, what does it matter?' sighs a familiar voice. A miniature mother has popped up and is sitting on my shoulder. 'As if knowing the exact spot will make any difference. The weather's filthy. Just leave it.'

'No!' The rain trickling down my face suddenly feels warm. 'I told you, I want to know their every threshold. Through and out of life.'

The guide had mentioned another main deportation point – the goods station at Putlitzstrasse. A blustery walk from Westhafen S-Bahn in the Moabit district takes me there. The memorial is visible from far away. Above the railway tracks in the middle of the bridge – Putlitzbrücke – a grey, crooked silhouette topped by a massive Star of David climbs like a crazy staircase into a swirling sky. Below and to the left is an industrial complex with two sets of three tall chimneys, innocent chimneys rendered sinister because they are close to the rails, and we all know where those rails once led. The area is deserted.

VOM BAHNHOF PUTLITZSTRASSE
WURDEN IN DEN JAHREN
1941–1944
ZEHNTAUSENDE JUEDISCHER
MITBUERGER BERLINS
IN VERNICHTUNGSLAGER
DEPORTIERT
UND
ERMORDET

(FROM 1941 TO 1944 TENS OF THOUSANDS OF JEWISH FELLOW CITIZENS WERE DEPORTED FROM PUTLITZSTRASSE AND MURDERED IN THE EXTERMINATION CAMPS)

As I suspected, the same tens of thousands are commemorated in both stations, and I am still none the wiser.

In 1992 someone blew up the memorial, and a separate plaque marks its restoration:

SCHULD
die nicht verjährt
betroffen sind wir alle
NIE WIEDER

(GUILT
has no time limit
and affects us all
NEVER AGAIN)

I prepare to take a photo, and big spots of rain splatter my head. Out of the corner of my eye I see a middle-aged couple approach along the bridge. I crouch down, put my left hand on the plinth to steady myself and my fingers sink into a glutinous mass. Phlegm or bird shit. I think phlegm. The two people are getting closer.

I stretch my dripping left hand as far away from the rest of me as possible, try to keep the camera straight and squint through the viewfinder. The eyes in the back of my head focus on the couple as they draw level. Was it them? Have they turned round to take a second shot?

'Of course,' the man says mildly to his partner as they walk past, 'it's nearly 9th November.'

Near the bridge is a tiny Turkish café. I scour my hands at its washbasin, heartened that *Kristallnacht* is remembered not only by Jews, and the anonymous bastard who gobbed on the memorial joins Dr Mathwig down the drain.

I take stock of what I know so far and of what I'm trying to find out. It seems to me I'm acting out of character, or what I always thought my character was: methodical, working out what I want to do, then doing it. Since stumbling upon Max and Mally's memorials, that seems to have gone out of the window. I'm now acting on impulse, sure of one thing only: the best information comes by chance, and I don't always recognise it straight away. So my eyes, ears and antennae are on perpetual alert.

While drinking strong coffee by the blustery bridge overlooking the rails and chimneys, I feel like an odd kind of pilgrim, one without religion, shared cause or geographical goal. Unlike those heading for Jerusalem, Mecca or Santiago de Compostela, destination is beside the point, in fact the opposite of the point. The purpose of my journey is the journey itself, my quest to pinpoint the stages unique to Max and Mally along their road to nowhere.

Returning to Bleibtreustrasse, I glance up at the building's elegant pink-and-grey façade. First floor left, third floor right or fourth floor left. My grandparents looked out of one of those sets of windows.

'Who cares?' My tiny mother is back on my shoulder, drumming her heels into my collarbone. 'What's the point?'

'Because I'm getting a sense of them just by being here.'

'So you discover which flat and which railway station, what good will that do you?'

'Shut up, Mum.'

I'm committed now. I shall continue to let information seep through my whispery void and follow Max and Mally further along the paper trail through their public world.

TRANSGRESSION

I am sitting on a bench in the middle of the rush hour waiting for Gerda, whom I met at a stumble stone dedication ceremony. She is on her way home from work. After telling me her mother was a Holocaust survivor, she asked about my family, then about Max's tie business – what was the company called? I thought no more about it till this morning when she rang me, triumphant. *'Ich habe die Akte in der Hand!'* ('I'm holding the file in my hand!')

'What are you talking about?'

'Your grandfather's file. But it has to go back first thing tomorrow. Meet me tonight at Friedrichstrasse.'

Now I feel like a character conjured up by John le Carré about to meet my mole.

A train arrives. People stream past. No Gerda.

In 1975, with Germany still divided and the Wall fully functioning, my parents and I took the S-Bahn and crossed into East Berlin here at Friedrichstrasse. Border control was like an unsettling Punch and Judy show. We had to place our passports in the small opening of a wooden structure. A tiny red curtain swished across it, and our passports were gone. Minutes passed. We saw no one. What on earth were they doing? Then the curtain whisked open – that's the way to do it! – and we were free to go.

Everything I know so far of Max's business life is based on my mother's childhood memories. She liked visiting his office with Mally. The secretary let her bash a few keys on the typewriter before meeting her aunt Marie, who ran the workroom. Max, who organised the sales team, provided each salesman with his own colour-coded order pad. He used to bring home *das bunte Papier* (the coloured paper) for my mother to draw and paint on.

Another train. Still no Gerda.

The tight grip Max kept on family finances was a recurring theme. Once he mistakenly gave Mally double her housekeeping money because two crisp new banknotes had stuck together, and my mother was beside herself when Mally gave one back. Yet he never hesitated to support family in need, both his and Mally's.

Mally's aunt – Tante Findel – had opened a school for young ladies in Vienna but lost everything in the 1921 Austrian hyperinflation. She arrived in Berlin penniless.

'I can still see her sitting across from me the day she came,' my mother recalled in our talks. 'She had a very interesting face, good-looking with sharp blue eyes, white hair and a slight hunchback. "Tante Findel, how old are you?" I asked. "I'm a hundred," she replied, and I believed her. I was nearly six. She was then seventy.'

Findel stayed with them until Max set her up in a flat of her own. All paid for by his industry.

Yet another train and a disgorging of passengers. At last Gerda stands in front of me, brandishing her briefcase.

'It's all in here. Come on.' We charge along passageways to another line.

It's the last day of October, Hallowe'en, and in their flat Gerda's husband has a tub of sweets ready for trick or treat. Their excited children rush in and out. Their excited dog leaps up and wags his tail. On the dining table are bottles of lemonade, beer, glasses and plates of nibbles. Into the middle of it Gerda places my grandfather's file. Any moment now there'll be a disaster of puddles and sodden papers. I make notes as fast as I can.

On 12 August 1901 Max and his brother-in-law Siegfried Greiffenhagen each stumped up 161,000 Reichsmark to found their company Rewald & Greiffenhagen. How proudly German it was. The logo depicts a black eagle with 'R' under one outstretched wing, 'G' under the other, joined mid-body by a white ampersand.

When Siegfried died, Marie took his place, and in 1924 their son Manfred became a partner. The documents at this time are plastered with stamps to the tune of millions of Marks. The great inflation doesn't seem to have harmed their business, though. Maybe men who saved on a new suit still splashed out on a tie. Maybe exports kept them buoyant. By 1927, as Julia had discovered, Max and Marie were able to buy the Bleibtreustrasse block of flats, and in 1930 the company merged with another tie manufacturer to form Krawattenunion. Gone was the German eagle, replaced by a Bauhaus-style logo.

Only after the Nazis came to power did the company begin to decline. Mounting restrictions included a ban on the manufacture of brown and black ties, colours sacred to Hitler's Stormtroopers and the SS.

I am struck by two signatures. They are both Max's: one when he co-founded the company in 1901, the other in 1940 when he was forced to liquidate it. The first is confident, eager, an extravagance of swirls and tails straining towards the future. The second, with the addition of 'Israel' to his name and a Jewish identity number, reveals shakiness under the old flourish and is heartbreaking.

It is time to pack up. Gerda's friend who works at the archive and 'borrowed' the file will return it tomorrow, and no one will be any the wiser.

Once again, I change trains at Friedrichstrasse, buzzing, if baffled by this unusual evening. Taking the file was an act of transgression, of generosity, of bravado. It was also unnecessary. It's not as if the file is top secret. It is publicly accessible. I could have consulted it by applying in the normal way. Still, then I'd have been just like any other member of the public doing research. There would have been request slips to fill in and reluctant counter staff. It wouldn't have been just Max and me, the two of us locked in our own little bubble as I got to know his life's work from beginning to end amid the comings and goings of excited children and one dog.

I am left wondering why their company never carried his name. Why was it called Rewald, not Rychwalski & Greiffenhagen? Who was Rewald? Given the patriotic eagle logo, at first I thought 'Rewald' might be a Germanised version of the family name – 'Rychwalski' too Polish-sounding for such a solid German company. But that theory was scuppered when the man himself surfaced in the Krawattenunion merger – 'as a partner with limited liability. He has no authority to act for the company' – only to sink without trace one month later: '*The businessman Georg Rewald has left the company.*' Max had supplied half the original capital, Mr Rewald his name.

My train arrives, and I get in.

I see Max much more clearly now. Man of business. Family man. The twin pillars of his life. Thank you, Gerda. Who knows, perhaps the cloak-and-dagger tactics also fulfilled a need of her own. A chance to thumb her nose at authority – less the authority of now, more of then, when the few who dared oppose it risked violent reprisal. Whatever the reason, I am just glad she took the trouble.

A woman sitting opposite stares at me as if she knows exactly what I've been up to. I stare her out. Transgression long overdue, I think, as look where being so obedient had got my poor old grandfather. The spy born into the cold that overwhelmed In-Between and froze After may finally be finding a way to defrost it.

CROSSING THE ROAD

Unable to sleep, I get out of bed and look across the dark courtyard.

What a man of discipline Max was. Everything planned. He waited two years for the business to be up and running before finding a wife. My mother's anecdotes painted an unhappy picture of his and Mally's marriage – effectively another business transaction involving a dowry of which Mally never saw one Pfennig. Early on she wanted to leave him, forcing her mother Hulda to hot-foot it from Hamburg and make peace.

Their first child, Ernst, was born in 1905. Soon afterwards Max established his position in both Jewish and German society. He joined the board of the Jewish Institute for the Profoundly Deaf in Weissensee and turned his attention to the Freemasons, a brotherhood until recently not only closed to Jews but also regarded as suspect by some branches of Christianity. Max and a dozen other *Brüder* marked this enlightened new century by founding a new Lodge, open to Jew and gentile alike.

In 1908 Mally gave birth to a girl, a beautiful little thing with curly black hair and dark eyes. Like every first-born girl in the family, she was given a name beginning with an

'L', after Max's late mother Lina. Their daughter Lotte would later rebrand herself as Charlotte.

Family complete and status established, in the space of one year Max's well-ordered life shattered. In 1914 Germany was at war, Mally fell pregnant again and his business partner died. What did Max do? Donated to the Kaiser's war effort, joined forces with his sister and grafted his way through the First World War.

In 1924 he moved the family to 96 Kurfürstendamm, on the corner of Markgraf-Albrecht-Strasse. 'That was a beautiful flat,' my mother recalled. 'Four large reception rooms, four bedrooms, two maids' rooms. Centrally heated. Double windows. Enormous.'

All Max's hard work had finally paid off. He had arrived.

The Kurfürstendamm flat was the last family home Charlotte had known. After the war she drew a plan of it to accompany the family's restitution claim. So far I haven't bothered to search out whatever glass-and-steel structure replaced the old building, as it can't provide a true threshold. 'A lot of the houses had gone,' my mother told me, recalling her return to Berlin in the 1970s. 'We didn't visit any of my homes. On the Kurfürstendamm I saw the corner where we had lived, but the house was no longer there. It was bombed.'

Here in Bleibtreustrasse a light goes on across the courtyard. I must have been standing at the window for ages, as by now I can make out branches outlined against the sky and patches of cloud. Shall I go back to bed? No, it's too late for that. Both too late and too early.

Before I've thought through what to do, I've had a shower, dressed and am on my way out. As an afterthought,

I put Charlotte's plan in my bag. Perhaps the not-quite-day-light will help me imagine what's no longer there.

Kurfürstendamm is full of people heading to work, pouring in and out of the U-Bahn, getting on and off buses. I keep out of their way and walk in the direction of Halensee, passing boutiques draped with furs, several shoe shops, an internet café. I arrive at Markgraf-Albrecht-Strasse. Their corner. The building on the other side of the street must be number 96. It doesn't strike me as especially modern. I wait for the lights to change and go round to the front.

The ground floor is taken up by a restaurant. A man wheels out a stack of chairs and starts placing them around pavement tables. Stationed outside the main entrance are two police officers. Then I look up. Bloody hell.

'At the front was a very big balcony, a covered one, a "loggia" as Mally called it. We used it quite a bit in summer . . .'

Above the restaurant are three storeys of covered balconies framed by pillars, exactly as she had described.

I pull out Charlotte's plan. Number 96. Third floor. The library and smoking room opened onto the *loggia*. On the corner of both streets was the *Herrenzimmer*. Overlooking the side street were sitting room, dining room, plus the bedrooms.

'. . . but the house was no longer there. It was bombed.'

I don't need to imagine anything. I'm looking at the very flat my mother had thought of as home. That's the balcony she used to lean over to wave to her friends. Where Mally sat in the shade to shell peas. Suddenly I have been given two more thresholds to cross: from the street into the building, and the front door of their flat. I know exactly where to aim my camera.

A policewoman approaches and waves me away. She is one of the two officers I noticed by the entrance. *Verboten*.

'Please let me. My mother once lived here.' I show her the plan.

Strictly *verboten*, and she won't say why.

Frustration propels me back the way I have come, past cafés, furs and shoe shops to Bleibtreustrasse, where I am no closer to knowing which flat was theirs, whereas at number 96 Kurfürstendamm, magically resurrected, I know exactly but am prevented from so much as taking a photo. How could even the greatest forgetter of all time have failed to see such a distinctive building?

I turn into Bleibtreustrasse and pass a few *Stolpersteine* here and there in the pavement. Arriving at number 32, I step over Max and Mally's to open the front door of the block my mother had never thought of as home but which for decades was unable to deny existed. She lived here for three years before escaping to London, my grandparents for a further six. When the time came for the building to be made *judenrein* – cleansed of Jews – they would have to move again. But not yet. The chipping away at their rights and identities still had a long way to go.

1 January 1939: Jewish men must add 'Israel', Jewish women 'Sara' to their names.

In the same way as Max obeyed the law, he expected his family to obey him. I once asked my mother if she was frightened of him. No, she said, although she used to dread his inspections, stuffing schoolgirl mess inside her desk and sitting on the lid. 'He threw everything out and made me tidy up before checking my cash book. It didn't matter what I spent my pocket money on – a pencil, ice cream, sweets – as long as the total balanced. I always invented things so it worked out. Then he was happy, and I was happy.'

Max could have done with her creative accounting during the Nazi era instead of remaining deaf to his children. But when they were hit by another regulation –

21 February 1939: Jews must surrender all their jewellery and precious metals.

– one person emerged to whom he did listen.

'*Mallymax zealously handed over their gold and silver just as they did in the* [First World] *war, and this time I can even understand it as they are frightened,*' Charlotte reported to Ernst. '*But they would have given everything away had not Fräulein Kaiser phoned the evening the order appeared in the papers. You remember her, don't you? She used to do sewing for us before starting her own business with Gerti Meseritz.*'

Gerti Meseritz had married a cousin of Mally and, when widowed, went into partnership with Liesel Kaiser. They made classy silk underwear that involved regular trips to Paris to check out the latest fashions. Neither woman was Jewish.

I imagine Max and Mally's phone ringing late that evening. Which room is it in? Living room? No, the hall, where phones used to be when you didn't spend hours talking on them. Here comes Mally to answer it. 'Hallo. Yes, he's here.'

Max appears with his newspaper. 'Who is it?'

'Fräulein Kaiser,' she whispers.

He retreats.

'It's rather late, Liesel,' says Mally. 'Can't it wait?' Apparently not. 'Just a moment . . .'

She follows Max. 'She says she needs to talk to you urgently.'

'Whatever for?'

'She won't say on the phone.'

'Tell her to call round at a civilised hour. Oh, very well.' Max strides into the hall. 'Good evening, Fräulein Kaiser. What can I do for you?'

It's about what she can do for him. Has he read the paper?

'That's precisely what I was trying to do . . . Outside? Now? But it's gone ten o'clock!'

Charlotte's letter continued: '*At 10.30 she met him in the street, said she often travels to Paris on business, that she's willing to bring me valuables and he can trust her completely. She gave him no time to answer, said she would pick up everything the following evening and actually succeeded in extracting a few pieces.*'

Mally spreads out her jewellery on the bed. It's very good of Liesel to take the risk, but supposing she's caught? Even if she isn't, what's to stop Charlotte pawning the lot? Mally sighs. Still, there's no point keeping it here. The diamond bracelet had better go, the pearl necklace, her mother's gold watch. She adds two lockets, brooches, some loose gemstones.

Max joins her. Without a word he takes off his ring in the shape of a coiled snake with sapphire eyes and adds it to the collection.

The Berlin–Paris express stops at the border. A German officer slides open the compartment door and barely glances at the middle-aged woman with grey hair as he stamps her passport. The only other passenger has a large red 'J' in his. 'What's in this case? Open up.' He throws everything out, slits the lining and rummages around before leaving.

Fräulein Kaiser has to stop herself from helping the man as he fumbles for papers scattered at her feet. Trembling, he stuffs them back in his case. Police with dogs continue to patrol the platform. Some glance inside as they pass. She clasps her handbag and stares at the second hand on the station clock as it edges round. Click, click, click. The whistle blows. Only when the train moves do her hands relax.

The following afternoon at the Café du Dôme, she keeps glancing over the rim of her cup at her companion's hat: a jaunty number with black spotted veil and five cherries on a twig sticking straight up from the crown. On anyone else it would look absurd, but on Charlotte it is charming.

The café in Montparnasse serves as second home to local artists. A raucous few are sitting at a nearby table. One holds up a cartoon he has drawn of a tiny Führer acknowledging the salute of a flock of obese sheep.

'I wish I could stay here,' Fräulein Kaiser whispers.

'Why don't you?'

'It's not allowed.'

'Move your business to Paris, then.' Charlotte flicks ash from her cigarette in its holder. 'It should be easy enough for you. Bring out what you need.'

Fräulein Kaiser shakes her head. 'You don't understand.'

'*Her skills are considered essential to Germany,*' Charlotte's letter continued, '*and she can't simply stay abroad unofficially as she has her father and sister to support. I think I prefer being a Jew to a German who's against the Nazis, don't you agree?*

'*At least the parents are finally being more cooperative. I also told Fräulein Kaiser to prise cash out of them and to buy off them bits of old gold that can be sold by weight where you don't lose so much. She promised me she would. It's very touching; she's doing a lot and, when all's said and done, risking her life. Still, many people get a certain satisfaction out of helping Jews if it means they can give the Nazis one in the eye.*'

30 April 1939: Jewish tenants may be evicted for no reason; Jewish families are obliged to move into designated houses and districts.

* * *

I am sitting at Julia's desk, not thinking about which flat was Max and Mally's, not thinking about anything really, other than trying to tidy up the inside of my head by putting copies of the family papers and a mountain of scrappy notes into neat piles. That's when I see it. Hidden in plain sight. Their address on one document reads: *Bleibtreustrasse 32, III.*

Three small strokes. That's all. That's everything. The Roman number three means they lived on the third floor.

To make absolutely sure, I check the flat conversion dates. Third floor right: building work completed 17 November 1933. Third floor left: blank – that flat was never divided.

'After Ernst and Charlotte emigrated, the parents and I moved into a smaller flat . . .'

I dash downstairs, sprint across the courtyard, rocket up three flights, turn right and ring the bell. Scrabbling for my glasses, I try to catch my breath and read the brass nameplate. *Von* somebody or other.

The door opens onto a beautifully proportioned hall, large and square, with high ceilings and a twinkly chandelier. On the left a dark portrait in a gilded frame hangs above a side table displaying an ornate golden ornament. In the middle of the polished parquet lies a red Persian rug.

'Yes?'

My mouth is suddenly too small for teeth and tongue. 'Family connection . . . to this house . . . to this very flat.'

A blond secretary holds the door open, her arm barring entry. Behind her a framed coat of arms trumpets her boss's blue blood. I doubt my relationship to the two stumble stones will cut much ice here. 'What exactly is it you want?'

I try to explain. On most days I act sensibly. I weigh things up. I already emerged from the womb debating the pros and cons of staying where it was warm against slithering out into a harsh March morning. The obstetrician did a neat job when he cut and bound my umbilical cord. But an invisible part stayed attached and the scar tissue which covered the wound gradually thickened with a silence that grew out of outrage.

This is the flat they moved to willingly, the threshold they crossed daily when they still had choices. Choices are important, don't you agree? They're part of being human. And my grandparents were human. It's important to remember that they were two ordinary human beings.

Yes, yes, you haven't got all day. Bear with me.

What I want is . . . I want to search each room.

I want to rummage through cupboards, look under beds, climb up on chairs, shine a light into every corner.

I want to conduct a minute examination like a forensic scientist after a murder. I heard one interviewed the other day. A botanist. Did you know that, if buried before completely dead, a victim will have breathed in the soil of their grave? I want to discover Max and Mally as they used to be before their clock stopped. I want to get down on all fours, stick my nose to gaps in the floorboards and sniff. I want to breathe in their outbreaths. I want to fill my lungs with their normality.

The lips have tightened. The pale eyes flicker.

'What I'd like . . . is . . . Could I come in . . .?'

Incomprehension.

'. . . and stand in the hall?'

'You just want to come in?'

I nod.

'That's all?'

'Yes.'

'And stand in the hall?'

'Please.'

Violently, she releases the door and steps back. 'Come and stand in it, then.'

A few steps across the parquet takes me to the rug, thick and soft underfoot. I glimpse several doors with intricate mouldings, high and wide enough to allow big items of furniture through, some with glass panels at the top to let in light. All have the etched brass handles once touched by Max and Mally as they went from room to room, as they welcomed visitors and showed them out. I shuffle over the rug, trying to see round corners

'I don't suppose . . . Could I take a photo?'

But I have already outstayed my welcome it seems.

Back at Julia's I perform a speeded-up 'Knees Up Mother Brown', followed by 'Don't Dilly Dally':

My old man said, 'Follow the van
'And don't dilly dally on the way.'
Off went the van with me 'ome packed in it,
I walked behind with me old cock linnet.
Well, I dillied and dallied, dallied and I dillied,
Lost me way and don't know where to roam.
You can't trust the specials like the old-time coppers
When you can't find your way home.

'I'm English as well as British, remember?' I shout. 'I'm also very much a Londoner.' And I launch straight into the music hall number 'Maybe it's because I'm a Londoner'. Loud and raucous, my voice bounces off the walls and echoes through the large room.

I run to the window. Now I know exactly where to look. Across the courtyard, third floor right. Through one window I catch sight of a metal-backed chair next to a white slab of fridge. Was that always a kitchen? Is it where Mally arranged Ernst's tulips and carried them through to the *Wintergarten*? Where she catered for the out-of-town family?

On 22 June 1939 Max wrote to Ernst: '*We have had a lot of coming and going recently. Both boys from Tirschtiegel* [his nephews Kurt and Horst] *have been spending a lot of time in Berlin in order to push ahead with their emigration. Then we had Ruth from Betsche staying with her delightful little girl, 3¼ years old.*

'*Helga is staying alternately with us and with Lina . . .*'

The wind has got up. Trees in the courtyard bend and sway. A leaf lands on the stone window ledge. Another sticks to the pane, slides down, then another, and another. The whole shadow family whirls past me in leaf form.

There go my mother's uncles and aunts and cousins. That leaf with a large black spot? Cousin Alfred and his eye patch. Another small leaf hovers – young Heinz carefully signing his name – before it is whipped away.

A door clangs. I look down. A young woman walks across the courtyard and lets herself into the side wing.

The afternoon is gloomy, and a few lights already glow in the windows opposite. One illuminates the chair next to the fridge. A shadow walks past it. That was their home.

The side-wing woman reappears with rubbish bags and goes down the steps to the garage, once Herr Steinke's kingdom that used to stink, or did Alex mean that the man himself stank? Maybe both, and maybe this woman lives in the flat once inhabited by old Frau Steinke, who spent her last years dreaming of her glory days working for Joseph and Magda Goebbels. Memories that died with her except for the few she confided to a neighbour and that chance has passed on to me. I am the keeper of other people's memories.

I cross into Julia's office and sit at her desk. I like the brightness of this room and the open outlook over the back of Knesebeckstrasse. It's a street I often walk along. Opposite its junction with Lietzenburger Strasse, the main throughfare just visible through a gap in the buildings, there's a massive post office.* Postamt W15 had become the focus of my grandparents' lives, their main means of contact with the wider world.

1 September 1939: Germany invades Poland. Curfew for Jews – 8.00 p.m. in winter, 9.00 p.m. in summer.

The more isolated they grew, the more desperate they were to communicate. This became increasingly difficult after 3 September 1939, when Britain and France declared war on Germany.

12 September 1939: Jews may only frequent a few accredited shops.

20 September 1939: Jews are forbidden to own radios.

It became safer to stay home and become invisible in what was no longer the family's building. They began to rely more and more on Gerti Meseritz and Liesel Kaiser to run errands for them.

4 July 1940: Jews may only shop between 4.00 and 5.00 p.m.

19 July 1940: The telephone connections of Jews must be cut off.

---

* The post office, which was still standing during my early visits to Berlin, has since been pulled down.

But they could still send letters within Germany and to neutral countries, which, for the time being, included the USA. That had set me thinking.

Mally was close to her brother Fritz – 'Mally called all her menfolk "Fritz"', according to Charlotte – and Fritz's daughter Ursula had found refuge in Los Angeles. Highly likely, I reckoned, that Fritz would mention my grandparents when writing to her.

Mally and Fritz

I contacted Ursula's daughter in California to ask if she had any of her grandparents' letters. Yes, she did – a whole boxful – and I was welcome to make copies. It is these letters I have brought to Berlin to help me follow Max and Mally further into the fog of In-Between.

It has started to rain. A medley of reflections twinkles in the chink of wet tarmac visible in the gap between buildings. Amber, green – brake lights off – and back to red.

I spread Fritz's letters out on the desk. But first I must read another letter in very familiar handwriting. My grandparents wrote to their niece Ursula when they could no longer send letters to their own children. And, with no twenty-five-word Red Cross limit, Max poured out his heart:

'*Berlin, 15th December 1940*

'*My dear and so very distant niece Ursula,*

'*Given the prevailing circumstances under which we are forced to write, let my lines to you today be imbued with even more than usual affection. Their purpose is to congratulate you on your birthday; the third time you are celebrating it apart from your family.*

'*How can I enumerate all the things I wish for you! Health, luck and happiness; and let us not forget the economic side, which also has its part to play in life. May you also always retain your beauty and lovely figure; they are qualities which are likely to attract people to you and from whose number it is entirely possible that a suitable husband will be forthcoming.*

'*In the meantime, you have made friends amongst a circle of like-minded people in a country which is as rich in natural wonders as it is enlightened. And so at your young age the world is open to you; it beckons you towards a very happy future, something we wish for you from the bottom of our hearts.*

'*We are very grateful to you for keeping us constantly in touch with Hilda.*

'*With all my love*

'*Uncle Max*'

In an accompanying note Ursula's mother had scribbled: '*In the last few years Uncle Max has really become very nice – he doesn't make scenes any more, is always willing to help out and do good, not just once, but time and time again.*'

Not only the purse strings had loosened. As the situation worsened, the stern old man grew softer and offered his young niece the only birthday present still in his power to give: appreciation, encouragement and love.

Here's the warmth I used to reach for through my floral wallpaper all those decades ago. I hadn't simply imagined it. Well, I had – in my efforts to find that comfort my mother had such difficulty providing. Here, finally, is the confirmation that Max didn't entirely fit her picture of him, and the proof that she had once known a lot more than she later admitted to.

It is getting dark, rush hour judging by the build-up of cars I can see through the gap in the buildings, and still raining. I switch on the desk lamp.

While the war thundered on, Fritz, in Hamburg, reported on how 'the Berliners' were doing.

'*Aunt Mally had the joy of hearing from two of her children for her birthday. A Red Cross message from Ernst, which was 6 months old. Charlotte and husband are now in the south of the country* [France]. *It's not much, but these days one is grateful for anything. Have you heard any more from Hilda?*'

On 2 March 1941 Fritz announced: '*Provided nothing stops me, I intend going to Berlin for Uncle Max's 77th birthday. He is in remarkably good shape, has barely one grey hair, is all there mentally and in almost as good physical shape.*'

I'm surprised to discover that Jews could still travel. But not for much longer:

24 March 1941: Jews may only use public transport to get to and from work.

On 12 May 1941 Fritz reported: '*The Berliners are obliged to leave their flat at the beginning of June and will be moving into two rooms of the flat of an acquaintance in Sächsische Strasse. Charlotte and husband have also endured many hardships. His relatives have paid their passage to the USA. Once there, the parents hope they might be able to join them.'*

What mad fantasy is this? Forget Palestine. No longer possible. But Charlotte's on her way to the USA, so we'll go there instead . . . How exactly? While still within their own four walls, they clutched at straws and dreamed.

It is now completely dark. I am lulled by the rhythmic squeal of hydraulic brakes and reflected patterns of red, amber, green as the traffic stop-starts along Lietzenburger Strasse, the road my grandparents would soon have to cross to their last address.

I feel like James Stewart in Hitchcock's *Rear Window*, piecing together a murder from snatches of life flitting across the windows of the apartment block opposite. Not that any visible life is going on behind my Knesebeckstrasse rear windows, nor is much illuminated other than the chink of main road I can see through the gap. The flash of cars. The changing lights. And whereas James Stewart, immobilised by a plastercast, had Grace Kelly floating about in a glorious but impractical frock, I am immobilised by a dragging-down feeling as old as me, exhorting me not to move, not to think, not to breathe, then it'll go away . . . Only it doesn't. It never went away for my mother either, frozen on the landing at Madame Tussauds with two little girls digging away at her mind, clamouring to see unspeakable horrors.

Unbearable feelings sometimes give advance warning before they rise through the layers. They allow me to duck and do something else to bypass them. I could do that now. I want to do that now. But I don't. I force myself to stay put. At the same time, I won't let myself sink into them. I remain sitting at Julia's desk, staring at the dark building opposite, waiting.

In my early days of ferreting into In-Between, I used to take my washing to the launderette. There I sometimes met an old man who groaned as he transferred laundry from washer to dryer: 'It's bad today, moving about.' Shrapnel, journeying around his body ever since the war, had begun to surface. 'Look,' he said one day, rolling up his trouser leg to reveal a bubble shifting under papery skin.

That was in the 1980s, when the world of In-Between started opening up. Survivors who had been silent began to speak about their experiences. Claude Lanzmann's film *Shoah* was screened. I watched, listened, read and secretly investigated, my pendulum always swinging between the compulsion to find out until I could stand it no longer and turned my back on it all.

I realise I have been holding my breath, so take deep, shuddering lungfuls while watching the building, the rain, the lights, still struggling with the urge to get up and move for the sake of it. But this time I shall let whatever it is come to me.

In his haunting memoir *The Story of a Life*, Aharon Appelfeld wrote:

For many years I was sunk deep within the slumber of oblivion. My life flowed on the surface. I grew used to the cramped and moldy basements within me. True, I was always afraid of them. It seemed to me, not without reason, that the dark creatures seething there were growing stronger, and that someday, when the place became too narrow for them, they would burst out onto the surface. And, indeed, such outbursts did occur from time to time, but the powers of suppression held them in, and the basement was again shut up under lock and key.*

I can sense those days in every part of my body. Whenever it rains, it's cold, or a fierce wind is blowing, I'm taken back to the ghetto, to the camp, or to the forests where I spent many days. Memory, it seems, has deep roots in the body.†

When I read those words, they resonated in a way which made no sense. With no direct, personal experience of the Holocaust and therefore no memories of it, I distrusted that feeling of recognition. Yet could something else have taken root in my body? I was conceived and born when the Nuremberg war crimes trials kept the atrocities in the news, the cells that eventually became me multiplying along with my mother's rage. Only recently I had read an article about how a mother's harrowing experiences could affect her baby in the womb. Could that possibly have happened to me? Suppose rhizomes of my mother's rage had burrowed into me and caused the tension between her need to stifle – don't ask, don't talk, don't think – and mine to know? What she 'forgot', I absorbed without knowing what it was until it solidified into that lump of ice – the unknown unknown, later transformed into the known unknown. I have been trying to dislodge it and dig it up ever since. The

---

* *The Story of a Life* by Aharon Appelfeld (London: Penguin, 2006), p. viii.
† Ibid. p. 50.

only way I can do that, the only way open to me, is to sift through the evidence.

Entering all the forbidden places, raking and digging deep, is heady stuff, overwhelming at times, and seems to trigger extreme physical reactions – projectile vomiting, jangled teeth – all connected to my Berlin visits. While disentangling my roots from my mother's, not only have I gained a clearer picture of Max, Mally and the whole shadow family, but also of my young mother, who knew so much more than she later allowed herself to remember.

Another of my mother's cousins – yet another Ernst – had stayed in Germany and survived in hiding. A few months after liberation, on 28 November 1945, he wrote to Cousin Kurt (who had squeaked into England on the eve of war) explaining how he and his wife had managed it: *'From the summer of 1938 the head of the Stettin Jewish community was Paul Hirschfeld, a Gestapo agent. We watched carefully how the way was being prepared for what was to come, and on 29 January 1940 we thought it prudent to leave under cover of night and without the knowledge of the community. We travelled to Berlin and stayed first with Uncle Max and Aunt Mally, then with Lina (Uncle Louis had died one month previously). That was our salvation. Exactly two weeks later all the Jews in and around Stettin were deported to Poland, the first case of its kind in Germany.*

'After Stettin we were on our guard and didn't register with the Jewish community. That saved our lives yet again, for once the deportation of Berlin Jews really got going, it was done according to the lists the community was obliged to draw up, and we did not exist in the community's files . . .'

Through the summer of 1941 Fritz continued to send his daughter news of Max and Mally. On 2 July he reported: *'The Berliners are now living in two rooms, but they dislike it so much that, providing it's possible, they want to move again. Their current address is Berlin-Wilmersdorf, 27 Sächsischestr., second floor, c/o Singer.'*

The time has come to follow them.

* * *

Sächsische Strasse is the continuation of Bleibtreustrasse on the other side of the Lietzenburger Strasse divide. Here elegance gives way to simplicity. Front doors open onto small squares of grass and a few splashes of geraniums. The buildings further down look shabbier.

As I continue walking, a vast complex of flats comes into view across the street. Steel window frames painted white. Plain, functional, straight lines. The reddish-brown exterior appears cracked and stained.

On 21 August 1941 Fritz wrote to Ursula: *'Max has always defied his years, but now he has really aged. Unfortunately, Aunt Mally's heart isn't too good, and she certainly can't get the rest she needs, nor is she able to go away anywhere to recuperate.'*

Then, on 11 September 1941: *'Aunt Mally has been very ill. She suddenly had a severe stomach haemorrhage and had to be rushed to hospital. The doctors believe it's a perforated stomach ulcer, but can only make an exact diagnosis once the condition of the very weakened patient allows for an X-ray to be taken. Perhaps, dear Ursula, you could drop her a line.'*

19 September 1941: All Jews aged six and over must wear a yellow star sewn above their left breast bearing the word 'Jude'. Jews wishing to leave their district need written police permission.

When that order came through, Mally was still in hospital. I imagine Max fetching their coats and a needle, then Liesel Kaiser turning up with some shopping. She takes the coats from him and sews on both stars.

Fritz's last letter is dated 20 October 1941: '*At long last Aunt Mally seems to be on the road to recovery. Today, after about eight weeks in hospital, she should be on her way home. Uncle Max kept house for himself without any proper help, as well as making the long journey to the hospital in the Iranische Strasse. I should have liked to go to Berlin to be with Mally and talk to her but sadly that's no longer possible. We live a very secluded life.*'

Envelope with letter from Fritz to Ursula opened by German censor

One week later my mother wrote her brother Ernst a postcard: '*Charlotte might be on her way to USA by now. Ursula Los Angeles expecting a baby end of this year.*

'*The last news from Max and Mally were from May, they have changed their address, but are in the same district, otherwise they seem to be alright.*'

Number 27. The street number is visible from far away and displayed twice: on a black-and-white enamel plaque on the wall, and in peeling black paint on a light cube above the entrance.

According to Wolfgang – my one-man database – number 27 was the final address of eight Berlin Jews. Three avoided deportation by taking their own lives. The first to do so, on 15 November 1941, was Max and Mally's landlady, Margarete Singer.

I feel the pull of the millions. This is no good. I must think only of my grandparents. Of Mally recently out of hospital. She and Max stuck in two rooms they hate. One morning they find the flat strangely silent. The kitchen cold and empty. Frau Singer's bedroom door shut. Mally knocks softly. Then Max . . .

I am now directly opposite number 27. Three steps lead up to the front door. Scabby grab-rails on either side are sunk into lumps of concrete. On the wall to the right is a dark oblong patch marking the spot where a sign used to be.

While logging those facts, I grapple with two others.

The faded red door is ajar. A threshold has been handed to me on a plate. All I have to do is push the door open, walk up to the second floor and Max and Mally's last home.

My eyes are also fixed on another detail. Walls and door are smeared in graffiti. One seems to spell a word. Surely it can't say what I think it says.

I cross the street for a closer look.

Three letters on the wall proclaim *JUD*. However much I try to make them into a different word or an abstract, they stubbornly refuse to change. 'JEW' they shout out in red paint with an arrow pointing at the door.

My grandparents were to spend another nine months holed up in their dead landlady's flat. How on earth did they manage? I can't imagine. Actually, I can. All too well. That's the problem.

12 December 1941: Jews may not use public telephones.

But still they could write letters. To the family in Germany, if no longer to America. For on 7 December 1941 the Japanese had attacked Pearl Harbor, and the USA entered the war.

Three weeks later, in far-away Los Angeles, Ursula gave birth to her daughter. A Red Cross message with the news reached Hamburg too late for her parents, Fritz and Olga, to receive it. For on 12 December they had been deported to Riga's Jungfernhof camp. An eyewitness would later report to a liberated Cousin Ernst in Berlin: '*Herr Meseritz was shot. Frau Meseritz died of a lung infection.*' After the war, in a letter dated 6 January 1946, Cousin Ernst would ask Kurt in London to give my mother the wretched message, explaining: '*That's Aunt Mally's brother, a wonderful man. In 1940 I visited him twice in Hamburg. He suffered from detached retinas. So he was shot immediately.*'

In Hamburg someone picked up the Red Cross message announcing the birth of Fritz and Olga's granddaughter. Someone who knew where to forward it. To Berlin. To my grandparents. To this very door.

All I have to do is push it open.

Red Cross messages leave space on the other side for a reply, and this reply is in handwriting I have come to know very well: *'Parents gone on a journey. Trying to find out their address; our letter there came back. We send love. Are well. Warm wishes. Mally Max 5 May 1942'.*

20 June 1942: It is forbidden to sell eggs to Jews.

10 July 1942: It is forbidden to sell fresh milk to Jews.

By July 1942 Max and Mally's messages to Ernst mainly contained the names of family members who had 'relocated'. From their Berlin hiding place Cousin Ernst and his wife watched helplessly as deportations intensified along with the air raids. They may well have welcomed the bombs along with *'the broadcasts from London which we listened to as often as ten times a day'*, as two and a half years later a pulverising daytime attack would encourage them to become more 'official' – papers conveniently destroyed – and take cover in public shelters along with other *'Volksgenossen'* (patriotic comrades). But for the time being all they could do was observe and record. *'Our cousin Lina was taken away, as were Aunt Marie, Uncle Max and Aunt Mally . . .'*, they reported in their letter to Kurt of 28 November 1945.

Did it happen at dawn? At night? In broad daylight? Who saw? Who looked away? I really don't want to know the details. Except that's why I'm here. To learn, rather than turn my back. For by turning away, my murdered ones will always remain numbers on a list, perpetually in oblivion. They deserve, at the very least, what can be known to be known. They deserve to be brought back into the light.

'Believe me, I shall be only too happy to divest myself of all

the splendid furniture,' Mally had done her best to reassure Ernst, and herself, once Max had finally decided to leave Germany. *'I hope to live as unencumbered a life in my old age as has <u>always been my wish</u>.'*

'And your wish has been granted,' replied her Fascist fairy godmother.

> *For the journey you shall take with you:*
> - *80 Reichsmark*
> - *1 well-equipped case or rucksack with no locks*
> - *complete set of clothing*
> - *sturdy shoes*
> - *bed linen and blanket*
> - *plate or pot with spoon*
> - *one week's provisions.*

A few days before departure they received their final instructions:

> - *All cupboards and other containers in the flat to remain unlocked with keys left in the locks.*
> - *All rooms to be left clean, all dirty crockery and cutlery washed up, shutters closed.*
> - *Before collection, electricity, gas and water bills to have been paid and supplies turned off.*
> - *The building's manager/owner to be advised it is being vacated.*

Once again I am trying to grasp the ungraspable. I must be careful. By reaching too far into the fog, I could be sucked right in and lose both my grandparents and myself.

August temperatures were soaring into the thirties as Max and Mally emerged from the flat wearing coats to avoid carrying them. They left the door unlocked, dragged their luggage down two flights of stairs, and stepped into a beautiful late summer morning. Wan faces in the back of a truck stared out at them. Mally too weak to climb up. Shouts of '*Schnell! Schnell!*' ('Hurry! Hurry!') Hands tugging and bundling her and Max in. The truck jolted its way eastwards, swerving to avoid bomb craters. All around them were the smoking shells of buildings, here and there a lime tree covered in ash. They tried not to breathe. Worse than the stench of last night's raid was the reek of fear – their own and the fear of those crammed in the truck with them. Get through this day, then the next one, and the one after that.

Amongst Charlotte's papers is an envelope Gerti Meseritz posted to her after the war and stamped on arrival *16 July 1948, Grand Central Station, New York*, containing three sheets of paper folded one within the other; three letters signed by Max and Mally. Before I learned the old German script, the only words I could make out were their signatures. Later I realised all three are identical – one addressed to Ernst, one to Charlotte and Nepo, one to my mother.

'*August 1942*

'*Dear Ernst/Dear Children/Dear Hilda*

'*Before our departure to Theresienstadt we just want to bid you a fond farewell. Let us hope that we manage to come through everything safely and are granted the good fortune of seeing one another again.*

'*Gerti and Liesel have looked after us with the utmost*

kindness and have also assured us that they will love and care
for you in our name.

'May God protect you and us!*

'With love and kisses*

'from*

'Father*

'& Mother'*

The same farewell letter to each of their children, written
by Max and signed by him and Mally. Entrusted to two brave
women who never stopped caring for them and who *'have*
also assured us that they will love and care for you in our name'.
All three letters look as though they have never been touched.

The significance of finding them together hit me like a
brick. By not forwarding Ernst's or my mother's, Charlotte
had denied them their parents' last goodbye.

I tried to understand. In 1948 Charlotte's own life was
in turmoil . . . recently separated from Nepo . . . about to
return to Paris . . . Max and Mally's deaths already old news.

Even so. This wasn't nice. In fact, it was horrible. After lifelong battles with her parents, with one final shrug of her shoulders Charlotte had had the last word.

Those letters mark the moment the ice began to form. From then on Charlotte would ride her wave of anger, Ernst tuck himself into the folds of Mally's linen, my mother seal the edges of her mind and begin the long retreat inside it.

JUD. The red arrow points. The door opens wide. A thin man comes out smoking a cigarette. He sets off down the street, and the door slams shut.

* * *

Grunewald or Putlitzstrasse? I was still no closer to nailing Max and Mally's exit point to Theresienstadt and thought I never would. Then a third station rose out of the fog, and the fog cleared.

A heavy brick portico is all that remains of the Anhalter Bahnhof in Kreuzberg. The station used to provide the setting for international arrivals and departures. Newsreels from the Third Reich show it draped in swastikas, lines of police keeping ecstatic blondes from mobbing Hitler's train.

It also had other purposes, vividly described by Dietlinde Peters in *Der Anhalter Bahnhof als Deportationsbahnhof* (*The Anhalter Bahnhof as a Station of Deportation*). Three years after Kindertransportees had taken leave of their parents on its 'platform of tears', an ordinary train with ordinary passengers began to carry extra cargo. In 1942 two more carriages were linked up to the regular 6.07 departure for Dresden and Prague; third-class carriages with wooden seats that looked exactly the same as the others, except that their doors and windows were kept locked. These small 'privileged' transports were reserved for elderly Jews who had to pay for their 'resettlement' and, like real passengers, had to buy their tickets. But the fares bypassed German Rail and went straight to the Gestapo.

In the archives I had seen the deportation list with Max and Mally on it, but no mention of the station from which they had left. All I knew was that they were numbers 84 and 85 out of a total of one hundred Jews – a tiny shipment compared with most transports containing one thousand or more. Now I learned that a hundred was the number of deportees that fitted exactly into those two extra carriages – fifty in each – attached to the regular train which left the Anhalter Bahnhof early every morning for Prague, a mere hop and a skip from the concentration camp. The final piece of Max and Mally's jigsaw had slotted into place.

Not a cattle truck, but a passenger train. Not one thousand Jews, but one hundred. Almost cosy, I think with relief, then shudder at having been conned, if only momentarily, as had the deportees themselves, by a regime keen to present a veneer of humane treatment to the outside world.

When the first of those transports stopped in Dresden, the local Jewish community brought the passengers food to strengthen the impression of normality. Only on arrival at Theresienstadt did reality hit them.

'Not the worst camp,' my mother had said. 'At least they weren't killed there.'

And for many survivors it was the good camp, heaven by comparison to what came later – killing centres such as Chelmno, Sobibor, Majdanek, Treblinka and Auschwitz.

A favourite photo from the old shoebox shows a middle-aged Max with two of his brothers at a bathing resort taken, at a guess, shortly before the First World War. They are posing in a line and as usual resemble the Kaiser except for one detail: behind strategically draped towels all three are stark naked. There is something familiar about Max's shoulders, squarish with a dip at the collarbone. They are like mine.

Stubborn, stern, penny-pinching, long-winded – Max was all those things, as well as naked, vulnerable, increasingly generous to family and friends stuck in Germany, but ultimately unable to let go of his role as decision-maker. He refused to *pay attention to your children's advice*, as Charlotte instructed, and tragically ignored his wife. For one all-too-brief moment after *Kristallnacht* Mally took charge and received sound emigration advice from Benno Cohen at the Palestine Office. By the time Max followed it, it was too late.

In a letter to Ernst two weeks before war was declared, Mally had mentioned the birth in Palestine of a new family member. '*I hope to meet the young man soon. You know how fond I am of children, especially babies. My own children are letting me down by not having any.*'

'One did,' I whisper, standing under the brick arches that once led into the Anhalter Bahnhof's entrance hall. 'Well past babyhood, but here at last. I've come to see you off.'

The air is still relatively cool on that late August morning as one hundred elderly Jews file along the platform under armed guard. They drag their luggage to the furthest carriage and wait their turn to board. Numbers 84 and 85 of Transport I/49 to Theresienstadt take their places on the wooden seats. The carriage is locked. Dogs and uniforms patrol the platform. A whistle blows. Further down the train the last doors slam. The 6.07 to Dresden and Prague pulls away dead on time.

Transportliste

169

Lfd. No.	Name	Vorname	geb. am	Ort	Beruf		mdg	vch	Alter	arbeits- fähig	Wohnung Ort Straße		Bankenkto. Nr.	Devisinkto. Nr.
76	Rosenthal	Martin Israel	29.11.78.	Berlin	ohne			ja	70	x	N5, Gaydekstr.3			07217
77	Rosenthal geb.Silberman	Antonie Sara	4.5.77.	Oesel	ohne			ja	65	x	do.	AG24608	07210
78	Rothauer	Therese Sara	10.6.65	Budapest	ohne	ja			77	x	Wilmdf.,Danckelmannstr.	A480012	07201
79	Rothauer	Katalina Sara	30.5.66.	Budapest	ohne	ja			70	x	do.		07202
80	Ruben geb.Hirschthal	Jenny Sara	19.9.67.	Myszile	ohne			ja	75	x	N065,Stallschreiberstr. 12	A27361	07207
81	Ruben	Max Israel	25.3.67.	Coeslin	ohne			ja	75	x	N20, Dolstr.34/35	300008	07205
82	Ruben geb.Rubert	Wanda Sara	9.1.69.	Königsberg	ohne			ja	73	x	do.		07209
83	Ruben	Joseph Sara	25.4.97.		ohne	ja			45	ja	W15,Pariserstr.11	A300921	07203a
84	Ryminski	Max Israel	19.3.66.	Tirschtiegel	ohne			ja	76	x	W15,Blücholmstr.27	A370717	07232
85	Ryminski geb.Mauritz	Amalie Sara	12.1.76.	Fürstenwalde	ohne			ja	66	ja	do.		07233
86	Saloman	Marie Malene Sara	30.1.65.	Gorlitz	ohne	ja			77	x	W30,Wittenbergpl.3a	A334625	07236

PART 4:

THE CUPBOARD IS AIRED

THE COST OF CLAIMING

When I talked to my father about war and the family, I rarely felt compelled to tiptoe around him as I did my mother, yet even he had his limits. One Sunday, several months after his own mother (the one grandparent I knew) had died, he was sorting through her papers and wanted a break. By then I was in my mid-twenties and had just plucked out of the wastepaper basket a bundle of wartime postcards he had thrown in.

Later, striding over Hampstead Heath, we stopped to watch the kite flyers on Parliament Hill and I asked him about the cards. But for once his usual willingness to launch into a story deserted him. Suddenly he burst out: 'You've no idea what it felt like in Nazi Germany, never able to breathe.'

How true. I hope I never shall know what that felt like. But my mother did. Every time a letter arrived from Berlin she absorbed the foetid spaces between her parents' lines just long enough to send them another injection of fresh air. Did she ever keep the letters for any length of time? I doubt it. But one did survive.

I found it amongst Charlotte's papers. Written in April 1940, seven months into the war, Max revealed its convoluted journey in a margin note: *'Fondest greetings to you, dear Ursula, and many thanks – Uncle Max'.* From Berlin to Los

Angeles, from Los Angeles to London, and finally from London to Paris. My mother had forwarded it to her sister just in time as, shortly afterwards, with Paris occupied, Charlotte was on the run.

'*9th April 1940*

'*Dear Hilda*

'*A year ago we had the great pleasure of speaking to you on the telephone to wish you a happy birthday, a pleasure this time sadly denied to us. So please accept our warmest wishes by this method, wishes that are all the more heartfelt for being sent to you under such difficult conditions.*

'*In spite of everything, we must not give up hope that one day we shall be able to celebrate your birthday all together once again. Until then may Heaven continue to protect you and bestow upon you a happy future.*

'*A few days ago we took a short break and travelled to the same place as last year. Mother is in need of some rest and recuperation, and I hope this will help her feel somewhat better.*

'*Let me now acknowledge your news which this time was really detailed; that always gives us special pleasure. We were delighted to hear how much your boss appreciates you. If only we could do something similar for you!*

'*In the hope that these wishes for a happy birthday will, with God's help, reach you in good health and without too much delay, I am sending you my fondest greetings. Please also give my best regards to the doctor, as well as to his wife – I hope his practice continues to thrive.*

'*Father*

'*My darling child!*

'*You have no idea how much pleasure your letter gave us,*

especially as it brought us your good news. We were also delighted about your pay rise.

'*It is once again wonderfully peaceful and relaxing here, which can't do either of us any harm. I have been particularly under the weather and in great need of a rest. But let me now come to the main point of my letter, which is, my darling child, to congratulate you from the bottom of my heart on your birthday. This time we are unable to phone you as we did last year and hear your sweet voice – we shall just have to make the best of things and wait for better times! As you can imagine, we only want the best for you.*

'*Be happy and enjoy your day. With greetings to all the family and friends, and a big birthday kiss especially for you,*
'*from Mother*'

On a first reading, Mally's letter appears much more loving than Max's. I might never have believed him capable of expressing more than buttoned-up affection had I not seen his effusive letter to Ursula. How I wish he could have expressed himself as freely and fervently to his own daughter, but after all the years spent resisting his children's entreaties to send money, Mally and himself out of Germany, he was writing from the shadow of a towering slag heap of missed opportunities.

On re-reading his letter, I change my mind. It actually reveals not a lack of emotion but an excess of it and is all the more heart-rending for containing inside his tortuous phrasing feelings so powerful that he must hold on to them in order not to break apart.

My mother followed his example, wrapped up her own feelings and pushed them down so deep inside her that by the time I screwed up my courage to ask what had happened to Max and Mally, she had made herself forget details she might once have known. Over the decades, growing ever smaller and harder, and hidden beneath a narrative of parental coldness, was a tiny compressed kernel of love. Theirs for her and her love for them.

* * *

Towards the end of the war my mother had got fed up with my father not popping the question and decided to join Charlotte and Nepo in New York. Only when the USA granted her a visa did my father grasp that she meant business, and in November 1945 they married.

Hilda and Ernst Kohnstamm on their wedding day

With the war over and Hitler defeated, life was all about looking ahead. My parents bought a 1930s semi behind a thick privet hedge in Hampstead Garden Suburb. They had me.

Sadly, they didn't have my siblings – my mother suffered two miscarriages. My father started a textile-importing business with a partner he had met during internment.

Meanwhile Max and Mally's three children tried to pick up the pieces and reconnect. Charlotte, back in Paris after the collapse of her marriage to Nepo, wrote to Ernst:

'What exactly do you do as "officer of the state"? Is it admin? Couldn't you spend your holidays in Europe? And are you living on your own or have you shacked up with a woman? It's really hilarious to think how little we know about one another when we're not on bad terms or in any way estranged. So write, for goodness' sake!'

There was another reason for Charlotte's letter, which is dated 21 May 1950. The Federal Republic of Germany had announced it would pay reparations to Jewish survivors for their losses, and to make a claim in the names of Max and Mally the three siblings had to work as a unit.

In 1950 the process was still in its infancy, and I am surprised to discover that both Ernst and Charlotte had been reluctant to make a claim at all. Her letter continues:

'*I felt much the same as you. I didn't want to touch anything that had belonged to Mallymax as I always had the impression that they never wanted to give us anything. However, as they are now beyond helping, and anyway Kohnstamm* [my father] *doesn't understand such sentiments, while I was in London over Christmas I pulled myself together and began to deal with it.*'

Ernst, unlike Charlotte, had bathed in Mally's love, so he would probably have been reluctant for a different reason. Some survivors shuddered at the idea of accepting what they saw as 'blood money'.

What of my mother? I am sad to think she quite possibly shared those feelings and never expressed them. Claiming meant wading through all the shit but, like Mally before her, she now followed where her husband led. My father simply wanted to nail the bastards and get what he and my mother were due. He didn't '*understand such sentiments*' because no one close to him had been murdered. Both his immediate and extended family had made it to the UK.

The main problem facing Ernst, Charlotte and my mother was how to provide supporting evidence. They had all left Berlin well before the confiscations started.

Charlotte's letter continued: '*I wrote to Gerti Meseritz/ Fräulein Kaiser, our "safekeepers", and what do you know, a folder Max had entrusted to them came to light. It contains an inventory of assets and the contract of sale for 32 Bleibtreustrasse. We put in an application for the three of us. Although restitution for Berlin is still a long way off, we need to apply now.*'

* * *

The Landesarchiv Berlin, which holds the restitution files, is in Eichborndamm, a long S-Bahn ride away in northwest Berlin. At the main entrance I'm greeted by massively blown-up photos of the blown-up city. Isolated buildings stick up like lone teeth in an expanse of gums, with muffled-up women searching for anything edible, valuable, burnable amongst the rubble.

If Max had misjudged the Nazis, the Nazis also misjudged Max. Give him receipts for what was stolen, and he filed them. Take away his name, give him a number, and he made sure that records of his and Mally's identity, of their last will and testament, of their assets and title to the Bleibtreustrasse block of flats, were preserved. Their Finance Ministry files had been bombed and the Gestapo destroyed all their records, but in the folder entrusted to those two brave women, Max's documents survived.

I know that folder. I still have it. It had fascinated me as a child, the way it opened like a concertina. Covered in grey linen, the word *Dokumente* is imprinted in gold lettering on the front. And here, on the table in front of me, are some of the items it once contained. I'm drawn to a draft list in Max's handwriting of confiscated possessions. They are set out in neat, pencilled columns, together with the receipt for their surrender:

1 grey Persian lamb collar and 2 cuffs
1 vacuum cleaner with attachments
1 large sun lamp
1 hairdryer
2 opera glasses

When, I wonder, did my grandparents last sit side by side to look through those opera glasses, absorbed by the drama, swept away by the music?

4 ties

2 dresses. 1 blouse.

1 suit. 1 jacket. 1 hat.

Those were their very last possessions to be confiscated on 4 July 1942. Six weeks before deportation.

To make their claim, the three siblings had to pick over a family battlefield still soaked in frustration and anguish. Charlotte did the donkey work. '*Soon I'll be marching through the Brandenburg Gate back to the city of my birth*,' she wrote to Ernst on 4 April 1953, '*and I must admit, that makes me feel pretty apprehensive.*'

She made a detailed inventory of the contents of each room to accompany her plan of the Kurfürstendamm flat. I walk through them with her, starting in her bedroom furnished entirely in oak, with a large wardrobe, desk and day bed, two chairs and a Singer sewing machine. We cross into Max and Mally's bedroom (cherry wood), where a fur rug is draped over the sofa at the foot of their beds. Persian carpets cover the floors. In the drawing room (mahogany) a Bechstein grand piano stands next to cabinets displaying porcelain animals. Several oil paintings hang on the walls, and there are silk curtains at the windows. I count the chandeliers, Biedermeier chairs, polished tables, and peek into cupboards stacked with bed and table linen. Sideboards in the dining room contain silver cutlery, a twenty-four-piece KPM dinner service and acres of crystal glasses. I circle the *Venus de Milo* on a plinth and peer into the cabinet displaying a collection of antique coffee cups.

By contrast, my mother's list of the contents of the Bleibtreustrasse flat is terse and to the point. Get it down and over with.

Surviving witnesses confirmed that nothing was missing in any of my grandparents' flats; they had kept all their furniture and possessions intact. That fact was stressed time and time again. Nothing was missing. And time and time again, their claim was refused.

The lawyer's letters are plastered with underlinings and illegible comments. While trying to make them out, I've started to itch. Like I've been here before. Like who were these anonymous bureaucrats ignoring every receipt and witness statement? Old Nazis, by any chance?

Plus ça change, plus c'est la même chose . . . Take the administration of France after the Revolution. Officials who collected taxes for the new regime were often the same ones who'd served Louis XVI. *Le Roi est mort. Vive la République.* But let's not rock the sacred boat of bureaucracy. *Hitler est mort. Vive Adenauer.* But I bet the stonewalling file notes I'm struggling with were made by the same gang who hoovered up Jewish property in the first place.

The siblings' lawyer protested: '*I find it incomprehensible that the only evidence on which the Finance Minister is prepared to base his offer is a single note written on the final settlement of accounts in the Finance Ministry's files: "Otto Genz RM 787.50".* * Does the Finance Minister really consider the household and furniture of such well-to-do people to have*

---

* This final settlement of accounts is the only surviving piece of paper from Max and Mally's files in the Brandenburg Landeshauptarchiv. The rest were destroyed in air raids. How convenient for the restitution authorities, keen to pay out as little as possible.

been worth a mere RM 787.50? Everybody knows what went on in those days and the manner in which assets were calculated and disposed of.'

On 25 June 1960, fifteen years after the end of the war, it was Fräulein Kaiser's turn to testify. Was she now the only witness still alive? Or had the lawyer calculated she would be a better bet than the others because she wasn't – let's whisper it – Jewish?

Yes, Fräulein Kaiser confirmed, she had definitely always seen all their furniture and possessions in every flat they had lived in. '*Nothing was missing. Herr and Frau Rychwalski had kept everything in preparation for emigration.*'

Still the Restitution Department would not budge.

Six months later, on 4 January 1961, Fräulein Kaiser made a second sworn statement: '*Shortly before the couple Max and Mally Rychwalski were deported to Theresienstadt, between 19 and 26 August 1942, I visited their flat in Sächsischestrasse and ascertained that the items of furniture described in my declaration of 25 June 1960 were still there. I can say that with certainty because the truth is that I went round to the couple practically every day in order to care for them in their plight and bring them food. It is a well-known fact that those who wore the yellow star were forbidden to frequent shops open to the general public.*'

My one and only glimpse of humanity amongst these godforsaken papers.

I picture Max opening the folder labelled *Dokumente*. Every section on the contents page is filled in, all compartments full. Here the children will find his and Mally's birth and marriage certificates, their wills, synagogue and Kulturbund membership cards, bank and house details, his war certificate of merit, and the receipts for all their confiscated property.

He hasn't filed the last ones yet, for the items surrendered six weeks ago. He must do it now. Max hates crossing things out, but clarity outweighs neatness. He must separate the surrender

Inhalts-Verzeichnis

1	Familien-Papiere	*Schul-Urkd. Heirats-Urkd. Photokopien*
2	Urkunden	*Polizeiliche Abmeldungen*
3	Mietverträge	
4	Persönliches	*Testament, Bank-Vollmacht Mally*
5	*Hilde = Geburts-Urkunde Impfschein / Mally Impfschein*	
6	*Silber-Schmuck-Abgabe / Pelz-Abgabe, ... Abgaben*	
7	*Auswanderungs-Papiere ...*	
8	*Juden-Abgabe - R'Fluchtsteuer*	
9	*Kriegs-Verdienst-Kreuz u. andere Ehrenurkunden*	
10	*Bank-Aufstellung, Vermögens-Aufstellung / Kinder-Ausstattungs-Verzeichnis*	

(*Abgabe*, singular) of furs from the very last lot of *Abgaben* (plural) of several different items. It is important not to let grammatical standards slip, even now. Especially now. Keeping order helps. He blots the entry, then slots in the last receipt.

There is a knock, and Mally gasps. 'Not yet,' Max puts his hand on hers. How thin she has become. 'We don't leave till tomorrow. This will be Liesel.' He closes the folder and goes to answer the door.

*   *   *

I take the S-Bahn back to the city centre. By the time we pull into the main station, I have sunk into a trance. Doors open. Passengers get out and get in. Tannoy announcements distort and echo. Arrows point: *U-Bahn – International Departures – Arrivals*. The doors hiss shut, and once again my eyes lose focus. Rails run parallel, cross and diverge. Berlin's transport system, always good, had helped the handful of Jews who stayed and survived to disappear into the crowd. They travelled light. They kept on the move.

I feel weighed down by all Max and Mally's stuff, by their inability to let go. I'm swamped by lists.

Of chairs and beds, tables and desks, lamps and chandeliers.

Of porcelain ornaments and one silver samovar.

Of linen on shelves, silver in drawers, crystal in cabinets.

Of carpets on floors and portraits on walls.

Of 2 dresses.

Of 1 blouse.

1 suit.

1 jacket.

1 hat.

RECONNECTING

Farewell, Berlin. But not for long. I have arranged with Wolfgang that next summer we will place a *Stolperstein* for Cousin Lina. Wolfgang is going to find out where it should go, as Lina's final address won't do – 22 Heilbronner Strasse, her aunt Marie's *Judenhaus*, and one of the gateways to death. Lina's *Stolperstein* must be placed where she last lived in freedom.

I wheel my case along the street. After all the massive Berlin doorways, my own home seems to have shrunk to the size of a doll's house. I turn my key in the lock, take one step inside and get no further. A rare feeling is washing through me, so rare it takes me a moment to pinpoint what it is: utter satisfaction.

I am standing on a rug that came from Berlin. 'Remember Mr Gerson, who played tennis with Dad?' my mother said when she gave it to me. 'He and his parents lived in our house in the Bleibtreustrasse. This little rug came with the Gerson possessions.'

In the summer of 1939 Max wrote to Ernst: *'We've been busy helping the Gersons, our neighbours across the landing. They left early this morning to join their son in England.'*

So the Gersons lived in the undivided flat. Third floor left. My grandparents helped them prepare for life in London. Back and forth across the landing. 'Would you like to give us something for your daughter? There's room in the trunk.'

They fetched this rug and carried it over the same threshold I only recently crossed myself.

Never mind the dark and drizzle, I don't want to shut the door. A maelstrom of particles have joined into a chain stretching across the night sky, linking my grandparents in their hallway to me in mine. Unbroken.

* * *

I am about to book my flight to Berlin for Lina's *Stolperstein* dedication – we shall hold it in eight months' time, next July – when an invitation arrives. Hans and Dieter are going to celebrate their civil partnership the very same month. What perfect timing, and I know instantly what my gift will be.

Jugendstil. Or, if you prefer it, Art Nouveau. In 1903, when Max and Mally married, their cutlery had been the latest fashion. My mother had regularly used these large spoons, and their pattern is a family refrain. Later, when I visited Charlotte in New York, I recognised knives and forks from the same set. The teaspoons eventually turned up in Tel Aviv amongst Ernst's possessions, although I doubt they had done much stirring there; stainless steel was more his style. They surfaced after his death, along with Max and Mally's letters.

The spoons need a good polish, but I soon give up on the cream cleaner. It sticks inside every groove and swirl.

The other one is better. 'Apply with a wet sponge.' I work up a pink foam. Rinse, repeat, rinse, repeat . . .

With each application the blackness relents, revealing entwined leaves and stems which overflow onto the back, as though the exuberant silversmith did not know how to stop. One last flurry with the duster. There. That will do. More than do. The spoons sparkle and wink. Soon they will find a new home in their old one.

Or so I think when I check in at Heathrow, pleased with how well prepared I am. I have even finished a course of antibiotics after an insect bite on my ankle looked as if it might be infected. The swelling's gone down, and I'm fine, all set to dedicate Lina's stumble stone and celebrate Hans and Dieter's big day.

I've never had a suitcase go missing, but what's the betting that the first time I do, it will be the one with the spoons?

'You can't take knives or forks into the cabin,' says the girl at check-in.

'What about spoons? These are big.'

'Spoons are okay.'

'Are you sure?'

'Absolutely.'

My case disappears along the conveyor belt. The spoons and I head for passport control.

Security is slow and very busy. Shoes off. Belt off. Frisked. Boy, is it hot. I pad barefoot into the electronic archway. Nothing beeps. I go to collect my bag. It isn't there.

'Spoons!' As though he had found Semtex.

'I was told spoons were all right.'

'Who told you?'

'The check-in desk.'

'BA? What do they know? Spoons are NOT ALLOWED IN CABIN LUGGAGE.'

'So what do I do?'

'You'll have to leave them behind.'

'Can I collect them on my return?'

'No. They'll be destroyed.'

This simply cannot be. After all the spoons have been through, to survive the Nazis only to be blown up by the so-called free world?

Behind me crowds of spoonless passengers mutter and kick their bare heels. I hold my ground, face running with sweat, tears and snot, sobbing about wedding presents and sentimental value and how the hell do you scoop someone to death?

A supervisor arrives. He offers a solution. It means going back through security and passport control and checking in all over again. I am in a film running backwards, the only one in it.

The crowds have grown; queues snake around one another. At this rate, I'll miss my flight. I grab an official. 'Don't stress, don't stress,' he keeps saying as he delivers me to a desk.

I wrap the spoons in a scarf to stop them rattling in their plastic bag and watch the tiny parcel disappear between two juggernaut cases. They might as well have exploded them in front of me there and then. How can they possibly ever arrive? How can they fail to fall down a crack in the conveyor belt? What I need is support, a listening ear, reassurance.

I ring my friend who's psychic. She apparently gets wind

of things that haven't yet happened. 'Although sometimes I'm wrong.'

I need certainty. 'Will I ever see the spoons again?'

'Yes.' Soothing, confident.

'No, I mean really.'

'Yes!'

'You're just saying that.'

She laughs. 'They'll be fine. Calm down.'

I sit rigid in the departure lounge. The trouble with normally being calm and sensible is that when I do have a wobble it feels like full-blown derangement. All the more galling not to be taken seriously. High time that changed. What is the point of being calm and sensible, anyway? Look at my ankle, or rather ankles, plural. When it comes to Berlin, my body has a mind of its own. The insect, or two insects working in tandem, bit me on each ankle, leaving puncture marks either side of the Achilles tendons. The antibiotics may have zapped a swollen left foot, but as I board the plane that baking July afternoon my right one starts to throb.

Next day finds me in A&E in Dahlem, foot the size of a melon. As the colour changes from pink to red to puce, I try to imagine it belongs to someone else. More antibiotics are stuffed into me, plus antihistamine and instructions to return immediately for intravenous treatment if my temperature shoots up.

From the hospital I ring Wolfgang, who has to shout through hammering. Gunter Demnig is placing stumble stones. 'But one is missing. It got left behind.'

'Lina's?'

'Possibly.' A tiny hesitation before the 'possibly' has given the game away.

Oh great. In a few days' time my new German friends and acquaintances are going to join me, who might be in hospital, to dedicate a stumble stone which might not be there.

'Dahlem, did you say? That was the SS hospital . . .'

Shut up, Wolfgang.

'. . . till the Americans took it over.'

Back in my sweltering hotel room I try to unpack without moving, swat mosquitoes and examine my mutating foot. Two kidney-shaped blisters over the bite marks are swelling with yellow liquid. I am starring in my own monster movie.

I extract wedding paper from a side pocket of my suitcase. Might as well wrap the spoons.

Oh yes. The sight of that little package jiggling towards me along the conveyor belt was worth a hundred insect bites.

A DIFFERENT
ROLL OF THE DICE

It is so hot on the morning of Lina's *Stolperstein* dedication that the air has given up circulating. I lie on the floor to cool down. Not that it makes much difference. With rivulets of sweat running off me, I calculate the last possible moment I can get changed. I should like to dress up for Lina. This is her day, and I want to look my best. Some hope. My bandaged foot will eventually have to be squeezed into sandals. As for tights, forget it.

Thinking of tights makes me think of Auntie Hedy and how, with a different roll of the dice, I might have grown up with Lina and be placing a stumble stone for Auntie Hedy. Max's niece v. Mally's niece, both born at the tail end of the nineteenth century, both single and under the cut-off age (fifty-five) for a domestic work permit and visa to the UK. Yet Hedy was the one who escaped and played such a large part in my childhood. How come she made it and not Lina?

Tights had not quite arrived when Auntie Hedy gave 12-year-old me my first holiday job at Madame Lieberg's, a long, narrow corsetière shop in Golders Green. She looked after the stocking counter. Wolford, Berlei and Aristoc were her holy trinity.

'Which ones shall I give Mum for her birthday?'

Aristoc, of course, the ARISTOCracy of stockings.

From my position behind the counter, I watched breasts wobble in and sail out. The suspender belts and skimpy bras worn by my mother would not fit most of Madame Lieberg's customers. They had themselves bolted into all-in-one contraptions that pushed everything in and thrust it up. Fierce elastication and underwiring were orchestrated by Ollie, pins sprouting from pursed lips and a tape measure hanging round her neck. She bustled in and out of cubicles, pulling, pinging, pinning and tweaking before disappearing into the sewing-machine whirr at the back of the shop.

I sat high up on a wooden stool at the glass-topped counter and didn't move – there was no room to – other than to write price labels. Beneath my pen lay shallow drawers of fifteen, twenty, thirty denier; more were stacked on floor-to-ceiling shelves behind me. Auntie Hedy could put her hand to any make, size and shade with her eyes shut. She did the accounts for the whole business, but over the stockings she ruled by divine right.

My parents and I were her closest family in England. One year we returned from holiday to find framed birds-of-paradise winking at us all the way up the stairs; a surprise treat from Auntie Hedy, who didn't understand that even a naturalised Englishman's home is his castle, just as my father failed to appreciate how she, in a rented room without a proper home of her own, could have such a big stake in his.

My father raged, the birds disappeared and Nothing More Was Said. If there was an atmosphere, I doubt it lasted long. Auntie Hedy and my father soon returned to playing Beethoven piano pieces for four hands from a beautiful edition she had given him.

I often think of her decked out in green and purple, her favourite colours, preferably worn together. She was our own Mrs Malaprop, ordering from a surreal menu at the local Italian – *sôle manure* followed by the hot wine cream dessert, *zambezi*. Once the German restitution kicked in, there was no stopping her, and her travels broadened the family vocabulary:

Blumenthals
classy New York department store (Bloomingdale's)
Kenneth
Israeli Parliament (Knesset)
Albatross
prison island off San Francisco (Alcatraz)

I try to imagine growing up with Lina instead, but doubt that had ever been even remotely on the cards. Hedy had always needed to work; Lina didn't. Hedy was a fighter; Lina wasn't. After *Kristallnacht*, as Charlotte reported to Ernst, Lina was *'helpless and traumatised'*. Hedy, on the other hand, looked for a way out.

Her first attempt to Holland failed, and I never knew how she finally made it to the UK until I read Ernst's cache of letters. A friend of my mother's had found her a job. *'She's already got her permit and will hopefully arrive soon'*, my mother wrote to Ernst on 4 February 1939. During those crucial pre-war months, when Max and Mally failed to emigrate and it seems that Lina never tried, my mother and her friend engineered Hedy's flight to England and saved her life. Over the following decades, none of them ever mentioned it.

Through retirement, heart disease and cancer, Auntie Hedy kept her fighting spirit until the day she died. A few hours earlier I had visited her in hospital, and only then, looking stricken, did she raise and lower her arm in her first and last gesture of resignation.

I know so much about her, so little about Lina, and both feel out of kilter. If we'd been a normal non-murdered family – I think as I continue to lie on the floor and drip – Auntie Hedy would simply have taken her place in the general back-drop of great-aunts, uncles and cousins whom we saw now and then. Her existence wouldn't have been such a big deal.

Hedy

Lina

Wolfgang drives, Barbara sits holding a flower, and for once no one talks. We turn down Sächsische Strasse, and as we pass number 27 I see its front door has a fresh coat of turquoise paint. The graffiti, arrow and word *JUD* remain untouched.

Lina and her father Louis lived at number 48, further along on the other side of the street. A small group of people are waiting. Lina's shiny memorial has joined two older dull ones, all three looking somewhat adrift on a wide section of the pavement as the original building was destroyed. I look more closely and see the cement around her stumble stone is still damp. No wonder Wolfgang was quiet on the drive; he must still have been catching his breath.

Frau Lenck has come, and I remind her of her first email: '*In this city where your family suffered so much, they are not forgotten.*'

'That's why I wanted to be here today,' she says.

Given the scale of war damage, I find it remarkable that three out of four family homes should have survived more or less intact. Apart from my mother's birthplace, which now accommodates a tree, the other thresholds are the original ones and theoretically available to my exploding feet. 96 Kurfürstendamm, I have meanwhile discovered, remains out of bounds for security reasons – it is the residence of the current mayor of Berlin.

Wolfgang reads out the stark facts surrounding Lina's deportation. On 13 January 1942 she was one of 1,034 Jews loaded onto transport No. 8 bound for Riga. The journey took three days, and many froze to death on the way.

A few people are dabbing their eyes. Yet I don't feel at all like crying. Her life is at last being acknowledged. People have put themselves out to make this gesture. Julia is here with a friend. Hans has taken time off work. Someone I met at the conference has come specially from Hamburg. This is Lina's moment, and I'm glad.

I hand round copies of the only photo with her in it; the 1908 family one taken at Cousin Ernst's bar mitzvah. This photo represents the entire fate of German Jews under the Nazis: those who died before deportation, fled, took their own lives or were murdered. Lina, aged sixteen, sits on a rug at the front, surrounded by her little girl cousins. The bar mitzvah boy – the only one who would hide in Germany and survive – stands between his seated parents.

After the war, Cousin Ernst – by then a man in his forties – gave an insight into Lina's last months and weeks. In a sworn statement to the Entschädigungsamt Berlin (Berlin Compensation Office), he declared: *'My wife and I fled from Stettin at the end of January 1940 and, to begin with, stayed with my cousin Lina in Berlin. She did forced labour, like all Jews, peeling potatoes in an Aschinger canteen kitchen. The Gestapo summoned her several times to Burgstrasse. There they threatened her and extorted money and property from her. Before she was deported, a Gestapo officer seized her grand piano for his own personal use. My wife and I were witnesses . . .'*

A young woman is examining the photo. 'Which one is Lina's father?' she asks.

'That's Louis, third from the right, back row.'

'And her mother?'

'The short one standing next to him.'

The woman tells me she teaches at a nearby Polish school. Her class is doing a project on the Holocaust. Might they 'adopt' Lina's stumble stone? And who are the others in the photo?

I offer to email a key to who is who. Perhaps she even knows the town where the photo was taken – Trzcianka, which is now in Poland. Before the war it was still part of Germany and called Schönlanke.

'Could we also have a photo of you?'

'Of me? Why?'

'Of today. Lina's stumble stone day. Then we'll have both you and Lina.'

The shadow family has had nothing to do with me for so long that I still struggle with the connection obvious to everyone else.

A gust of wind has thrown my cupboard doors wide open and blown its contents out into the world.

MEETING MYSELF

The Berlin Compensation Office, I was told, is a gold mine of information. Well worth a visit because you simply never know what you'll find there.

I walk the whole length of Sächsische Strasse until I reach Fehrbelliner Platz, a huge intersection of several streets encircled by official buildings designed for the thousand-year Reich – vast grey structures pockmarked by rows of square windows. Number 1 Fehrbelliner Platz was seized by the SS in 1943, requisitioned by the British after the war, then handed over to the municipality of West Berlin. Since the 1950s it has housed the Berlin Compensation Office.

'We're not an archive,' Frau Schmidt warned me on the phone. 'We don't have the facilities. We're a working office and can only accommodate one researcher, maximum two, at any one time. You need to make an appointment. Frau Beck handles the old files, and she will prepare them for you.'

Stone reliefs of toiling, heroic figures frame the entrance. Just looking at them is exhausting. I push open the door and enter Kafka-land. Corridors of beige lino, cream walls and yellow doors stretch away in all directions. Office numbers don't follow any particular order. 'This floor, keep turning left,' a passing worker bee instructs. Some offices have a row of green chairs outside so that alive-and-kicking claimants have somewhere to sit while waiting.

There are no chairs outside mine. I knock and enter. The room is light and airy. Frau Beck is sitting behind a tower of folders. She indicates a table in the corner with a heap of files waiting for me. As for photocopies, they will take weeks, an invoice has to be raised in a far-flung department and, by the way, the machine is currently out of order – clearly she doesn't hold with the extra work researchers into past cases generate.

In my bag, *verboten* in normal archives, is my camera. The atmosphere immediately changes. Frau Beck is delighted. She even allows me to undo tight bindings to free documents as long as I do them up again. If she keeps the window open, would I mind if she smokes? We have a deal.

I open Max's file and recognise my father's handwriting. He completed the section of the claim form listing different categories of loss: (A) Life, (B) Health, (C) Freedom, (D) Property, (E) Career, (F) . . . The last time I was aware of these documents will have been in the 1950s as they were gathering signatures and witness statements on their travels between New York, London, Tel Aviv and Berlin. In front of me are all the whispered words from long ago.

Sitting on the floor with my storybook, I would yearn to be read to, but the bubble of intensity around my parents put me off asking. Instead I traced the red-and-black pattern in the Afghan carpet and listened to the rhythm of their voices, the repetition of the German categories of loss as familiar and strangely soothing as my bedtime ritual.

Good night
Schaden am Leben
Sleep tight
Schaden an Freiheit
Watch out that the bugs don't bite
Schaden an Körper und Gesundheit

In those days the enormity was still fresh, the concepts hard to grasp, the vocabulary to deal with it new.

The task of the Restitution Department was straightforward by comparison. It dealt with losses that had a clear monetary value: houses, furniture, jewellery, gold and silver, works of art, bank accounts, stocks and shares. At the Berlin Compensation Office, however, someone had to calculate the value of a life shortened, an education uncompleted, career prospects down the toilet. The whole Nazi period of harassment, expulsion and murder was broken down into these categories to make the process manageable.

I open Mally's file. My mother had filled in the claim form when she knew, or claimed to know, very little; neither the date her parents were forced to move out of their own flat, nor of their deportation.

As far as I can understand from the lawyer's deposition, damages were only claimed from 19 September 1941, the date '*she was obliged to wear the yellow star*'. Is that all, I think? What about damages suffered before then, such as the loss of her civil rights, her nationality, home, the right to walk the streets without fear, to walk the streets at all, in short the right to live as a human being?

I'm flummoxed by the categories and legal language, which would be perplexing enough in English, let alone in

German. Category A: Loss of Life. Well, that's clear enough, and we have the exact date Mally died: 13 November 1942. But what about the relentless build-up of anti-Semitic measures she and all Jews were forced to comply with ever since 1933? Aren't they relevant to Category B (Damage to Health) and Category C (Loss of Freedom)?

All the time that I'm struggling with these bloody categories, I realise that actually I don't want to know which loss belongs where. I don't want to play their game. I don't want to divvy up the unending awfulness into neat compartments. It offends me.

Once again fury erupts through my feet, one still discoloured. It is clear where Max and Mally's claim had to end, but where did it begin? Surely long before 19 September 1941 and the introduction of the yellow star.

I am also aware of a strange paradox: Max, if not Mally, would have felt completely at home here. Columns were his milieu, ruled lines his support. Think of the contents page in the old linen-covered folder in which he gave each anti-Semitic regulation its own section.

Enough. I need to get out of these files and out of the building.

On the way back I pass Lina's stumble stone. The sun hits the brass surface at an oblique angle and clearly shows up the inscription. I crouch down to take a photo.

A walking frame and pair of knobbly feet stop next to me. 'That's new.' Feet and voice belong to a woman of about eighty.

'Yes, it was only placed the other day.'

'I didn't notice. It's very small.'

'That's the idea. To commemorate ordinary people. She was my cousin.'

We stand together for a moment. I reckon my companion would have been a child when Lina's turn came. I imagine her waking up in the early hours hearing boots on cobbles, an engine revving, and peeping through lace curtains to glimpse Lina being taken away. A sudden daytime round-up would have had her mother quickly pulling her down a side street. 'Come away! Don't look!' Of course she looked. She saw the fear and never forgot.

'I think it's very good,' she says.

The following day Frau Beck has acquired an assistant who spends a lot of time talking to her pot plants, a strategy which must work as they look healthy.

Against a background of bored banter ('I'm not opening that file today, madam.' – 'Fine by me, madam.') I open Charlotte's file.

Her claim for Loss of Career was difficult to prove. No official record survived of the jewellery business she had run from home, so she cobbled together what evidence she could, including an old letterhead:

═══════ A T E L I E R ═══════
FÜR MODISCHEN SCHMUCK
LOTTE RYCHWALSKI
BERLIN-HALENSEE KURFÜRSTENDAMM 96
H 2 UHLAND 1084 • POSTSCHECK: BERLIN 112478

On the other side of this crumpled scrap of notepaper I come face to face with my schoolgirl mother-to-be:

'*Dear Fräulein,*
'*Here is my last will and testament.*
'*TO EAT you will find:*
'*one artichoke (plus sauce)*
'*stewed fruit*
'*tomatoes, butter, eggs and lemons (in cupboard)*
'*There is NO BREAD.*
'*1000 greetings.*'

And a very faint pencilled reply from Charlotte:

'*Sweetheart, that was <u>absolutely delicious</u>! The sauce plus the stewed fruit! How about that!*'

An undated note kept as a reminder of her sister's light-hearted spirit.

Finally, I turn to my mother's file. In the hierarchy of suffering, she denied her own. To the question *Were you yourself persecuted?* she had answered *No*.

Picture the lawyer's weary sigh as he dictated the accompanying letter: '*Furthermore, let me point out that the applicant has inadvertently completed the covering sheet incorrectly. Given her Jewish origins, the applicant was herself also persecuted.*'

My mother's claim for Loss of Education trundled on for years. By the time she was paid out, my own education had gone further than hers ever did. To celebrate she bought each of us a fantastic pair of shoes.

I flick through all the pieces of evidence she had been obliged to supply: her own curriculum vitae; a sworn statement from Auntie Hedy; a certificate from her old school. Finally, they required a document with her maiden name as well as her married one as proof of identity.

A worn, buff envelope clamped to the binding holds a folded piece of paper. I straighten it out. *CERTIFIED COPY OF AN ENTRY OF BIRTH*, I read, *Pursuant to the Births and Deaths Registration Acts—*

Good heavens, it's me. I have just been born. *Mona F. Taylor, Interim Registrar for HENDON in the COUNTY OF MIDDLESEX*, certifies the fact that I exist and who my parents are. The clincher for the Berlin Compensation Office is the red penny stamp with the profile of King George VI stuck in the bottom right-hand corner to give the official seal of approval. My former monarch and I have spent half a century in a building seized by the SS, then by the British, finally given back to the city of Berlin.

'Frau Beck! I've found my birth certificate.'

The assistant stops talking to her plants and stares at me. Frau Beck stubs out a cigarette and hauls her top half in from the open window. The office falls silent as dead files spring into life.

Frau Beck says something I have difficulty grasping. 'I can ask Frau Schmidt. Then you can take it home.'

'What?'

'The original. We can keep a copy for our files.'

While trying to absorb her meaning, I hear another voice, very close and familiar. 'That's nice of you, but really not necessary. After all, I already have a copy of my birth certificate, I know when I was born, ha ha . . .'

What's going on? Rational default mode has kicked in.

I re-read my mother's pencilled note. '*There is NO BREAD. 1000 greetings.*' All the burrowing and following in Max and Mally's footsteps I have done for myself, true enough, but also for the sake of that light-hearted girl who also appeared in my world before the walls began to close in. She might suddenly turn a somersault or fashion false teeth out of inside-out orange peel and threaten my father and me with a kiss.

I kick the old me out of the way. 'Forget what I just said. Yes, please, I'd like to take it home.'

Ever since Max and Mally first popped up on my computer screen my actions have been instinctive, fuelled by a desire to find out, find out, find out. Here in Berlin, where I feel not exactly at home but at ease, not only does no one question these needs, they do their best to help fulfil them.

Frau Schmidt, a gentle butterfly of a civil servant, flutters over the file to release the binding. 'I'll make a copy of your mother's note, too, if you like,' she whispers, 'then you can take home the original of that as well.'

Yes, I do like, Frau Schmidt. I like very much.

She has brought along an article from the local paper reporting Lina's stumble stone dedication with the unsettling description of the sponsor (me) as her *great-niece, a Jewish woman living in London*. I am not her great-niece, but that isn't what bothers me; being defined as Jewish, not British, does. It makes *'living in London'* seem incidental, as though I might up sticks at any moment and move somewhere else, for isn't that what Jews always do?

Frau Schmidt lingers. She has worked in the department a long time and remembers when the files were active, the claimants alive. She was very young then and had nightmares of her own parents being deported. 'It weighs you down,' she murmurs, then goes to make the copies.

I consider what other official documents my mother could have chosen to prove who she was and where she came from. Marriage certificate, British naturalisation certificate, her own birth certificate, even her old German passport – although that had probably long been shredded. Instead she opted for her baby messenger – me, via my birth certificate.

'*Yes, my dear, you have become an uncle,*' she wrote to Ernst shortly after my birth. '*We have called her Jacqueline (my father-in-law's name was Jacob, and anyway, we like the name).*

'*Little Jacqueline is lying in her basket in the corner and has just burped. She is very appetising for a new-born, not at all wrinkly, but smooth and pink with lots of black hair.*'

Neither Max nor Mally were remembered in my naming. Maybe 'M' names would have gone to my two younger siblings had my mother not had her miscarriages.

Frau Beck and her assistant are talking in lowered voices with the occasional glance in my direction, as though they half expect a queue to form in the corridor outside. For if the contents of one fifty-year-old brown envelope can turn up in the flesh, what's to stop a rush of others from doing the same?

After much agreeing, confirming and signing of papers in duplicate – we are at the heart of German bureaucracy, after all, but what a kind heart it has turned out to have – the two documents are mine.

THE LAST THRESHOLD

A year and a half after my first visit to Berlin, my fourth one is coming to an end. I have seen the city in every season, meeting Wolfgang for the first time in freezing midwinter and returning that spring to speak at the *Stolpersteine* conference. Autumn winds were whipping leaves off the trees when I jumped into the troubling waters of In-Between. Now it is high summer.

My last few days are a time to unwind. The weather is perfect. I take a boat trip. Meet Julia for breakfast at the Reichstag. Meet Wolfgang and Barbara for a concert and picnic. Dress up for Hans and Dieter's big day and deliver the spoons to their old/new home.

Passing an internet café, I go in to check my emails – and get a shock.

Evidence, like scum, keeps rising to the surface. A woman I barely know, whom I had met at the conference, has sent me a link to the National Archives in Prague. Death certificates of inmates who died in Theresienstadt are now online, and they are very detailed, containing information lacking in Charlotte's Red Cross copies.

I last saw Max and Mally as they took their seats on the train and I waved them goodbye. Suddenly I have been given the last piece of their jigsaw. But the one before it is missing, and that missing piece I shall only find in the memorial books in the Jewish Library (the ones the librarian suggested I consult with a companion).

Early next morning, before the heat of the day can take hold, I return to confront the stark details leading to the endgame for tens of thousands of German Jews. Lists of names and fates. Where each person came from and where they were sent. On what date. In which transport. I appeal to my body not to react and open the first volume.

In front of me, in alphabetical order, lies my whole shadow family. Just copy the facts, I tell myself. Don't think.

Don't think, indeed! Brain humming, synapses firing like mini machine guns, I copy furiously and, as I do so, family members appear and disappear in a jumble of scenes.

I watch Max and Mally arrive in the old fortress on that late August day in 1942, bewildered and exhausted, dragging their luggage. And when they get there, they are assigned different rooms, one for men, one for women, up in the attics – out of sight, out of mind. I hope Mally manages to join her sister-in-law Marie, who has already been there for six weeks. A familiar face. A scrap of comfort.

One week later Max's youngest brother Eugen arrives with his family from Tirschtiegel, plus Cousin Alfred and his girls from Betsche, all crammed into the same transport. Surely the family will now band together as they always have done, the young and resilient looking after their parents, aunts, uncles. Surely younger legs will carry bread and soup up all those stairs to Mally.

Suddenly Marie disappears. On 19 September 1942 Max's sister is one out of two thousand Jews loaded onto Transport Bo, bound for Treblinka.

Oh God. I freeze when I read that, deeply shocked. Although surrounded by the wholesale murder of most of my family, for some reason Marie's stands out. Perhaps because she lived such a successful, independent life. Or because I know a lot about her – her red hair and habit of hiding chocolate to resist temptation, then hunting for it; her second marriage to a no-goodnik whom she quickly divorced. Or because she had the opportunity to exchange her house for one in England '*but has ruled it out*', as Charlotte wrote to Ernst in the summer of 1939, '*as it would almost certainly be too small to provide her with sufficient income. So, even now, she prefers to risk everything*'. Or because Treblinka, where she finally lost her gamble, was obliterated. Everyone knows about Auschwitz. You can see the train tracks, the barracks and crematoria, the piles of shoes and spectacles. If you were fit enough to work, you even had a chance to survive Auschwitz. Not much of one, but still a chance. Whereas Treblinka was a death factory, pure and simple. And when the Nazis saw the war was lost, they razed it to the ground. Recently, though, Treblinka has started giving up some of its secrets. A button here. Part of a comb there. Streaks of whitish residue turn out to be human ash mixed with fragments of bone. And I shudder. That could be Marie, I think, my energetic great-aunt ahead of her time, the equal of any man, slaughtered in this forgotten place of utter desolation.

All the while Mally is still up in the attics. By now she may not have had the strength to leave her bunk. Does she just lie there on her thin straw mattress? Amongst fleas and lice and stench.

And what of Max? With his younger brother in a different building, he is all on his own.

Endless days. Airless nights that steadily get colder.

Of those who remain in Theresienstadt, the very old and very young – the ones with least resilience – succumb first.

15 December 1942: seven-year-old Emmi from Betsche.

3 January 1943: Max's brother Eugen.

Three weeks after Eugen's death, on 23 January 1943, Transport Cr ships his wife and young son to Auschwitz.

The Betsche Five are now reduced to three: Alfred, his wife Ruth and their remaining daughter Helga.

They are joined by Marie's eldest son, Manfred Greiffenhagen. He writes poems and lyrics for shows to entertain Theresienstadt inmates and contributes to the script for the notorious film *Der Führer schenkt den Juden eine Stadt* (*The Führer Gives the Jews a City*), designed to hoodwink the general public by showing what a great time the Jews are having in their glorious ghetto. (A Red Cross delegation is similarly duped.) No sooner is the film in the can than Manfred is bundled onto Transport Em to Auschwitz. One week later, on 6 October 1944, Alfred, Ruth and Helga follow in Transport Eo.

Alfred with his eye patch and open, flowing handwriting.

Alfred, who gave my mother her first orange.

Alfred, who has been nudging me ever since I started this journey.

Alfred finally disappears from view.

But I remember you, Alfred. You and your girls. I see you clearly now.

No onward transport for Max and Mally. They stayed put.

Mally died at 6.30 a.m. on 13 November 1942 in room 113 of Building L317. She was sixty-four.

Max died two months later, at 8 a.m. on 31 January 1943 in room 14 of Building L118. Death confirmed at 9.20 a.m. He was seventy-eight.

BACK TO THE BEGINNING

I leave the library and step out into the dazzling midday sun. I can't see a thing and veer into a shady corner, my heart thumping as if I have just run a marathon rather than sat motionless staring at lists.

Now what shall I do? I thought I had crossed every available threshold, but it seems I haven't. The old fortress of Theresienstadt still exists. So do plans of the ghetto. That means I could go and find my grandparents' buildings. I could stand in the very spots where their light went out for good. Room 113 of Building L317. Room 14 of Building L118.

Shall I do it, then? Shall I go there? Or shall I go somewhere else entirely?

In my mind's eye, clear as clear, is the photo from the old shoebox of Mally taken the day she and Max became engaged.

June 1903. Midsummer's Day. The two families have met at her parents' Hamburg home and set the wedding date for August. With the formalities over and the photographer gone, Mally is impatient to spend time on her own with Max. She's delighted to find him lingering in the hall, studying her picture of fishermen. She suggests showing him the spot on the waterfront where she set up her easel and painted it. With a bit of luck, their parents, floored by the heat, will stay behind.

They walk side by side, not touching. He could at least take her arm, Mally thinks. She glances round at her brother, their chaperone. Fritz grins, then pointedly turns to watch an old steamship leave its dock and lets them walk on.

Mally slips her arm through Max's, and immediately he pulls her closer. A gust of wind makes her clutch her hat. She laughs and pins it firmly back in place. With its spray of delicate flowers, it sets off her dress a treat – white lace down to her wrists and nipped-in waist. 'Come on!' She picks up her skirt and breaks into a run. 'We're nearly there.'

Max pretends to race her. They round the next bend, and Mally points to three fishermen standing on a rock. It is the same rock and a similar scene to the one in her painting. This is the spot where the water changes colour and becomes the sea. Next stop America. Here the horizon opens up and everything becomes possible.

She wishes she could explain that feeling to him, but doesn't know how to, especially now Max has put his arms around her, and any words she might have summoned up have flown out of the window. She is only aware of his closeness, maleness, a whiff of cigar, of cologne. She leans back against him, and together they watch the steamship chug past.

'Beautiful,' Max murmurs.

Me or the ship? Mally looks up quickly to reassure herself. Mind you, the ship has beauty too, its masts tall and elegant, sails still furled, smoke belching out of both funnels. She's about to say: 'Let's travel! Explore new lands!' – but stops short, struck by his expression. A mix of determination and hope for the future, also of vulnerability and a desire to please. Suddenly she feels she's the strong one.

Max is whispering. His beard and breath tickle her ear, the wind snatching away his words. '. . . a flat near the *Tiergarten* . . . children . . .'

Oh yes, children. Mally likes children. She pictures her niece, Hedy. She enjoys making the solemn little child giggle.

So that is how life will be. Running her own household. Becoming a mother. Inviting friends and family to her home in the capital. Together they will explore Berlin, walk along its rivers and around its lakes. She will take along her sketchbook and set up her easel to capture different images. Mally can already feel new horizons opening up.

The steamship is now no more than a dot. The inverted 'V' of its wake flattens and disappears into the sea, which sparkles all the way to where it meets the sky. Not a cloud.

* * *

For one moment I have touched the old world before it shattered. No longer are Max and Mally defined solely by wretchedness. As for standing in the spots where their lives ended? Maybe. Maybe not. For now I shall leave them on the brink of their future with years of normal life ahead of them, fresh and undefiled.

My old lump of ice has cracked. Meltwater seeps out of Before into In-Between and washes through After. Let it keep on flowing.

SOURCES

Walter Benjamin
The epigraph comes from Lisa Fittko's testimony to the USC Shoah Foundation Institute recorded in 1999, in which she recalls guiding Walter Benjamin to the French–Spanish border when he tried, and tragically failed, to escape.

Instructions for Jews before deportation
(Part 3, Crossing the Road)
No written instructions were found specifically for Berlin Jews. The ones quoted are dated 19 March 1942 and appear on a *Merkblatt* (instruction sheet) for the imminent deportation of Jews from Würzburg.

Private and public sources
Most primary sources are in German and, when quoted, translated by the author. Her grandparents' letters were initially impenetrable. Learning to decipher their handwriting and the old German *Sütterlin* script played a major part in the journey of the book.

Private sources

Author's:

From Hilda:
Post-war family letters and official communications relating to restitution.

From Charlotte:
Pre- and post-war family letters. Love letters. Official documents, including Max and Mally's birth, marriage and death certificates.

From Ernst:
More than fifty letters, postcards and Red Cross messages written by Max and Mally from 1933 to 1942.
Pre- and post-war letters from Hilda and Charlotte.
Official letters and documents covering his escape from Berlin and attempts to free his parents.

From Cousin Kurt Rychwalski:
Two letters written by Cousin Ernst and his wife Helene, dated November 1945 and January 1946, describing how they survived by hiding in Berlin. Copies are in the Wiener Holocaust Library, London, and the Silent Heroes Memorial Center, part of the German Resistance Memorial Center (Gedenkstätte Deutscher Widerstand), Berlin.

From Laure Wittner (Hannelore Greiffenhagen):
Video-recorded conversations between Laure and the author (2014) in which Laure remembers her Berlin childhood, father Manfred and grandmother Marie Greiffenhagen.

Lonnie Zwerin:

Wartime letters from her grandparents Fritz and Olga Meseritz in Hamburg to her mother Ursula in Los Angeles. Now deposited in the Leo Baeck Institute, New York.

Roni G. Ronen (Rosner), grandson of Max's sister Regina:

Archive of Rychwalski family photos and papers transported from Germany to Palestine in 1933.

Public sources

Brandenburgisches Landeshauptarchiv (Brandenburg Main State Archives):

Finance Ministry files containing pre-war correspondence and the final Declaration of Assets (Vermögenserklärung) each deportee was obliged to complete before transport to the concentration camps.

Deportation lists for each transport.

Rep. 36A Oberfinanzpräsident Berlin-Brandenburg (II):

File 32582 Cousin Lina Rychwalski

Files 5038 and **5039** Eugen Rychwalski

File 5040 Jacob Rychwalski

File 5037 Cousin Alfred Rychwalski

File 32580 Cousin Ernst Rychwalski

File 32581 Georg Rychwalski

No. 55125 (Deportation list to Theresienstadt with Alfred Rychwalski and family, Nos 3–7)

No. 55124 (letter from the Gestapo enclosing *Alterstransport* deportation list to Theresienstadt with Max and Mally Rychwalski, Nos 84 and 85)

Landesarchiv Berlin (Berlin State Archives):
Restitution Office (Wiedergutmachungsamt) files containing post-war claims for property losses in West Berlin – bank deposits and financial holdings, houses, furniture, businesses, jewellery, artworks.

> **B Rep. 025-05 (53 WGA 615/57) Page 41** (siblings' lawyer letter)
>
> **B Rep. 025-05 (53 WGA 615/57) Page 51** (Fräulein Kaiser first declaration)
>
> **B Rep. 025-05 (53 WGA 615/57) Page 65** (Fräulein Kaiser second declaration)
>
> **B Rep. 025-05 (53 WGA 616/57) Pages 7 and 8** (final confiscations)

Ausgleichsamt Referat E (Lastenausgleich) (Compensation Claims Office), Berlin:
Relates to losses suffered in the former GDR, namely Krawattenunion, the family's tie factory located in East Berlin. (Restitution made after 1990.) **File A10/EF 4831 BF USA *Teil* Ib** refers to the order forbidding the manufacture of black and brown ties.

Entschädigungsamt Berlin (Berlin Compensation Office):
Files of post-war claims for loss of life, health, freedom, education, career.

> **File 72.919** Max
>
> **File 72.922** Mally
>
> **File 353.241** Hilda
>
> **File 335.705** Charlotte
>
> **File 301.964** Ernst

SOURCES

File 72.659 Cousin Ernst Richards (formerly Ernst Rychwalski)
File 275.890 Cousin Lina

Handelsregister (Company Register), Berlin Charlottenburg:
Number 88 156 (11412)
Record of the family tie business Rewald & Greiffenhagen founded in 1901, merged with Berenhaut & Anker in 1930 to form Krawattenunion. Company dissolved 1940.

Weissensee Jewish Cemetery, Berlin:
Index cards containing details of an individual's death and burial service.

Grundbuch (Land Register), Berlin:
Record of a building's boundaries and all changes of ownership. Access restricted to the property's owners.

Bauamt (Planning Office), Berlin:
Contains requests to make changes to a building, including architects' plans, and the date work completed. Access restricted to the property's owners.

Yad Vashem Database of Holocaust Victims. Jerusalem:
Details of an individual's deportation, transport number and destination, plus survivors' testimonies.

Terezin Initiative (holocaust.cz), Prague:
Online database of death certificates issued for inmates of Theresienstadt/Terezin.

United States Holocaust Memorial Museum, Washington, D.C.:
Typescripts of poems and lyrics written by Manfred Greiffenhagen in concentration camp. (Accession No. 2011.270.5)

APPENDIX

Bleibtreu heißt die Straße

Vor fast vierzig Jahren wohnte ich hier.
. . . Zupft mich was am Ärmel, wenn ich
So für mich hin den Kurfürstendamm entlang
Schlendere – heißt wohl das Wort.
Und nichts zu suchen, das war mein Sinn.
Und immer wieder das Gezupfe.
Sei doch vernünftig, sage ich zu ihr.
Vierzig Jahre! Ich bin es nicht mehr.
Vierzig Jahre. Wie oft haben meine Zellen
Sich erneuert inzwischen
In der Fremde, im Exil.
New York, Ninety-Sixth Street und Central Park,
Minetta Street in Greenwich Village.
Und Zürich und Hollywood. Und dann noch Jerusalem.
Was willst du von mir, Bleibtreu?
Ja, ich weiß. Nein, ich vergaß nichts.
Hier war mein Glück zu Hause. Und meine Not.
Hier kam mein Kind zur Welt. Und mußte fort.
Hier besuchten mich meine Freunde
Und die Gestapo.

Nachts hörte man die Stadtbahnzüge
Und das Horst Wessel-Lied aus der Kneipe nebenan.
Was blieb davon?
Die rosa Petunien auf dem Balkon.
Der kleine Schreibwarenladen.
Und eine alte Wunde, unvernarbt.

Mascha Kaléko

ACKNOWLEDGEMENTS

My cousins Roni G. Ronen (Rosner) and Lonnie Zwerin generously gave me access to their own family archives to fill gaps in my story. I am also grateful to the late Laure Wittner (Hannelore Greiffenhagen) for providing a vivid picture of her Berlin childhood and of her grandmother, Marie Greiffenhagen.

Early interest and support from author A.L. Kennedy helped my project on its way, as did shrewd questioning from friends Pat Davis, Judy Gable, Jacqui Hutson, Elaine Sweet and Melissa Harman as it developed. Char March provided valuable feedback as the book came together, and I am indebted to Kathy Gale for her perceptive comments as it neared completion.

My childhood friend Philippa Trop, greatly missed, helped me crystallise a seminal moment we had shared fifty years earlier. And the late dear Edith Argy enabled me to decipher my grandparents' handwriting myself.

In Berlin many public officials, museum and archive staff went the extra mile so that I might dig deeper to find more information. I particularly wish to thank: Dr Monika Nakath (Brandenburg Main State Archives); Dr Ulrich Baumann (Deputy Director of Berlin's Memorial to the

Murdered Jews of Europe); Edeltraud Frankenstein and Gabriele Kühne (Coordination Office *Stolpersteine* Berlin); Sonja Miltenberger (Charlottenburg-Wilmersdorf *Heimat* Museum); Barbara Schieb (Silent Heroes Memorial within the Memorial to German Resistance).

For welcoming me into their homes and for sharing their own family experiences and memories, I am grateful to:

Annelie Thiemann; Helmut Metzner and Lutz Rambow; Juliane Rupp; Ilse Südmersen; Margot Loehr; Dr Dietlinde Peters; Christine Holzkamp; Dr Gabriele Riebensahm; the late Charly de Wolff; Hans-Hermann Fouquet.

The Wiener Holocaust Library in London provided practical help and invaluable background information, especially Howard Falksohn, Senior Archivist, and Sonia Bacca, former Reader Services Librarian.

Special thanks go to my agent, Rowan Lawton of The Soho Agency, for her wholehearted commitment to the project, and to Jamie Byng and Jenny Fry's excellent team at Canongate Books for the care they have taken to realise it. I am particularly grateful to Simon Thorogood for his acute editorial insights, to Lorraine McCann and Alison Rae for meticulous attention to the text, to Claire Reiderman for her assistance and the production team for great work on the images. Vicki Rutherford patiently kept me and the book on track.

A final thank you to Wolfgang Knoll, who is sadly no longer with us, and Barbara Knoll for their help and hospitality. When Wolfgang, embracing Gunter Demnig's *Stolpersteine* project, commemorated my grandparents, he provided the key that opened my cupboard of loss.